MOTORCYCLE TOURING

IN THE

SOUTHWEST

The Region's Best Rides

MOTORCYCLE TOURING

IN THE
SOUTHWEST

The Region's Best Rides

CHRISTY KARRAS
STEPHEN ZUSY

gpp®

travel

Guilford, Connecticut

To buy books in quantity for corporate use or incentives, call **(800) 962–0973** or e-mail **premiums@GlobePequot.com**.

Stephen Zusy photos: pages ix, xi, xii, xiv, 5, 7, 8, 9, 10, 15, 16, 19, 23, 33, 34, 36, 44, 49, 51, 52, 53, 54, 58, 62, 73, 75, 78, 79, 85, 87, 94, 96, 99, 101, 103, 104, 110, 120, 123, 124, 130, 135, 138, 139, 143, 145, 146, 148, 152, 154, 156, 165, 166, 171, 173, 177, 179, 180, 182, 186, 189, 190, 195, 201, 203, 204, 205, 207, 211, 212, 214, 227, 229, 230, 237, 239, 240, 241, 243, 247, 248 (top and bottom), 254, 255 (top), 261, 262, 264, 268, 278, 279, 280, 285, 286, 287; Christy Karras photos: pages xxi, 18, 25, 29, 32, 40, 41, 46, 59, 67, 111, 112, 127, 129, 131, 163, 217, 218, 220, 221, 223, 226, 232, 276; National Park Service photos: pages 61, 70, 86, 172, 198, 255 (bottom), 270; PDPhoto.org photo: page 76; NSBO www.byways.org photo: page 256

Text design by Sheryl P. Kober
Text layout by Melissa Evarts
Maps by Sue Murray © Morris Book Publishing, LLC

Library of Congress Cataloging-in-Publication Data

Karras, Christy.
  Motorcycle touring in the Southwest : the region's best rides / Christy Karras, Stephen Zusy.
    p. cm.
  Includes index.
  ISBN 978-0-7627-4743-6
  1. Motorcycle touring—Southwest, New—Guidebooks. 2. Southwest, New—Guidebooks. I. Zusy, Stephen (Stephen M.) II. Title.
  GV1059.522.S68K37 2010
  796.7—dc22   2009030642

Printed in China
10 9 8 7 6 5 4 3 2 1

CONTENTS

ACKNOWLEDGMENTS

A heartfelt thank you to all the rangers and staff at national parks, national monuments, national forests, visitor centers, and BLM offices. There are too many to mention individually, but we'd especially like to thank those stationed in the most remote corners of the Southwest. They seemed especially glad to have visitors and almost without exception went out of their way to provide all the information we needed, and then some.

Thanks to the dealers and motorcycle shops that helped outfit us for the journey, especially Zion Harley-Davidson in Washington, Utah. It's a big dealership, but the customer service is second to none. Stop by if you're passing through. If it's Saturday, they'll have the grill going, so grab a burger and wander around.

Thanks to the people who graciously allowed us to photograph them for the book.

Thanks to motorcycle-friendly businesses like Ray's Tavern and the Green River Roasting company in Green River, Utah; The Taos Plaza Indian Hills Inn in Taos, New Mexico; and Ghost Town Gear in Jerome, Arizona. There are a thousand more. You'll know them by the bikes lined up outside.

We're grateful for our editors at Globe Pequot Press for believing in us.

Finally, thanks to every fellow biker who swapped stories, gave us advice, and otherwise welcomed us into the extended family the motorcycle world represents. Your friendship, fortitude, and spirit of adventure humble and inspire us.

Steve:
I would be remiss if I didn't thank my friend Tom Quinn for allowing me to store the bike in his garage during the winter and giving me a key so I could have access whenever I needed it. Thanks also to my friend and co-worker Hayden Andrews for storing the trailer at his house. I apologize for not providing a key before you had to cut the cable to use your smoker.

Thanks to my cousin Jon in Durango for giving us a tip on a road that is a favorite of local riders. We did end up giving out the secret, and other riders will be lucky to find it.

Thanks to my family in Wisconsin for their understanding when I repeatedly told them all my vacation time was allotted to the book. I appreciate them giving me the time and space to work during the cruise celebrating my parents' fiftieth wedding anniversary.

A blanket thank you to all my Park City friends who let me disappear from November to February while Christy and I were finishing the book and then graciously allowed me to return to their lives with a big "Welcome Back."

A huge thank you to Christy for trusting me as a pilot as she listened to podcasts and took notes while riding on what I understand is a relatively uncomfortable rear seat. Her trust seemed steadfast even when the weather was nasty or we had a "close call" with a vehicle of the four-wheeled variety. Thankfully, the weather was pretty good most of the time, and we only had one or two narrow escapes. We need to figure out a safety harness, though, so she doesn't fall asleep and off the bike.

Christy is one hell of an editor, and I can't think of anyone else I trust as much to take my notes, which at times probably read like the ramblings of a crazed motorcycle enthusiast, and craft them into readable chapters. This book would not have been possible without what I know was at times a superhuman effort on her part.

Christy:

I sometimes joke that the reason there aren't more motorcycle touring guide books out there is because most folks who would like to write one realize how much work it is and (wisely) give up. I'd like to thank, and apologize to, everyone I neglected during those long nights of trying to take piles of information from rides and condense them into something shorter than the Bible. That includes my family and friends and most especially my wise, patient, and long-suffering sweetie, Bill. Someday, we'll have the time to ride together for relaxation, I promise.

Thanks to my many friends in the outdoor industry, many of them riders, who gave advice on gear and places to go. A special shout-out to EK USA, a Utah company that heard we needed new tiedowns for our trailer and sent us some that matched our bike! Thanks also to Tom Olsen for the helmet, which you probably didn't consider a permanent loan at the time.

I'm grateful for the acceptance and camaraderie of all motorcycle enthusiasts. My fellow women bikers, whether on the front of the bike or the back, are an inspiration.

Saguaros are a common sight all over Arizona and can live at higher elevations than you might expect.

Thanks to Steve, the best bike pilot I know and the only one I would have agreed to ride (or write) with. I'm amazed at your ability to handle the unexpected curves we found on the road, in business, and in life as we tackled this massive and almost-impossible task. I wouldn't have—and couldn't have—done this project with anyone else.

INTRODUCTION

Motorcycle touring has always been a great way to see and experience a place. On the back of a bike, you become part of your environment: You see, feel, hear, and sometimes even taste your surroundings. And the American Southwest is one of the most rewarding destinations in the world, with breathtaking scenery, astonishing history, and innumerable chances for recreation of all sorts.

For the most part the Southwest's climate and roads are ideal for exploration on a bike. In some places, you can ride at any time of the year. Some sections are so hot in the summer that you think your tires might melt, but ride 30 or 40 miles into the mountains and you'll need to put on another layer of gear. That makes for a lot of great riding that deserves to be explored and we're here to show you the best of the region.

We had ulterior motives for writing this book. Christy is a compulsive writer who was looking for another travel-book project. Steve is a photographer and avid motorcyclist with an adventurous spirit who dreams of living on the back of a bike. Both of us are always ready for a road trip.

We also saw a need for a user-friendly yet information-packed guide for two-wheeled travelers. General guidebooks are great resources for planning a trip but don't give specifics on mileage, where you can find services, or which establishments are particularly motorcycle friendly. Other books about motorcycle touring, while helpful and worth reading, are outdated or lack crucial information.

Many existing guidebooks have a state-by-state focus, but riders don't tour one state at a time, especially in the Southwest. And who wants to flip through a half-dozen travel books while planning a trip, much less drag them along in a saddlebag? The Southwest has always been its own entity, both geographically and culturally, and there's so much tying the states in this part of the country together that we think it makes more sense to focus on the region.

While our book is not designed to tell you everything about everywhere we've been, we hope it will be useful for anyone who wants to explore the Southwest via motorcycle—whether you've been riding for three days or thirty years and whether you're on a day trip or a six-month break from everyday life.

Throughout this book, we've included bits of insight or interesting experiences we've had on our rides. We hope this will give you a taste of all the quirky, weird, and wonderful things that can happen when you set off on a touring adventure. With all

These are just a few of the hundreds of bikes lining most of the streets of Ignacio, Colorado, during the Four Corners Biker Rally.

of the attractions in this part of the country, there is much more to see and do than we can tell you about here, so we encourage you to do your own research while planning your trip. Part of being on a bike is the sense of adventure and discovery, and sometimes it's fun to fly by the seat of your pants (or leathers). With too much planning and scheduling, you can lose that feeling. Then again, without enough, you'll miss new discoveries. There's more in-depth information about almost everything we discuss in this book on the Internet or in the pages of more specific regional guidebooks. Find a balance that works for you.

One of the best things about writing this book was that it gave us a chance to meet other riders and ask them about their own experiences. We're grateful for all the advice from fellow riders and happy to have had the chance to experience the unique fellowship that can only happen among bike enthusiasts.

HELPFUL INFORMATION

Welcome to the Southwest! We love the spontaneity of touring by bike, but we also know that a lack of preparation can ruin a trip. Part of that preparation is having this book, of course, but there are a lot of practicalities to keep in mind. Here is some information, gleaned from various sources (including our own trial and error), that we hope will help you make the most of your trip.

ROADS

The Southwest presents its own challenges as well as opportunities, and sometimes one characteristic can be both. Long, open stretches of road offer a chance to open up the throttle, kick back a little, and check out the scenery; but your next shelter might be a long way away. The combination of mountains and deserts is unbeatable, but it can be blazing hot at lower elevations with snow right to the sides of the road or falling out of the sky at higher elevations.

A twisty, well-banked ride that drops off the Mogollon Rim in Arizona, US 60 clings to the walls of Salt River Canyon all the way to the bottom.

We did our best to avoid interstates unless absolutely necessary, since they can be windy, boring, and stressful—and because many of the best experiences happen on the back roads. A word of warning when riding twisty mountain roads: On the ascent, they are great fun as you power through turns with the throttles on, but the same speed on the descent could be hazardous to your health. You can easily approach a 25- or 30-mile-an-hour decreasing-radius curve moving twice as fast as you should. As always, be aware of your speed and your riding ability on these roads. Some of them will test your bike-handling skills, but all of them should make you smile.

The Southwest is covered with unpaved roads, many of them on public land and open to most bikes. Others are rough, rutted, or (worst of all) sandy. We recommend asking locally about unfamiliar roads before taking them. Ranger stations, Bureau of Land Management offices, and visitor centers are great about answering questions about road conditions—as are most biker hangouts.

WEATHER

Weather is a big deal in the Southwest. You might think summer means hot and dry. But in July and August, monsoonal moisture from the Gulf of Mexico spins up into virtually every area we cover in this book. That moisture, mixed with hot air rising over mountains, causes thunderstorms, especially at high elevations. Afternoons in August can change quickly from 98 degrees and uncomfortably muggy to cool or downright cold and rainy in the span of an hour.

Beware of the potential for flash floods. Be especially alert when traveling through any low-lying areas and anywhere where water appears to wash across the road. Storms in the Southwest can bring a lot of water in short bursts, and much of it doesn't get absorbed by the soil. The runoff can cause problems ranging from a minor inconvenience to a flash flood. The water can deposit debris, usually in the form of sand and small pebbles, across roads. Be very careful crossing them when they are dry and don't try to cross them if there is more than a couple inches of water. If

Christy: Because of the big change in elevation from valley to mountain, there's a good chance of encountering changing weather conditions. Be prepared with full rain gear. We passed a big, burly guy riding a Harley in northern New Mexico one day during a rainstorm. Boy, did he stand out: He was covered head to toe in bright yellow waterproof vinyl coveralls—and he was not ashamed. Sometimes, you have to choose between fashion and frostbite. ●

the water flows continuously, the pavement can be slick—and the last thing you want is to get swept downstream swirling in a mix of water, sand, and miscellaneous vegetation.

On the other hand, the sun here can be direct, hot, dry, and brutal. Use sunscreen to avoid burns. A breeze always feels nice, but wind gusts can happen pretty much anywhere, anytime (especially in wide-open areas) and can be strong enough to almost knock you off your bike.

Waiting out a torrential downpour in Española, New Mexico. The water in the road eventually rose to the top of the curb.

Just south of Telluride, Colorado, this rest stop has one of the best views of any in the Southwest. The clouds looked ominous but produced only a few drops of rain.

ELEVATION

Most of the rides in this book take you up and down through many elevation changes. That's one of the great things about them. But it also means a little advance planning can make things more pleasant. We usually tried to time our mountain/valley combination rides so that we would be in the valleys in the mornings and evenings and in the mountains during the warmest part of the day. It didn't always work out that way, but on the days it did, we enjoyed nice temperatures in the mountaintops while those in the valleys sweltered. Of course, this also meant we sometimes rode through mountain thunderstorms.

In technical terms, the temperature drops at a predictable rate as the elevation changes. This change, called the lapse rate, means a drop of about 6 degrees Fahrenheit for every thousand feet of elevation gain. You can often gain 4,000 or 5,000 feet in elevation on a given ride—we'll let you do the math.

GEAR

We can't overstress the importance of having the right gear. In the Southwest, where the temperature can vary by 50 degrees in one day and storms are fierce and unexpected, you'll want gear that can protect you and keep you comfortable in all kinds of weather. That means you will need several layers. Comfort, versatility, ease of use, and protection from the elements are all-important.

Christy: Silk and merino as lightweight base layers, socks, and tops keep me warm and wick away sweat when it's hot. Wool is a great temperature regulator.

I often wear nylon quick-dry pants, though I still like jeans—sometimes fashion overrides function.

I love my mesh riding jacket with pads and a zip-out water-proof liner that keeps me warm. It's like wearing no jacket at all on hot days, yet I always have some elbow and shoulder protection. I can pack the liner in a saddlebag and quickly zip it in when clouds arise. I occasionally ride in a leather jacket, a classic choice and very durable.

I usually ride in leather ankle boots, and I often think I should just break down and buy some durable and sexy motorcycle-specific boots. And since I like to explore things on foot, I try to bring along some hiking shoes.

I generally wear a helmet. I don't find them particularly comfortable (and Steve wouldn't let me get a pink one), but I already have enough brain damage to make writing a book difficult, so I wear one partly for the benefit of you, our reader.

Steve: I rode in leathers for years, but I have grown to love my textile riding suit. It has a zip-out liner, padding in all the right

HYDRATION

Staying hydrated is a big challenge. Wind, dry desert air, and sun can strip every drop of moisture from your body, especially when you're booking it on the highway or muscling the bike through miles of hairpin turns. And since you might go 50 or even 100 miles between towns, it's imperative to carry water with you. You will usually find Steve wearing a CamelBak, one of many hydration backpacks on the market. It's very compact yet holds 100

places, loads of zippers for ventilation, and a lot of reflective material that makes me more visible at night. I can wear it comfortably in anything except the 100-degree heat of summer in the Arizona desert. It is also (mostly) waterproof and dries quickly if I ride through a rain shower.

For those looking for one jacket that offers protection, versatility, and enough layers to wear year-round: I'm sorry to say there is no such thing. If you ride extensively, you will need more than one set of riding gear. When you shop for gear, try on many styles and designs. Take time in the store to remove the liner and see if you can get it back in the jacket quickly and easily. Whatever you choose must be easy to use or you'll find yourself not using it when you should.

Like Christy, I have a collection of light base layers, from T-shirts to socks, that wick away moisture.

I wear heavy leather boots that come two-thirds of the way up to my knees. Countless coats of mink oil make them virtually waterproof. I've ridden for hours in the rain and my feet stay almost completely dry. I like that they have a decent-size heel I can hang on the foot peg. They are comfortable enough to wear around town or on a short hike—a great mix of comfort and protection. ●

ounces. It can go under and over gear, and the drinking tube is convenient and allows you to sip from it regularly rather than having to stop to get a drink.

SUPPLIES

We tend to always bring supplies with us even on short rides, including maps, snacks, comfortable shoes, and a basic first-aid kit. Most modern bikes require premium gas, so make sure gas stations you find have high octane or carry octane booster. We tend to keep some on the bike, just in case. Bring along paper funnels and paper towels; both are valuable if you need to check or add oil and you are not at a gas station.

NATIVE AMERICANS

Throughout the Southwest, you'll see remnants of the ancient civilization called the Ancestral Puebloans (once called the Anasazi, now considered a pejorative term). For a thousand years, until about A.D. 1400, the Southwest was home to them and the Fremont (who also ranged north and west from here into much of what is now eastern Utah). The ancient culture shifted around A.D. 1300, resulting in a mysterious mass migration and an end to these civilizations. It's still not clear what happened, though widespread drought is a possibility.

But the people didn't disappear completely. They left behind amazing art and architecture, some of it preserved in this desert landscape. And their ancestors still live in this area, although they have changed over the generations. You will get a chance to meet them as you travel here. Some still live in the settlements their people have occupied for hundreds of years.

Modern American Indian groups have their own governments, rules, and customs that visitors are subject to on their land. Pay attention to things like speed limits and other signs. Never take photographs of people or their homes without permission. Do ask if you have questions; people are generally happy to discuss their culture.

FEE AREAS

Part of the region's appeal lies in its abundance of state and national parks and monuments. Unlike other parts of the world, the most impressive attractions here are publicly owned, which means less commercialism and lower entrance fees. Most parks require a small fee to enter, but motorcycle fees are about half those for cars.

If you're going to spend a lot of time here and want to see many national parks and monuments, you might want to invest in an annual pass (available at most visitor centers). Since there is no motorcycle discount for the pass, it takes visiting a fair number of parks for it to pay off. But it is convenient to pull out the card rather than cash or a credit card, especially when you intend to visit multiple parks or monuments in the same day. In this part of the country, the annual pass can easily pay for itself in a week to ten days of riding (and with so much to see and do, you've barely scratched the surface in ten days). Plan for fees of about $3 to $12 for most of the attractions we mention and decide accordingly.

WILDLIFE

Most of the terrain we talk about is good habitat for animals both wild and domestic. We've seen deer, elk, moose, horses, sheep, goats, cows, dogs, cats, rabbits, snakes, and even eagles on or near the road. Luckily (knock on wood) we didn't have any sudden encounters with any animals, but the quantity of roadkill we saw reminded us of those who did. In short, while you are enjoying the scenery, keep your eyes peeled for furry or feathered friends. They can pop out of the forest or underbrush at remarkable speed and cause great harm to you and any passengers should you meet them head-on.

HELMET LAWS

Whatever your view on helmets, you should know the laws in the states you'll be visiting. As of the writing of this book, all the states we cover require helmets for those under age eighteen (New Mexico also requires reflectors). Even though many unadvisable behaviors (prostitution, gambling, smoking) are legal in Nevada, no one can ride there without a helmet. Go figure.

The American Motorcyclist Association (AMA) is an excellent source for information on motorcycle laws by state. The AMA Web site, www.amadirectlink.com, has information on helmet laws plus everything from eye protection requirements to the legality of lane splitting. Check for specific and updated requirements before you go.

TRAILERING YOUR BIKE

With the long distances between cities in this region, trailering your bike can be a good option, especially if you're coming from far away or are pressed for time and want to focus on the best rides.

Regulations regarding trailers vary from state to state. In Utah, where we were based, trailers under 750 pounds don't require registration. But we got pulled over in Arizona where, no matter the size of your trailer, you need registration. Even if you're not from Arizona, you can get ticketed for not registering your trailer in your home state. Registering your trailer might be a good idea even if it's not required, because it might help you get it back if it's stolen. (Not that theft is a big issue. We use common sense and have never had a problem.)

BIKE TYPE

What's the best bike for touring? We rode a Buell Ulysses because, for the purposes of this book, we wanted a bike that could go pretty much everywhere any bike could go. Most of the rides we discuss are perfectly doable on any road bike (we note those that aren't).

There are some things we love about the Buell. With a 1203cc engine and the optional tour kit, we can load it with gear and still have plenty of power. Because of its design, it takes curves like a sport bike. Buell is owned by Harley-Davidson, so parts and service are easy to find. The Ulysses lacks some of the bells and

Bikes of different feathers flock together at Gila Cliff Dwellings National Monument in New Mexico.

whistles of the bikes it's designed to compete with, but it's considerably less expensive than some we considered, especially its main rival, the BMW—another popular touring bike.

Every bike will have its pluses and minuses, but the short answer is: The best bike to tour on is the one you have. We've encountered people riding everything from full-on sport bikes with stuff tied on with bungee cords to the most modern (and

Steve: I quickly got used to the simplicity of the Buell and figured out ways to make my time in the saddle as comfortable as possible. It wasn't pleasant for Christy on long days as a passenger. A memory foam or gel seat might have provided a little more comfort. For the most part, it is a great bike for the kind of riding we did and the distances we wanted to cover. ●

expensive) touring bikes pulling trailers—and everything in between. If it's running and can hold enough gear for your trip, it's the right bike.

Enough advice, warnings, and introductions. This book is about the adventure that comes with getting on the back of a motorcycle and finding places to explore. So get out there, keep the rubber on the road, and enjoy.

Steve: I stopped at a gas station just north of Española, New Mexico, to fuel up and get a snack. As I sat at the side of the parking lot eating, an attendant was sweeping the lot with a well-worn broom. He deftly used it to work his way over to me and the bike.

He seemed shy, but he commented on my bike and wanted to know why I would wear a CamelBak on the motorcycle. I explained that I spend most of the day on and off the bike, and if I'm not constantly drinking water, I'll get dehydrated and tired. He asked me where I had ridden from, and I told him I started in Park City, Utah, and would be doing a big loop back through New Mexico and Arizona.

That's when the truth came out. He grinned shyly and said he had an old Gold Wing at home that he kept in decent working order. He rides it around the area on a pretty regular basis, but he had always wanted to take a long trip. I said the Gold Wing is a good bike for that, and I encouraged him to do it.

He looked down at the ground and mumbled, "Yeah, I know, but it's hard." His voice trailed off. There was a moment of silence, and then he said he had to get back to work and I said I had to hit the road. I fired up the bike and roared off.

Yeah, I thought, a long trip can be hard to do, but man, is it worth it! ●

NORTHERN UTAH

Northern Utah is our home base and we couldn't resist introducing you to it. Although this part of the world is more alpine and dry highlands than red-rock desert, it has its fair share of nice rides. The nightlife isn't the best, although a couple places—like the Shooting Star in Huntsville, one of the oldest bars west of the Mississippi—are worth checking out.

You do get a variety of landscapes—from lush forest to dry, flat desert—all within reach of whatever city or town you choose as a home base. Endless chances for recreation are part of the appeal of living here. Relatively short distances between towns makes loops easy and if you were to pull out a map and draw a circle with a radius of four or five hours of riding, using any of the cities or towns along the Wasatch front or back as a base, you would be amazed at the diversity of landscapes you can ride through.

One word of caution—and this is purely personal opinion and we have no research to back it up other than having traveled extensively throughout the country by car and bike—Utah drivers are perhaps some of the least considerate when it comes to motorcycles. A saying goes something like this: "You know you're driving in Utah when the slowest-moving vehicles are in the left lane, the fastest are in the right, and everyone in the middle wants to get off the road."

This is especially true if you find yourself on an interstate trying to get from point A to B. You may be riding in the middle lane going at or a little over the speed limit and have a pickup or SUV pass you in the right lane going much faster than the general flow of traffic. This may explain why Utah riders are often eager to take the back roads. Always be aware of your surroundings and assume that car drivers don't see you whenever you ride—but be especially careful in Utah. ●

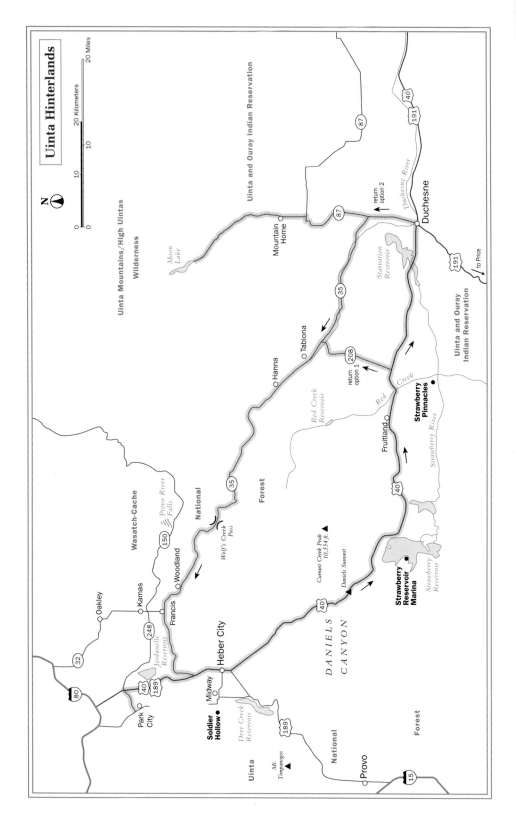

Uinta Hinterlands

Uinta Hinterlands

Directions:

east on US 40 from Park City or Heber City
north on UT 208 or UT 87 to UT 35
west on UT 35 to Francis
west on UT 32 or UT 248 back to Heber City or Park City

Distance:

from Park City to Duchesne: 89 miles
from Duchesne to Hanna: 30 miles
from Hanna to Park City: 55 miles
from Park City to Evanston, Wyoming, via UT 150: 93 miles
each way

Time:

a half day for the loop, more if you want to explore further

Services:

at Park City, Heber City, Duchesne, and Hanna

Best Time of Year:

late May through September

Highlights:

high mountains and meadows; high-desert sightseeing with
rivers, reservoirs and rock formations; out-of-the-way, historic towns; a beautiful, curvy mountain route home

This is a major biker loop and, as a one-way, one of the best routes to southeastern Utah. It offers a combination of desert and mountain riding while covering a lot of territory. We'll start this drive in Park City. From there, head south on US 40 through Heber City.

Heber City is a combination of traditional Mormon town and modern sprawl. In a verdant valley at the base of the Wasatch Mountains, Heber's residents and tourists enjoy fly-fishing and ultralight gliding. Traces of the old-fashioned life linger; you'll even see the occasional sheep pasture. In fact, national sheepdog events are held just up the hill at Soldier Hollow, site of the 2002 Winter Olympics cross-country skiing competition.

South of town, at the intersection of US 189 and US 40, continue on US 40. To the west is Mount Timpanogos, and if you take US 189 toward Provo Canyon, you can connect with the Alpine Loop of ride 3. A mile and a half later, you leave farmland behind and pass aspen-decorated campgrounds. At first, the road is a flat and narrow two lanes. Entering Daniels Canyon, it starts to climb and twist (watch for rude RV drivers), and soon the mountains stretch right down to the side of the road.

The road is in good shape, although still only two lanes most of the time until Daniels Summit. Passing opportunities are frequent; just be alert to traffic (sometimes passing illegally over a double-yellow line) in the other lane. US 40 leads to many recreation areas, so a lot of the traffic consists of pickup trucks hauling boats, ATVs, and dirt bikes. The road comes out of the canyon into high alpine meadows dotted with a few stands of trees. It's usually windy, but the road is easy and wide open.

About 23 miles east of Heber City, 8,400-acre Strawberry Reservoir is a major destination for recreation, including fishing (especially cutthroat trout—someone caught a 30-pounder here in 1930), boating, and off-road motor sports. There's lots of RV-style camping, and not a lot of trees or shade—in other words, typical Utah reservoir–style outdoor living.

There's a U.S. Forest Service visitor center (open 9 a.m. to 3 p.m.) on the western edge. A paved road, FR 131, runs along the forested western shore past the Strawberry Bay Marina with year-

There isn't much shade, but the fishing is great at Strawberry Reservoir.

round services, including a restaurant and lodge. Shortly before the Renegade Marina boat ramp is the turnoff for Indian Creek Road, about 10 miles of good graded dirt and gravel until it hits pavement that leads south to US 6. Don't try it without inquiring at the visitor center about road conditions.

Back on US 40, the road is mostly straight and easy, with gentle curves. Traffic can be heavy here, especially on weekends as people head back and forth from their recreational exploits in northeastern Utah. Frequent passing lanes let you get away from the worst offenders.

The eastern side of the summit is drier and warms up quickly. The terrain changes rapidly ten or fifteen minutes past the reservoir from alpine to arid juniper-covered mesas that look more like southern Utah. Depending on your opinion, the stretch is either not very exciting or quintessential open desert riding.

For a nice paved shortcut to our return road that lets you bypass the often windy desert plains of the Duchesne area, take UT 208 (the turn is a few miles past the town of Fruitland) north to UT 35. UT 208 starts off in desert and eventually drops down into the relatively lush river valley that characterizes UT 35, one of the best motorcycle roads in the state.

Christy: Civilization came late to this part of the world, which was generally ignored by authorities in Utah, Wyoming, and Colorado. When a Mormon expedition checked out this remote area separated from the Wasatch Front by mountains, they returned with a verdict of "Don't go there." But as early as 1837, Fort Uintah was a trading center for fur trappers. Traditional homesteaders lay claim to their allotted 160 acres before coal mining took off in the nineteenth century. Since the 1940s, oil has been big here—which means in Utah, the oil in your ride may have come from somewhere under your tires.

This route also takes you past several tribal areas. American Indians (specifically, members of the Ute tribe) were living here long before there was such a thing as a reservation. In the 1860s and '70s, after some skirmishes between whites and several bands around Utah, the federal government forcibly moved many bands to this area. (In 1886 black buffalo soldiers from the U.S. Cavalry were sent here to keep the peace.) ●

If you keep going on US 40, you still meet up with UT 35 eventually via UT 87, which intersects with UT 35 north of town. Or you could continue on the straight, easy road toward Vernal (see ride 2). Most people go to Duchesne on their way through it to some place on the other side, but the locals who staff the visitor center on the west end of town are very helpful and knowledgeable, offering brochures for tourist attractions in addition to a display of locally mined honeycomb quartz.

As you ride through the town of Myton, between Duchesne and Roosevelt, you'll see a turnoff for Nine Mile Canyon. While the canyon is rightfully legendary for its collection of ancient rock art, the road to it is unpaved and often rough.

Roosevelt is a cute little town with a quaint Main Street, featuring small businesses such as Marion's Variety, with its old-

The Strawberry Pinnacles are about 6 miles off US 40 via a partly paved road with a couple miles of decent unpaved road at the end.

fashioned lunch counter. A local biker recommended Kim's on the east end of town. It serves burgers and a mix of ethnic food. It's closed Saturday and Sunday.

Eventually, you'll want to discover the beauty that is UT 35 through Wolf Creek Pass. Seasonal closures usually end by April or May; check in with the Utah Department of Transportation Web site (www.dot.state.ut.us) or a ranger station for updates. Things can get scary at elevation and you really don't want to have to take the rare shelter available along the way: Aside from the little towns of Tabiona and Hanna, your only option would be a hole-in-the-ground potty.

Head north on UT 87 (turn left at Center Street in Duchesne), which will connect you to UT 35. On any of this area's beautiful summer or fall days, this is a great ride. The road dips and turns just enough to keep things lively while leaving you some brain power to appreciate the natural beauty that surrounds you on all sides.

There are lots of possible little side trips in this area. For a breath of cooler air and maybe a splash in the water, head north to Moon Lake—the road is paved all the way, starting in suburban desert badlands and eventually surrounded by forest. Many other roads north toward the Uinta Mountains turn rough before they reach anything truly scenic.

US 6 to the south of here is called Utah's deadliest highway, mostly because drivers seem to lose their common sense on it and end up running into each other. US 191 from Price to Duchesne is a great alternative. This is a designated scenic byway and for good reason. Not only is this a less-crowded drive than US 6, but at its best it is also one of the prettiest drives in the state. Even better, it's a great road for a bike, with lots of curves and something new around every bend. Surprisingly, many motorcyclists aren't familiar with the route.

The turn for US 191 in Duchesne is easy to miss. It is in the center of town and appears to be just a turn into a neighborhood, so watch for signs. Make the turn south and within minutes you will be climbing out of Duchesne into Indian Canyon. The road continues to climb gradually for about 28 miles to beautiful mountain vistas at Indian Creek Pass, then drops over the next 19 miles to the town of Helper, just north of Price. ●

US 191 is a fun ride and a great alternative to the madness of US 6.

The Hanna Lounge is a popular stop for riders and locals alike.

UT 35 rises into relatively lush forest about the time you're hitting the bucolic town of Tabiona. This is the southern flank of the Uinta Mountains, the state's highest, and you can tell: The air gets cooler, aspens blanket the roadsides, and cliffs rise on the hilltops above the tree line.

In the hamlet of Hanna, the Hanna Lounge is a popular stop for bikers. Maybe it's the "lounge" part—the owner seeks to provide the kind of real bar experience you usually don't find within Utah's borders. This is not a swanky joint and you wouldn't want it to be. The attached cafe serves burger-type fare. Another popular hangout is Defa's Dude Ranch, just before you get to Wolf Creek Pass. Go to www.defasduderanch.com for information and directions.

Back on UT 35, the road just keeps getting better. You may encounter a slow vehicle or two, but who cares? You will soon easily find your way around them on well-banked asphalt that seems to have been laid out just for you.

The road rises and falls with the mountains, following the Duchesne River. The western slope gradually drops down into the mountain valleys where we started this ride. UT 35 takes you

Mirror Lake Scenic Byway tops out at an impressive 10,759 feet as it winds its way from Kamas, Utah, to Evanston, Wyoming.

through the picturesque little towns of Woodland and Francis, former farming towns that are now playgrounds for the rich (this part of UT 35 is accessible year-round). Residential roads carve their way up the hillsides, lined by extra-large "cabins" with great views of the peaks to the west.

At Francis, you can either head south toward Heber or north toward Kamas, Marion, and Oakley. Either way, you'll end up connecting back with US 40, then I-80 back to Salt Lake City.

These towns are also the gateway to UT 150, the beautiful high-elevation Mirror Lake Scenic Byway through the Uinta Mountains. Rising into the mountains and passing glorious peaks in one of the country's few east-to-west oriented mountain ranges, it reaches heights of 10,000 feet or so before dropping into biker-friendly Evanston, Wyoming. The road is usually open from Memorial Day until the first heavy snowfall (usually in September or October). Be sure to take the short, paved hike to Upper Provo River Falls, 24 miles into the byway. Return the way you came or hit I-80 out of Evanston for a fast, windy ride home.

RIDE
2

Dinosaurland

Directions:
east on US 40 from Vernal to Dinosaur National Monument
and back
north on US 191 from Vernal
north on UT 44 from Flaming Gorge and back

Distance:
from Vernal to Dinosaur, Colorado (Dinosaur National
Monument): 34 miles
from Dinosaur to Harpers Corner: 35 miles
from Vernal to Manila: 64 miles

Time:
at least half a day, more if you pull over to see the sights

Services:
at Vernal, Dinosaur, and Manila

Best Time of Year:
spring and autumn, winter can come as early as Labor Day
at high elevations, summers are usually nice

Highlights:
fierce geology, outlaw hideaways, ancient civilizations,
Flaming Gorge Reservoir

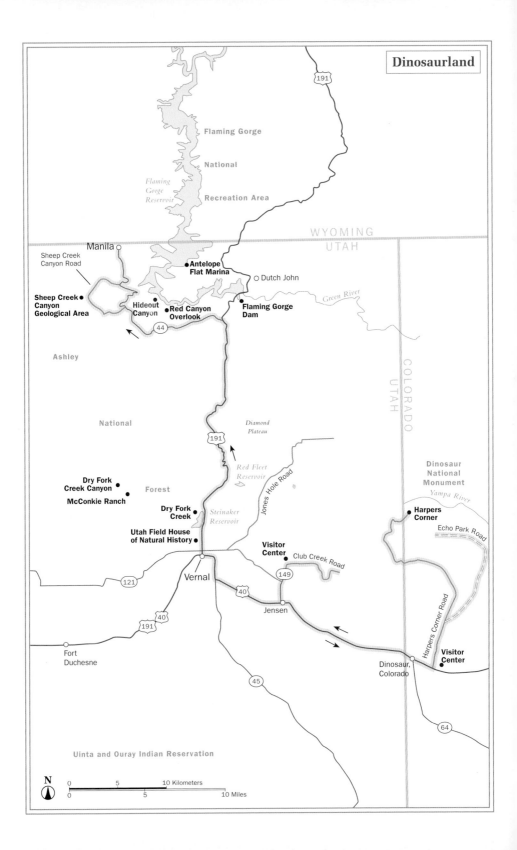

Dinosaurland

191

Flaming Gorge

National

Recreation Area

Flaming Gorge Reservoir

WYOMING
UTAH

Manila

Sheep Creek
Canyon Road

**Antelope
Flat Marina**

Dutch John

Green River

**Sheep Creek
Canyon
Geological Area**

**Hideout
Canyon**

**Red Canyon
Overlook**

**Flaming Gorge
Dam**

44

Ashley

COLORADO
UTAH

National

*Diamond
Plateau*

191

*Red Fleet
Reservoir*

Jones Hole Road

**Dinosaur
National
Monument**

Yampa River

**Dry Fork
Creek Canyon**

Forest

McConkie Ranch

**Dry Fork
Creek**

*Steinaker
Reservoir*

**Harpers
Corner**

Echo Park Road

**Utah Field House
of Natural History**

**Visitor
Center**

Club Creek Road

121

Vernal

149

40

Harpers Corner Road

**Visitor
Center**

Jensen

40

191

45

Fort
Duchesne

Dinosaur,
Colorado

64

Uinta and Ouray Indian Reservation

N

0   5   10 Kilometers
0   5   10 Miles

This area, encompassing far northeastern Utah and northwestern Colorado, was for a long time one of America's most remote outposts—or at least it felt that way. And visitors for ages have thought this a good thing. About a hundred years ago, outlaws hid out here while on the run from the law; these days, folks use it as a getaway from their everyday lives.

Vernal makes a good base for exploring. Hotels, especially of the lower-end variety, are plentiful here, although it might be wise to make reservations in advance—you've got oil and gas workers, tourists, and Green River boaters all vying for rooms. Coal, oil, and natural gas are fueling a major economic and population boom and the influx of workers means hotels fill up quickly with part-time residents. (This will also be true of mining or drilling towns throughout the Southwest so be careful when making reservations and demand that you get what you ask for.) Although Vernal has a number of restaurants, most of them are of the fast-food or family-restaurant variety. It's pretty much a matter of take your pick.

Just as the signs of oil and gas drilling are obvious, it's hard to miss Vernal's pride in its heritage. It seems every hotel and restaurant makes some kind of reference to either dinosaurs or outlaws, sometimes going so far as to sport life-size pastel fiber-glass dinosaurs in front of their businesses.

For more dinos, as well as a real taste of their role in this region, stop by the spiffy Utah Field House of Natural History State Park Museum, right on Main Street (as US 40 is called in

Steve: This is big-game country. Perhaps the largest bull elk I've ever seen was in the section of US 40 between Vernal and Dinosaur National Monument. It was late fall, and it came charging out of the sagebrush and ran across US 40 about a half-mile in front of me. Its head was thrown back, and it was bugling to ward off interlopers. There are also lots of mule deer in the sage. It grows high and thick in this part of the state, so deer are very difficult to see. ●

town). Opened in 2004, it boasts easy-to-understand exhibitions about the various prehistoric ages and what lived here during those times. It's also a respite from the sometimes oppressive sunshine outside or rare rainy days, as well as a great complement to a ride through Dinosaur National Monument. Most of the tourist sites around here offer free brochures with suggestions for short road trips. (To find out more before you go, check out the region's Web site at www.dinoland.com.)

Ride to Jensen for the turnoff to Dinosaur National Monument. The monument has no services at either entrance and there's not much to Jensen besides an RV park, so be sure to stock up on any needs, including food and fuel, in either Vernal or Dinosaur, Colorado, before you head into the park. (This is very dry desert, so we will remind you again to bring water.) The road into Dinosaur National Monument is worth the ride. We gave up breakfast at Betty's Cafe in Vernal to get an early start. Betty's was recommended by a few of the locals at the Dinosaur Brew Haus, which serves up actual beer on tap.

One of the best things about Dinosaur National Monument is how much you can see from the road. Two paved "auto tour" routes take you through it (one of them, Harpers Corner, is closed Jan through mid-Apr). A little way into the monument, visitors used to be able to get close to excavations in a working dinosaur quarry, but it's been closed for a few years. It's supposed to reopen at some point, but funding issues make its future uncertain. Still, the visitor center has plenty of information and the park's ancient rock art, outlaw cabin remnants, and millions of years of rock formations and fossils are on permanent display. The helpful and knowledgeable rangers offer walking and bus tours as well. This desert was tropical or even covered with water at one point, and the red and yellow striped escarpments all around are layers of rock and sediment from throughout the ages.

The road into the monument from Colorado, Harpers Corner Road, is in excellent shape. It climbs quickly from the desert floor at the visitor center through piñon, juniper, and sage to high mountain meadow. The posted speed is 45 miles per hour, and while big sweeping turns and undulating hills urge you to pull back on the throttle, the curves want to be ridden much faster. A good portion of the road is open range, so cattle graze very close to the side of the road. Take your time and watch your pace.

According to the driving tour brochure, Harpers Corner Road is about 35 miles long (32 miles according to our odometer). At the end of the road, Harpers Corner Road Trail is about a 1-mile hike each way. It takes you to an overlook of the confluence of the Yampa and Green Rivers. This is an easy hike and

Petroglyphs like these are a short distance from the road in Dinosaur National Monument.

the first 100 yards or so are the steepest part. It's well worth the walk: The views are incredible as you look out over a section of the river popular for rafting, judging by the boats on the river below.

Steve: Rangers can give speeding tickets; I was checking my speed on the way out of the monument and almost got tagged. I also almost ran over a 3-foot-long snake. It looked like a rattler but when I stopped to check it out and encourage it to leave the road, it quickly made its way under a good-size sage bush without making a sound. I was doing a good deed by helping the snake from the road but I assume the rangers frown on anything even remotely approaching harassment of the wildlife. ●

Mitten Park Fault is visible from the Harpers Corner overlook in Dinosaur National Monument.

The other scenic drive, Echo Park Road, reminds us of the unpaved road out of Tortilla Flats in Arizona, although this one was perhaps a bit steeper and more rugged at the beginning. It drops quickly through classic red-rock sandstone—which becomes soft dust when crushed. There are two signs as it starts to descend: PASSENGER CARS NOT ADVISED. TRAILERS PROHIBITED. and IMPASSABLE WHEN WET. Once you get below the red rock, the road is packed gravel that takes you to Echo Park campground and boat ramp. Continuing on Yampa Bench Road will take you to Deerlodge campground and boat ramp.

If you're interested in ancient rock art, make the short detour on your way into or out of Vernal to the McConkie Ranch site in Dry Fork Creek Canyon. From the center of downtown Vernal, head west to 500 West, turn north (right) and ride UT 121 to 3500 West. Turn north (right) and head about 10 miles up the road until you reach a major fork in the road and turn right (you're following signs for Red Cloud Loop). Cross the bridge and continue for another 2 miles until you reach a canyon and Dry Fork Creek.

Up the canyon, on a 200-foot-tall rock face, is some of the world's most spectacular rock art: haunting figures pecked into the canyon wall by the Fremont people as long as 2,000 years ago. The owners of this land, on the McConkie Ranch, believe people should be able to see and study the wonders here, so they allow respectful visitors onto their property despite potential problems with vandalism and noise.

Now we'll explore the area north of Vernal. Nowhere is the geological uniqueness of this land so evident as along US 191 from Vernal north to Flaming Gorge Reservoir. The highway has markers noting which time period's rock you're passing through at any given moment (stop by at the turnoff just north of Vernal to get the full explanation of what you'll be seeing).

About 12 miles north of Vernal on US 191, you'll pass Red Fleet State Park, named for a group of bright red rock formations that supposedly look like the masts of a ship.

We don't often get chances to see actual dinosaur tracks in the places they walked, but you have one here. If you want to take a short detour and a little hike, here's your chance (warning: Unless you're really hardy or crazy, don't try it in riding boots). Go 2 miles past the Red Fleet turnoff and take a right turn just past the phosphate plant on your left. There is a small sign pointing the way to the dinosaur trackway. Take the road about 2.3 miles to the parking area on your right. The hike is 1.5 miles each way. Remember to take water. At the parking area, borrow a *Red Fleet Dinosaur Trackway Trail Guide* for more information. You can jump into the lake at the far end of the trail, where dino tracks about a foot across lead down into the water. The water may partially cover them if the lake level is high).

US 191 north goes through yet more geologic ages and climbs into forested mountains. You'll eventually hit close to 9,000 feet before dropping again just a little at Flaming Gorge Reservoir, one of Utah's most popular recreation areas. The reservoir is 90 miles long, has a capacity of 3,788,900 acre-feet, and produces state-record lake trout that can weigh up to 50 pounds.

At the intersection of US 191 and UT 44 just south of the reservoir, you'll have to decide which route to take. It will be a long time before roads converge again around this long north-

Platter-size fossilized dinosaur tracks lead to the water's edge at Red Fleet State Park north of Vernal.

south stretch of water. Unless you have a lot of time or have already gone on UT 44 and want to try the other side, we recommend taking US 191 the short distance to the dam and visitor center and then going back to UT 44. The dam is staffed with enthusiastic tour guides who are happy to give information. The visitor center next door can also give you updates on regional attractions and conditions.

For a very different view of the reservoir from the one you will get at the overlooks along UT 44, go a little bit farther on US 191. This is the flatter side of the reservoir (thus its name, Antelope Flat), which means you'll be looking at the water with mountains rising behind it. If you continue up this side, you'll reach Dutch John, used as a base for dam-building operations.

Back on UT 44 take the Red Canyon overlook turnoff (about 3 miles beyond the intersection with US 191). The Red Canyon Recreation Complex includes a lodge and some decent dining options of the burgers-and-fries variety. Another couple miles, and you're at the Red Canyon Overlook. The name's origin is obvious: The canyon walls are bright red, creating quite a contrast with water and sky. You're on the edge of a cliff, looking down 1,700 feet to the reservoir. Another overlook, Hideout Canyon, is named for the outlaws who used to frequent this remote area.

From here, the road goes through the hamlet of Manila, where you can fill up on gas. If you want a long and blustery ride back to the Salt Lake City area, you could continue north through high-elevation desert dotted with oil rigs, the mountains receding off to the south, to the junction of I-80 (it is 231 miles from Flaming Gorge to Salt Lake City if you go this way). Otherwise, backtrack to Vernal.

While you're here, consider taking the quick Sheep Creek Canyon loop from UT 44. This short, paved byway's compact, dramatic landscapes vividly portray the natural forces working to create the geological wonders of the whole Southwest. In the canyon a piece of the earth rises almost vertically in a dramatic multilayered fold pushed up by earthquakes along the Uinta Crest Fault. We also saw Rocky Mountain bighorn sheep just off the side of the road, which reminded us about the abundant wildlife around here. While it is paved all the way, the road is not well maintained, so it may be very rough in places. Take care, especially on tight curves, and ask at the visitor center if you have any questions. ●

If you're lucky, you might glimpse some of the Rocky Mountain bighorn sheep that call the Flaming Gorge Reservoir area home.

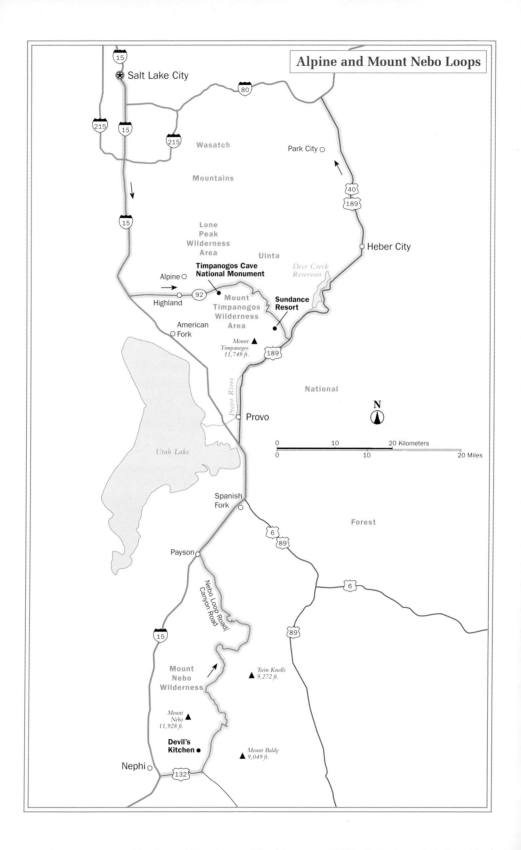

Alpine and Mount Nebo Loops

Alpine Loop Directions:
south on I-15 to Highland and Alpine
east on UT 92
east on US 189 to Heber City
north on US 40 to Park City and Salt Lake City

Mount Nebo Loop Directions from the North:
south on I-15 to Payson (exit 254)
east (left) onto Main Street (SR 77)
south to 100 North (SR 198)
east (left) to 600 East, then right on 600 East. Stay on this road, which eventually becomes Canyon Road, south to the entrance to Payson Canyon and the beginning of the byway (CR 015)

Mount Nebo Loop Directions from the South:
north on I-15 to Nephi (exit 222)
east (right) onto SR 132 for about 6 miles to the entrance of the byway on your left

Alpine Loop Distance:
124 miles from Park City

Mount Nebo Loop Distance:
167 miles from Park City (38 miles of which are the Mount Nebo Scenic Byway)

Time:
half a day or more for both loops; each can be done in
three hours or so, including stops

Services:
Alpine, Heber City, Provo, Payson, and Nephi

Best Time of Year:
any time but winter, when scenic byway roads are closed
(check in advance; usually both are closed until at least
Memorial Day and sometimes into June)

Highlights:
forests, peaks, Sundance Resort, changing elevation and
scenery around Mount Nebo

These two rides can easily be combined into a day trip from Salt Lake City, Provo, or Park City—or they could be side trips if you're passing through and have the time. They have a lot in common: Both take you around the flank of big, dramatic, iconic mountains—Timpanogos and Nebo are the highest peaks along the Wasatch Range. Both rides give you lots of glorious alpine scenery. Both start at low elevation, climb, then come back down. And you can't get to either of them without passing through some very boring urban territory. If you're at all into hiking, bring some comfortable shoes.

Because we started and ended at Park City, we'll do the Alpine Loop first. Wherever you're coming from, you'll want to find your way to the Alpine-Highland exit and go east toward the mountains. After a lot of suburbia, enter American Fork Canyon and breathe a sigh of relief. There's a $6 fee to enter the canyon.

Not far up the canyon, you'll see signs for Timpanogos Cave National Monument. The caves are full of colorful formations called helictites. They're open May through October. There's a $7

Tibble Fork Reservoir, at the top of a short leg off the Alpine Loop, is a great place to stop and wet a line if you have one.

fee to enter the caves, which are at the top of a short, steep hike that gains 1,200 feet in elevation. Once you get to the top, tours last about an hour. Tours are limited to twenty people at a time, so you might have to get a ticket a few hours or even days in advance during busy summer weekends.

Continuing through the canyon, roads are very narrow, twisty, and slow. You'll see lots of people recreating, since this is so close to Salt Lake City and Provo. The loop continues through quaking aspen forests, giving an occasional view of the steep slopes and cliffs of Mount Timpanogos, the second-highest peak in the Wasatch Range.

Toward the Provo Canyon end of the Alpine Loop and nestled at the base of the mountains, Sundance Resort (owned by actor Robert Redford) is a nice place to stop and have lunch or just relax and take in the scenery.

Once you're back on US 189, you can either go connect with the "Wasatch Back" (the communities on the east side of the Wasatch Range) or go back down to Provo and I-15. Go south for the Mount Nebo Scenic Byway. Before the byway, as with the Alpine Loop, you'll pass through a lot of town to get to the country.

Steve: I didn't know exactly which I-15 exit would get me to the Mount Nebo Loop. I was getting closer to Mount Nebo, so I took the Nephi exit. It became obvious that I had taken the correct exit when I saw one of those brown and white state signs for the MOUNT NEBO SCENIC BYWAY at the end of the off-ramp. There are times when it feels as if Utah is trying to keep certain things a secret and you had better know where you're going, because if you don't already know, no one will tell you.

We came into the loop from the south. The loop takes you around the back flank of Mount Nebo, the southernmost and highest mountain in the Wasatch Range. The ride is scenic and it is a byway, but it was not particularly impressive after some of the riding we did in the rest of the Southwest. This isn't helped by a 2007 fire that torched thousands of acres through here. The road is fairly narrow and winding, mostly through open range, and not in very good shape. In addition, there are parallel ridges running the direction of travel for most of the length of the ride, almost as if someone had driven on the road with a multi-wheeled trailer while the asphalt was still hot and soft. ●

The road reaches its summit about 14 miles from the turn onto the byway off SR 132. The road climbs from a little more than 5,200 feet above sea level in Nephi, slices its way through the Uinta-Wasatch-Cache National Forest and reaches just over 9,000 feet at the road's summit (the top of the mountain is 11,928 feet). The first couple of miles are pretty mellow, but once the road starts its ascent, it climbs quickly, so you'll notice a relatively rapid change in the vegetation as sagebrush gives way to aspen, cottonwood, maple, and stands of pine and spruce. Plentiful overlooks allow you to stop often and take in the scenery. Don't miss Devil's Kitchen, where a short hike takes you to a stand of bright red-rock formations that would look more at home in southern Utah.

Devil's Kitchen, a geological anomaly on Mount Nebo, looks as if it should be in southern Utah.

Pay heed to the black and yellow speed limit signs that seem to be placed before almost every curve. Do some rapid mental calculations (open range plus ridges in the road plus sand, gravel, and rocks from any recent rains, multiplied by too much speed going into a turn) and you realize conditions are not in your favor. This is also a popular area to hike and camp, with quite a few large pickups towing campers. We don't enjoy coming around a blind curve to find them taking up half our lane, so we stuck pretty close to the suggested speed limit.

Steve: I guess when you're on two wheels, you tend to pay attention to things that can do you harm. I tend to notice roadkill—not for its ability to harm me but for the potential abundance of those things that are still alive and can run out in front of me. I saw three dead mule deer in the 6 miles from the highway off-ramp to the Mount Nebo Scenic Byway turnoff. Ride this area with caution. Wildlife viewing is one thing, but you don't want to take these guys head-on. The wilderness around here is also great habitat for bobcat, bear, and cougar, but the chances of seeing one of these predators deep in the woods is slim, so don't expect to see them hanging out by the road waiting for you to come along and snatch a glance.

About two-thirds of the way to the summit, I found an abundance—even an overabundance—of insect life. My windshield and face shield were covered in so much bug juice that I had to stop to remove the semi-liquid insect remains so I could see. When I stopped to clean up, I was amazed and saddened to realize that most of the insects were butterflies. As I cleaned their dead brethren off my face shield, several good-size butterflies landed on the upper edge of my windshield (if they only knew how ironic that was), handlebars, and tank. It appeared many were in various stages of courtship—which may account for their apparent lack of concern about the danger Plexiglas might pose.

I was surrounded by wildflowers galore. I'm no biologist, but summers are short at these elevations, so if you are a moth or butterfly on a warm summer day, with flowers in bloom and the opposite sex flitting about, you would make hay while the sun shined, so to speak. I feel a little bad for being the last thing many of them encountered; I'm just glad I didn't hit that convergence of nature at two or three times the speed I was traveling. Large butterflies hitting your face shield at 30 miles per hour is undoubtedly much less disturbing than it would be at 60 or 70. ●

RIDE

4

The Loneliest Highway

Directions:

southwest on UT 68 from Lehi

south on US 6 to Delta

west on US 50 to Great Basin National Park

north on US 93 to Wendover

east on I-80 to Salt Lake City

Distance:

550 to 570 miles, depending on trips into Great Basin National Park from Baker

Time:

two days or more, depending on time spent in the park

Services:

at Delta (Utah), Baker (Nevada), Ely (Nevada), and Wendover (Nevada/Utah)

Best Time of Year:

spring and fall; summer is very hot, and the national park's high elevations are not accessible in winter

Highlights:

old mining towns (and some new ones), Great Basin National Park, cheap slots at West Wendover, Bonneville Salt Flats

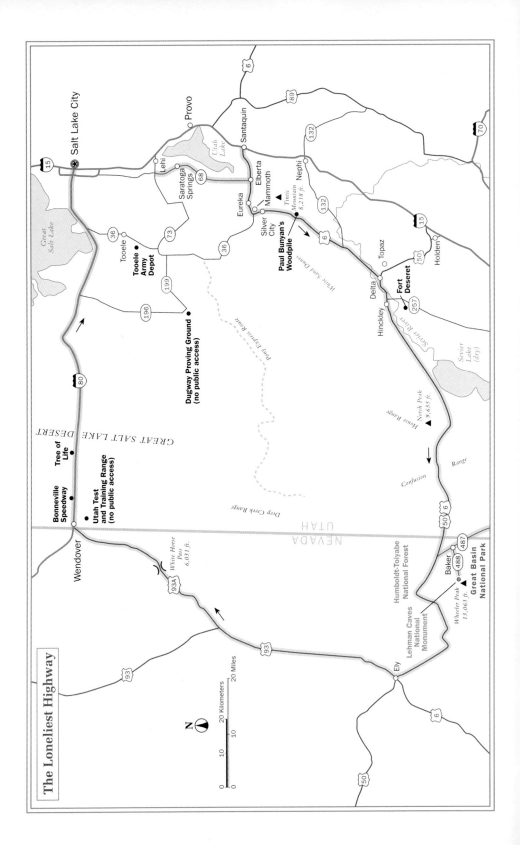

The Loneliest Highway

N

10   20 Kilometers
0
10   20 Miles
0

Salt Lake City

Provo

Santaquin

Lehi

Saratoga Springs

Utah Lake

Elberta

Eureka

Mammoth

Silver City

Tintic Mountain 8,218 ft.

Paul Bunyan's Woodpile

Tooele

Tooele Army Depot

Dugway Proving Ground (no public access)

Pony Express Route

Nephi

Topaz

Delta

Fort Deseret

Hinckley

Holden

Sevier River

Sevier Lake (dry)

Great Salt Lake

Tree of Life

Bonneville Speedway

Utah Test and Training Range (no public access)

GREAT SALT LAKE DESERT

Wendover

House Range

Notch Peak 9,655 ft.

Confusion   Range

Deep Creek Range

NEVADA
UTAH

White Horse Pass 6,031 ft.

Humboldt-Toiyabe National Forest

Baker

Great Basin National Park

Wheeler Peak 13,063 ft.

Lehman Caves National Monument

Ely

6   89   132   70   68   36   73   199   196   80   93A   93   50   15   257   487   488   6

You can reach Great Basin National Park from Las Vegas, Nevada, or Salt Lake City, Utah. Despite that, many Utah residents don't visit this isolated park just over the Nevada border and don't even really know what's there. They also might feel a little trepidation about the "Loneliest Highway," US 50, which stretches across miles of open desert with not a city in sight. That same wide-open wilderness is appealing to some of us, including many bikers. For solitude, with small rewards along the way and a big one at the end, there's nothing like this tour through the notoriously empty Great Basin.

We started off in Salt Lake City, though you could venture forth from anyplace along the Wasatch Front. We'll be heading in a generally southwestern direction toward US 50, and you have several options to get there.

You could stay on I-15 southbound until Santaquin and make a beeline westward, but we wanted to see less of the traffic

Eureka's Main Street must have been bustling once, but now it's just a sad reminder of better times gone by.

On your way through Eureka, notice the log cabin just off the main drag. This was once the home of Orrin Porter Rockwell, Mormon leader Brigham Young's notorious henchman. If you crossed him, violence was definitely a possibility. Rockwell was also the first beer maker in Utah. No doubt if he were around these days, he'd ride a Harley. ●

through Provo on I-15 and more of Utah Lake's freshwater shores, so went south on UT 68. If you're coming from the south, you can hook up with this route by getting on US 50 from I-15 at Holden.

UT 68 is a quick 65 miles per hour through desert grassland being covered over by the subdivisions of Saratoga Springs and Eagle Mountain, two of the nation's fastest-growing suburban areas. Farther south, it runs past sprawling fields and spread-out houses with hay bales, sprinkler wheels, and juniper scattered between. At Elberta (which may or may not have a working gas station), take the only major right turn heading out of town, and you'll be on US 6. Soon, the road starts to wind up into the hills toward old mining towns.

It's hard to tell now, but this region used to be full of busy boomtowns. You'll see the remnants of a few, both in the towns that still exist and in the hillsides surrounding them. A couple of them are accessible by partly paved roads.

Eureka imparts a sense both of the place's history and its current desperate situation. Most businesses and houses are boarded up. As its name suggests, this was once where people came to make their fortunes. But just as most of the gold is gone from the hills, the money didn't stay in Eureka. And all those slag piles of mining detritus have become a Superfund site. Once you know about the toxic dust swirling around, it's hard to feel inclined to stay for long. On the other hand, many of the locals are bikers and they're happy to chat.

From Eureka, UT 36 heads north toward desert land that's desolation not too far from civilization—a combination deemed suitable in the past for military forts and the Pony Express route and in the present a couple military weapons testing and demolition sites. We'll go southwest on US 6, through more old ghost towns that have mostly been denuded of anything interesting. Mining operations have recently started up again, so they might be fenced off.

You'll pass by the Little Sahara Recreation Area, packed on summer weekends with sand-loving dirt bikes and other wheeled vehicles crawling over the hills. For those of us on road bikes, it's worth a quick look from the paved entrance road.

Four or 5 miles north of Little Sahara on US 6 is the turnoff, heading east, for Paul Bunyan's woodpile (it should be signed, but thieves seem to steal the signs as soon as they get put up). A fire in 2001 also destroyed much of the vegetation and displays. But the woodpile, an uplifted section of horizontal volcanic basalt columns that look like logs, is still an interesting little side trip (don't bother if the unpaved road looks bad).

Delta, mostly a farming and ranching town, is your last stop before the desolate US 50. If you plan to proceed westward from here, you MUST fuel up in Delta. (If you decided to hit US 50 from I-15 farther south, you *must* fill up in Milford.) You will also want to load up on water and maybe snacks for the road ahead and be sure you check your tires and such. You're heading into a whole lot of nothing. Delta is home to a number of nondescript family

The people of Delta are happy to share their history and knowledge with you. For a compelling look at a sobering and sad chapter in American history, head northwest of town and follow signs for Topaz, a Japanese internment camp during World War II. And just south of town, you can prowl around remnants of Fort Deseret, whose thick mud walls could have defended the area but never really had to. For details on anything related to this whole region, stop in at the informative museum on the main drag in Delta. ●

US 50 may be the loneliest highway, but it has its share of pleasant surprises, including this rainbow east of Delta.

restaurants that are your last hot-meal options for a long time.

Soon, you're in wide-open country, on a good, fast road. There's no shade, no shelter, and no services for 80 miles. You'll see almost no other traffic (and what you will see is motorcycles). You will also see vast expanses of desert, punctuated by jagged, north-south-running mountain ranges that rise sharply up from the desert floor like the remnants of Egyptian pyramids. The whole thing starts to look surreal, with mirages appearing every now and then on the horizon. In summer temperatures here can get above 100 degrees, so this is not a good midday ride if you're bothered by the heat.

Just when you're getting really tired of the open desert, you cross the Utah/Nevada border and hang a right, following signs for Baker. Be sure to wear a helmet once you cross the border: In Nevada everyone has to wear one (riding without a helmet is one of the few risks you're not allowed to take in Nevada).

If you've followed our route, it's likely afternoon by now, so you have two options: Stay in Baker or keep going to Ely and return to visit Great Basin National Park the next day.

Despite being right outside a national park, Baker doesn't have much in the way of lodging. If you want to stay here, you'll want to make a reservation in advance. We stayed at the Whispering Elms, one of a few places resembling a motel in Baker. With a campground, RV park, and bar, it claims to have "recently remodeled rooms," but little appears to have changed since the 1970s. Try instead the Silver Jack Inn, a small, motorcycle-friendly establishment with seven guest rooms and a nice cafe attached.

Baker is oddly appealing, full of quirky artistic types who want to be close to natural beauty but away from everything else. Their work is everywhere, including lots of what they call "Post Impressionism"—whimsical handmade sculptures attached to fence posts all over town. There are also a couple surprisingly good restaurants. Every place is motorcycle friendly; they like individualists around here.

Ely is the only substantial town for hundreds of miles. It is a major ranching and mining center (the Ruth Copper Pit, just outside town, is one of the biggest open-pit mines in the world),

One example of the many odd and sometimes disturbing art pieces that dot the landscape around Baker, Nevada.

serving the vast territory around it with all the things modern people need to survive. Be sure to gas up before you leave, since there's a whole lot of nothing in all directions.

Ely has a good number of hotels, but since it's a mining town with workers coming in and out, you may want to reserve a room in advance. The stakes are high: If you don't get a room here, you have a long way to go for the next opportunity. At the national park, there is no formal lodging but lots of camping spots, which is actually your most scenic and pleasant option if you don't mind sleeping in a tent.

We're in the middle of the Great Basin, so-called because what water there is here doesn't drain into any ocean but either evaporates or disappears into the sand. Mountains popping up out of the desert are the result of cracks in the desert floor, which is actually spreading (unlike the Rockies, which were formed by tectonic plates crashing into each other). In contrast to the arid deserts all around, Great Basin National Park is an oasis of diversity. The Snake Range, with 13,063-foot Wheeler Peak in its midst, encompasses seven different subclimates, all determined by elevation.

The wood of ancient bristlecone pine trees is so dense and resinous that many of the trees will slowly erode rather than rot.

Before you embark on the scenic drive to the top of the mountain, stop in at the visitor center and see if you need to make a reservation for a tour through Lehman Caves. Full of strange rock formations, the caves are pretty interesting, and you might as well see them while you're

If you have some time and want to explore, you could visit the Wendover Airport (take a left, or south, turn off the main strip just across the state border in Utah), formerly Wendover Air Force Base. A small museum commemorates the former military base's role as the site where pilots practiced to drop atomic bombs during World War II. ●

here. At 50 degrees and 90 percent humidity year-round, they are also a reliable respite from the heat outside. Tours do fill up during busy times.

The winding road up the mountain is a fun ride, with lots of pullouts offering expansive views over the mountains and deserts below. Even if it's 90-plus degrees at the bottom, you might want to bring a jacket, since it'll be a lot cooler at the top. You start off with sagebrushes, then go through piñon pines, mountain mahoganies, aspens, and evergreens. The drive tops off at 10,000 feet. If you can handle it (and have brought some hiking shoes along), take one of several one- or two-hour hikes up from here to discover the mysterious bristlecone pine, which can live 3,000 years or more. If you do the main 2-mile bristlecone hike, take your time at this altitude, which can literally steal your breath away. Also, keep an eye on the sky and head back if storm clouds roll in.

There are a number of unpaved roads in the park, all of which could be in decent or questionable condition. If you're in the mood to try one of them, check in at the visitor center and ask about conditions.

You could return to Salt Lake City on US 50 (US 50 westward crosses Nevada, through more desolate territory). We wanted to head back via the gambling border town of Wendover, on I-80 to the north, so we took US 93 north from Ely. It's a slab of straight pavement along a desert floor with few people, no vegetation, constant wind, scorching heat, and toxic slag piles as far as the eye can see. We don't recommend it. Most people will go to

Fully clad in black leather, a rider awaits her turn to try for a record during Speed Week on the Bonneville Salt Flats.

Wendover via I-80, making it a day or overnight trip.

Wendover is a small town right on the Utah border (there are actually two towns, Wendover, Utah, and West Wendover, Nevada). West Wendover is where Mormons come to gamble, and that description says it all. It's a welcome change from the mind-numbing desert and a place to play some low-ante card games or nickel slots and eat a not-quite-Vegas buffet. You won't be alone as a biker out here; you'll see plenty of fellow touring aficionados along I-80.

The most interesting thing about the ride through the west desert on I-80 is the Bonneville Salt Flats, which really are something. White plains with purple mountains around their perimeter stretch out under skies that are almost always bright blue. It's a great place to take pictures. You can even ride on it a little if you want (the entrance to the Bonneville Speedway, where Speed Week races are held every August, is near Wendover). If you do, plan to wash the salt off your bike as soon as possible.

I-80 is straight and fast all the way back to Salt Lake City. Be careful: There are a lot of accidents along this stretch, most of them caused by drowsy or aggressive drivers. That giant sculpture you see on the north side of I-80, 25 miles east of Wendover, is *Metaphor: A Tree of Life*. Now a little decrepit, the 87-foot-high cement sculpture was originally created in the 1980s by Swedish artist Karl Momen, who financed it himself as an unexpected gift to the people of Utah.

SOUTHERN UTAH

Southern Utah contains some of the best riding in the country as well as some of the world's most scenic territory, thanks to five national parks—Bryce Canyon, Zion, Capitol Reef, Arches, and Canyonlands—plus a handful of national monuments and Utah's share of Monument Valley Navajo Tribal Park. Even when these special places are overwhelmed with tourists, southern Utah offers many ways to find solitude, and that appeals to a whole different crowd. Go to southern Utah to find some of the most remarkable places on Earth—or to find yourself.

The southern Utah desert holds a special place in the hearts of many who live in the Southwest. You must spend time exploring and uncovering this place to truly appreciate its special gifts. If you only have time to pass through, you will only get a small sense of what is distinctive about it. If you have the time and desire, find a location that speaks to you, get off your bike, and go explore. You will be amazed at the discoveries you make about what you thought the desert is, or should be.

Civilization generally arises when you need it but of all the regions we cover in this book, southern Utah is the shortest on great hangouts and has perhaps a greater distance between them than in any other area besides Nevada. We will try to point them out where they exist (sometimes in unexpected places) but in general, you're here for the roads and the scenery.

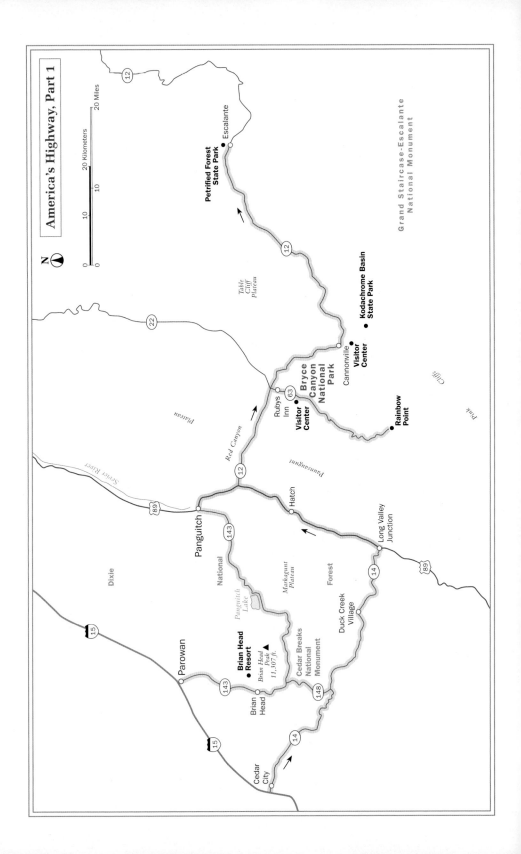

America's Highway, Part 1

N

0 10 20 Kilometers
0 10 20 Miles

12

Petrified Forest
State Park

Escalante

12

Grand Staircase-Escalante
National Monument

Table
Cliff
Plateau

22

Kodachrome Basin
State Park

Sevier River

Visitor
Center

Cannonville

Bryce
Canyon
National
Park

Rubys
Inn

63

Plateau

Visitor
Center

Red Canyon

Rainbow
Point

12

Paunsaugunt

Pink
Cliffs

89

Panguitch

Hatch

12

143

Long Valley
Junction

Dixie

National

Markagunt
Plateau

Panguitch
Lake

14

89

Forest

Duck Creek
Village

15

Parowan

Brian Head
Resort

Brian Head
Peak
11,307 ft.

Cedar Breaks
National
Monument

148

143

Brian Head

14

15

Cedar
City

RIDE
5

America's Highway, Part 1

Directions:
east on UT 14 from Cedar City to Long Valley Junction
north on US 89 to junction with UT 12
east on UT 12

Distance:
from Cedar City to UT 12/US 89 intersection: 40 miles
from UT 12/US 89 intersection to Bryce Canyon National
Park: 17 miles
from UT 12/US 89 intersection to Escalante: 45 miles

Time:
a full day

Services:
at Cedar City, Panguitch, Hatch, Bryce Canyon, Cannonville,
and Escalante

Best Time of Year:
late May through early October; snow can accumulate at
the many high-elevation areas on this ride as late as June
and as early as September, so check in advance

Highlights:
Cedar Breaks National Monument, Markagunt Plateau,
Bryce Canyon National Park, Grand Staircase-Escalante
National Monument

Some rides in the Southwest are about the roads—the curves, bends, twisties, or wide-open screamers, call them what you will. Other rides are about the scenery—the cliffs, forests, deserts, or canyons. Still others have history going back hundreds, thousands, even millions of years. Very few of them pack all three into such a relatively short stretch of pavement as America's Highway, UT 12.

UT 12 is also called the Most Scenic Road in America and America's Road, and it runs through an area that deserves more time and attention than most people give it. This is some of the world's most spectacular country, and if you are passing through this region, UT 12 is a must-do ride. It is certainly worthy of a detour no matter your ultimate destination. There's so much going on, we've divided it up into two rides (see ride 6), though you can't really do one and not the other.

Home base for this ride depends on where you are and where you're headed. This is primarily a one-way ride from point A to B and points beyond, not a loop, but it could be (returning to US 89 after Torrey, for example) depending on where you want to end up. It doesn't matter whether you come down from the north or up from the south; you are in for a treat. Either way, you should allow for at least a couple days to see all the national parks and monuments on both this ride and ride 6.

Home to Southern Utah University, Cedar City is a medium-size college town with a few decent restaurants and coffee shops as well as a slew of inexpensive motels. For our purposes, it's the start of a long and wonderful ride through some of the Southwest's best roads. Head east from Main Street on UT 14, which goes into a canyon and soon starts to climb. The road gets steeper and steeper into switchbacks that cover a lot of elevation in a short time, giving you views of verdant mountain slopes and, eventually, the red rocks of Cedar Breaks National Monument. In early summer, waterfalls cascade down the mountainside's steep slopes and wildflowers pop out everywhere.

Because it's a principal route to the other side of the Markagunt Plateau, which divides the Great Basin valley below from the beauty that awaits on the other side, the road is generally well maintained, although you could encounter some debris after bad weather. You may also have to deal with RVs chugging up the mountain, but passing lanes at regular intervals should help you zip past them.

To get to Cedar Breaks, a short must-do side trip, follow the signs and make the jaunt north on UT 148. Another option to get here is to take UT 143 from Parowan, a small town a half-hour north of Cedar City on I-15. That road is shorter than UT 14, even steeper, and with some of the tightest switchbacks you'll anywhere. It reaches the mountaintop at Brian Head Resort, a small, old-fashioned ski resort that tops out at 11,000 feet. This road, too, connects with UT 148.

UT 148 is a fairly narrow two-lane road along the top of the plateau through beautiful high-alpine meadows flanked by evergreen trees. Cedar Breaks is a smaller version of the red-rock hoodoos and carved-out valleys of Bryce Canyon National Park, with views of the Great Basin valley beyond to boot. Overlooks are only a short walk from the pullouts.

UT 14 peaks out a little over 10,300 feet above sea level. From Cedar Breaks, you have several options, all of which are official scenic byways. You could continue to take UT 143 from Brian Head over the plateau to Panguitch. Or you could go back to UT 14 and take it the same direction but a little to the south, ending up at Hatch. They're both two-lane highways with nice scenery, and you should do both sometime if you can. In fact, you could do all of the roads we've just mentioned as a 123-mile loop.

We take UT 14, which wins out over UT 143 only because its scenery is slightly more dramatic. If you take UT 143, you'll go past more rolling meadows and Panguitch Lake before reaching US 89. UT 14 descends a bit into Long Valley, which is full of the lava-flow remnants that serve as reminders of this area's volcanic past. The cabins and shops of Duck Creek Village, a spot of privately owned vacation land in the middle of national forest, pop suddenly out of the forest and disappear almost as quickly (unless you need a break from riding through nature and stop).

The sun sets over Panguitch Lake, just off UT 143 northeast of Cedar Breaks National Monument.

The road's gradual curves and lush surroundings make this a relaxing section between attractions.

UT 14 empties out at Long Valley Junction, one of many small towns along US 89 where the road parallels the Sevier River. From here, you start to see views of colorful cliffs off to the distance; you'll be there soon.

Our goal is the legendary UT 12, the turn for which is about 13 miles north of Hatch. Finally!

Shortly after turning onto UT 12, you'll go through scenic (and aptly named) Red Canyon, its dark green pines juxtaposed against bright canyon walls, then climb to the Paunsaugunt Plateau on your way to Bryce Canyon National Park. The park is named after Ebenezer Bryce, one of the area's early pioneers. Don't be put off by the relatively small scale of the entrance; this isn't a massive, in-your-face national park.

Enjoy Bryce Canyon from the lookouts along its scenic drive, which is 32 miles round-trip. The park's most famous views are from the rim, which rises above a giant amphitheater filled with pink and orange rock formations and surrounded by towering

UT 14 climbs through aspens and evergreens toward the red rocks of Cedar Breaks National Monument.

pine trees. Some folks say that to really appreciate the drama and scale of the geography, you must immerse yourself in it. There are about 60 miles of trails in the park, so go for it if you have the time, gear, and inclination.

Steve: I made my way out to Bryce Point, at an elevation of 8,300 feet, and worked my way back, stopping at Inspiration Point with additional stops at Sunset and Sunrise Points. If you don't have the time or energy to hike, I suggest stopping by the visitor center to view the large-format photography of Frank Sirona. It might seem a bit odd to be viewing photographs of the very park in which you happen to be standing, but this display of stunning photographs will provide a level of detail that you will most likely only experience if you spend time hiking among the hoodoos and exploring the park on an up-close-and-personal level. ●

A summer storm creates dramatic light on the hoodoos at Inspiration Point in Bryce Canyon National Park.

After leaving Bryce Canyon, you'll continue toward Grand Staircase-Escalante National Monument on a road that starts dropping into drier territory. You will pass through several small farming and ranching towns. There isn't much going on in any of them, though Cannonville is the turnoff point for Kodachrome Basin State Park, named for the colors in its sandstone chimneys (if you have a dirty mind, one or two of them will look like, well, something familiar). The state park, worth a short detour if you have time to spare, is at the end of a short paved road.

Because of its size (1.9 million acres) and the fact that it was created on land locals saw as having potential for development or ranching rather than tourism and preservation, the national monument has been controversial in rural Utah since its creation by President Bill Clinton in 1996. (Adding insult to injury, the declaration ceremony was held at Grand Canyon National Park in Arizona.) Stop at the Bureau of Land Management (BLM) office in Cannonville for information from the people who manage this massive chunk of southern Utah. The map there shows several roads intersecting UT 12 that head into the national monument

Steve: According to a woman giving information at the BLM office in Cannonville, if I intended to take any of the main unpaved roads into Grand Staircase-Escalante National Monument, I would need a bike with "attitude"—by which she meant a full-on dirt bike. She explained that the roads are a mix of dirt, sand, rocks, and bentonite clay. Bentonite is hard as cement when baked by the sun but becomes slippery as snot when it gets wet. The area had been getting a lot of rain from summer monsoons, so some roads were impassable.

For a little adventure, she suggested the Burr Trail out of Boulder. It's about 75 miles long; about the first 30 miles are paved and the rest sometimes passable, depending on the weather. The Burr Trail cuts across the Waterpocket Fold of Capitol Reef National Park. If you are lucky enough to make it the entire 75 miles, you will eventually end up back on pavement at UT 276 just north of Lake Powell's Bullfrog Marina.

I decided to see what it was like, with no intention of traveling the full 75 miles. If UT 12 is the civilized, well-groomed, polite member of the family, the Burr Trail is the rude and unruly stepbrother. The asphalt was rough with lots of potholes, the shoulders were just barely finished, and plenty of sand was washed across the road in some of the corners. The beautiful scenery rivals some of what you'll see on UT 12, but don't expect any paved overlooks. This was asphalt where it seemed somehow unnatural and out of place. If you do plan to take the Burr Trail for the full 75 miles, check with the local BLM office or the ranger station in Boulder for updated road conditions—and good luck. ●

Narrow slot canyons like this one carve their way through Grand Staircase-Escalante National Monument.

and might allow you to do a little exploring. A word of caution if you plan to attempt any backcountry riding: It's probably not a good idea for a road-bike rider to tackle most of the unpaved roads that enter the monument from UT 12, including Hole in the Rock Road. They are remote and conditions can deteriorate quickly.

Continue on toward the town of Escalante. It's not much but it does have a few hotels and an increasingly diverse cultural scene, so it's your best bet if you want to stop for the night before heading on to Torrey. If you do stick around a while, take some time and walk the path through chunks of ancient wood at Petrified Forest State Park, just north of town. If you've made it this far with a few hours of daylight to spare, feel free to continue on. Either way, this ride connects with ride 6, the second half of America's Highway.

RIDE

6

America's Highway, Part 2

Directions:
northeast on UT 12 from Escalante to Torrey
east on UT 24 from Torrey to Hanksville
north on UT 24 from Hanksville to Goblin Valley

Distance:
from Escalante to Torrey: 55 miles
from Boulder to Torrey: 36 miles
from Torrey to Hanksville: 47 miles
from Hanksville to Goblin Valley State Park: 12 miles
from Hanksville to Green River: 57 miles

Time:
at least one full day

Services:
at Escalante, Boulder (limited lodging), Torrey, and
Hanksville

Best Time of Year:
late May to early October

Highlights:
riding along the flank of stately Boulder Mountain, dramatic
changes in landscape, Capitol Reef National Park, Goblin
Valley State Park

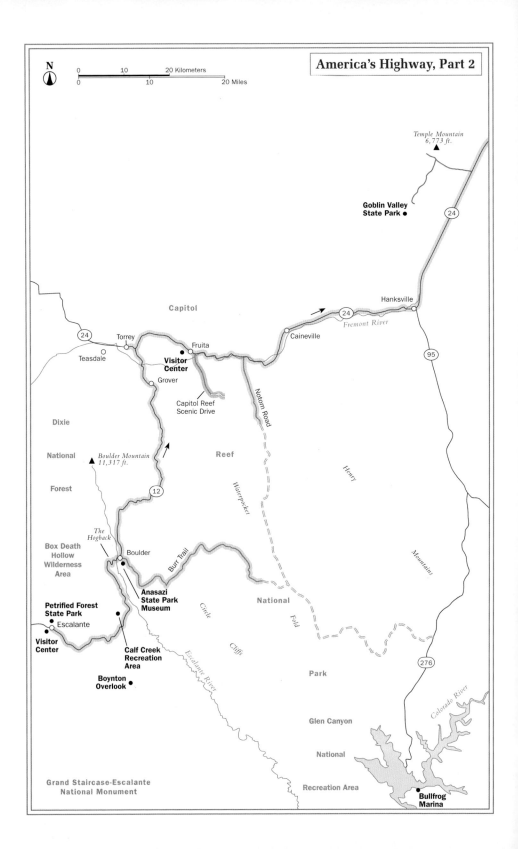

N

0   10   20 Kilometers

0   10   20 Miles

Temple Mountain
6,773 ft.

**Goblin Valley
State Park** ●

24

Hanksville

Capitol

24

24 Torrey
Teasdale

Fruita
Caineville

Fremont River

95

**Visitor
Center**

Grover

*Capitol Reef
Scenic Drive*

Notom Road

Dixie

National

Boulder Mountain
▲ *11,317 ft.*

Reef

Waterpocket

Henry

Forest

12

*The
Hogback*

**Box Death
Hollow
Wilderness
Area**

Boulder

Burr Trail

Mountains

**Anasazi
State Park
Museum**

Circle

National

Fold

**Petrified Forest
State Park**

●

Escalante

Cliffs

**Visitor
Center**

**Calf Creek
Recreation
Area**

Escalante River

276

**Boynton
Overlook** ●

Park

Colorado River

Glen Canyon

National

**Grand Staircase-Escalante
National Monument**

Recreation Area

●**Bullfrog
Marina**

Much of central southern Utah's best scenery is right off one road, America's Highway (UT 12), considered by some to be the most scenic highway in the country. While you are riding and gawking and oohing and aaahing, remind yourself that this road was not accessible to bikes until fairly recently. The highway, which was not even completely paved until the 1980s, is still somewhat off the beaten path. Despite all it has to offer, it is relatively little known, even in Utah.

This ride starts where ride 5 ends, in Escalante. About 10 miles past Escalante, you will come around a bend in the road and encounter Head of the Rocks. There are a couple of big pullouts and several overlooks just below the lip of the rim. It's worth getting off the bike and taking in the surreal look of pavement that seems to carve its way through and over the slickrock. About 4 miles farther, you reach Boynton Overlook, providing a view of the Escalante River Gorge near its confluence with Calf Creek. Displays tell the history of what you're seeing. Calf Creek Recreation Area, with its popular hike to beautiful Lower Calf Creek Falls, is about a mile and a half beyond the overlook.

The Head of the Rocks Overlook on UT 12 offers expansive views of the Henry Mountains and the Escalante basin.

Steve: Access the hike to Lower Calf Creek Falls via the Calf Creek Recreation Area campground. If you want to do the hike, wear comfortable shoes and lightweight clothing and bring lots of water. Pick up an interpretive guide at the campground. Matching with numbered posts along the path, the guide describes history, vegetation, and Native American ruins and pictographs you can easily miss unless you know where to look and what to look for. The 3-mile (each way) hike through a canyon to the falls is relatively easy, with little elevation gain. The most difficult part is the deep sand you will encounter along the way.

On the hike to the falls, I encountered families with school-age children, groups of teens, someone running the entire trail, and a trio of overweight folks who were flushed and breathing heavily while resting in what little shade they could find. I think they had one quart of water among them. I know this group didn't make it to the falls, so I can only assume they made it back to their car or campsite. It is sometimes startling how many people enter the wilderness or backcountry utterly unprepared for what nature might have in store.

You will feel moisture and hear the waterfall before you see it. The falls and the large pool of cool, clear water at its base are a much-appreciated respite from the heat of the desert. Put your things down at the base of a tree, take a dip, relax, look around, and stay a while. Remind yourself that you are in the heart of the Southern Utah desert in the summer. Amazing! ●

It's a short 12 miles from Calf Creek to the town of Boulder. The road climbs out of the canyon up to the Haymaker Bench and crosses the Hogback, where it tops the twisty ridgeline. At times, the ridge narrows to almost the width of the road. There are some pretty steep and nasty drop-offs on both sides. Watch out for cars and trucks coming at you from the north; drivers are entering a dramatically different landscape from the one they just left and may pay more attention to the scenery than the road. If you are so inclined, check out a couple of narrow unpaved viewpoints and pullouts, but use caution since some of them drop 4 to 6 inches from the pavement.

Coming off the ridge, you get a view from above into Boulder, one of the state's most beautiful locales. Sprawling farms and ranches lie in a broad valley surrounded by colorful rocks and hills, with the massive tree-covered pla-

The hike to Lower Calf Creek Falls is a relatively easy 6 miles round-trip.

teau of Boulder Mountain rising to the north. The town offers a couple restaurants and gas stations but not much lodging. It is also the site of Anasazi State Park Museum, once the site of one of the area's largest ancient settlements.

From Boulder north, UT 12 climbs into Dixie National Forest and meanders its way across the side of Boulder Mountain. The 36 miles from Boulder to Torrey could hardly be more different from the 80 miles or so you just came through. The road climbs quickly into high alpine terrain. Boulder Mountain rises 11,317 feet above sea level and the highway reaches an elevation of 9,600 feet before beginning its descent into the town of Torrey.

The road is in good shape but the curves on the north side tend to be pretty flat, so watch your speed. The mountain is open range and great deer and elk habitat—more reasons to be alert. Stop off at one or two of the many pullouts along the way for views all

A large and diverse population of wildlife thrives in the Dixie National Forest around Boulder and Torrey.

the way to Canyonlands National Park and beyond. You can see geography on a grand scale from here as the land slopes gently downhill, carved up by canyons to the Colorado River drainage.

Torrey is the gateway to Capitol Reef National Park, and it offers the full array of services. This is an increasingly popular choice for vacation homes as well as tourists, which may explain the number of good restaurants. Some fans consider Café Diablo one of the best in the state; for good, less-expensive food, try the Rim Rock Restaurant on the east side of town. From Torrey, hit UT 24 to Capitol Reef National Park.

UT 24 dissects the park from east to west, while the park runs north to south, which means you could almost ride right through and not really be sure why it's a national park. But if you get off the highway and start exploring, you will quickly recognize the beauty and significance of this natural wonder.

The park was created around the Waterpocket Fold, a 100-mile-long wrinkle in the earth's surface that starts north of here at Thousand Lakes Mountain and goes all the way to Lake Powell. If you are lucky enough to hike into the backcountry and reach the edge of an uplift, it will look as if the hand of God is breaking and peeling back the earth's crust. There is some great day hiking, with easy access to a beautiful panel of rock art just off the highway about a mile and a half east of the visitor center as well as Hickman Bridge, a natural bridge at the end of a moderately difficult hike that's 2 miles round-trip.

Even if you don't hike, you can get an idea of the park's grandeur via a couple short paved roads. Scenic Drive is 10 miles long, with short spurs into Grand Valley Wash and Capitol Gorge. Pick up a brochure explaining the sights along the ride. The wash is a narrowing canyon with Cassidy Arch (named for outlaw Butch Cassidy,

One of many red-rock slot canyons around Capitol Reef National Park.

who used many remote canyons around here as refuge from the law) at the end of a short hike.

The Capitol Gorge spur is a 2.2-mile narrow road that might occasionally be sandy (check at the visitor center). But it's worth the ride: The gorge is a narrow wash that was once used as a through road between here and the other side of the fold. Visitors can walk into the narrows and see rock art left by ancient people as well as more recent explorers. The tour brochure warns, "As wagonmasters did a century ago, carefully consider the weather before you proceed into the gorge." Rain even a hundred miles away can cause flash floods down below.

On the eastern end of the park, Notom Road is paved for the first 5 miles and gives wide-open views of the fold.

Christy pretends to push over one of the hoodoos at Goblin Valley State Park. Do not damage or destroy any of these wonderful formations!

UT 24 continues on to Hanksville and Green River. Whether you hit UT 24 from the Bicentennial Highway (see ride 9), Green River (see ride 7), or this one, be sure to stop at Goblin Valley State Park. The roads are in excellent condition all the way. A recent upgrade added new toilets, showers, and picnic areas.

Walk out to the main overlook at the end of the paved road to see why this is one of our favorite state parks. A valley is filled with bright orange-red rock formations, or hoodoos, that seem to sprout upright from the sandy bottom. Walking trails meander through them. Warning: In the summer, there is no shade and no water at the hoodoos themselves, so bring plenty to drink. There's a small admission fee (half price for motorcycles).

Just north of the park proper, the paved entry road makes a sharp curve, while a packed-dirt road continues westward through a sagebrush-filled valley up to the edge of the San Rafael Swell, a huge geologic uplift (those jutting crests of striped rock you see along I-70 are part of it). The road goes to Temple Mountain and the trailhead for Little Wildhorse and Bell Canyons, popular slot canyons (so named because they at times become nothing more than narrow slots). This fairly demanding loop hike takes about four hours. Still, it's one of the more accessible true slot-canyon experiences. Bring water! There is none on the hike and you'll need a lot.

The road is sealed dirt and any bike could handle it (double-check conditions if it has just rained) until after the slot canyon parking area. The Temple Mountain road is short and mostly paved, although it gets a bit rough as you reach the mountain and a ghost town where you can still see remnants of mines and the company town. Past here, the road is for ORVs and SUVs only.

RIDE

7

Arches and Canyons

Directions:

I-70 to US 191 to Moab

UT 313 to Canyonlands and Island in the Sky

UT 128 from Moab to Cisco (ghost town) and I-70

La Sal Scenic Mountain Loop from south of Moab to Castle Valley Road and UT 128

US 191 south to junction with UT 211 and south entrance to Canyonlands

Distance:

from Crescent Junction intersection (I-70) to Moab: 45 miles

from Moab to Arches National Park Visitor Center: 5 miles

from Moab to north Canyonlands entrance: 9 miles

from Moab to south Canyonlands entrance : 39 miles

from Moab to Dead Horse Point State Park: 32 miles

from Moab to Cisco (UT 128 ride): 37 miles

Time:

at least a day, more if you plan to do all the rides in this area and/or explore

Services:

at Green River, Moab, and Monticello

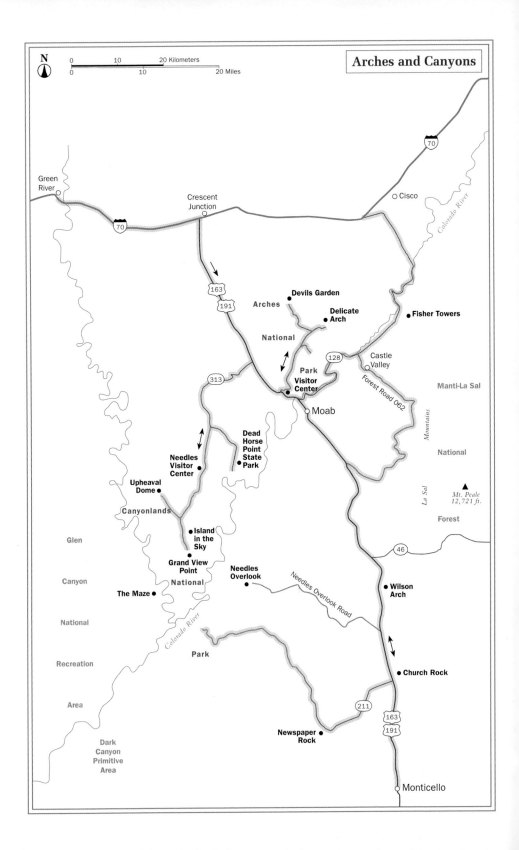

Best Time of Year:
spring and fall, though summer is not too bad

Highlights:
Arches and Canyonlands national parks, a rolling road
along the base of the La Sal Mountains, the Colorado River

Southeastern Utah is home to some of the most unique and spectacular scenery anywhere. Two national parks, Arches and Canyonlands, make for easy out-and-back rides offering short hikes to dramatic red-rock formations. The mountains, canyons, and rivers that dominate the landscape also serve as barriers, making large day-ride loops difficult to design. But possibilities for combining shorter rides are nearly endless—and welcoming and well-equipped towns keep you fed, housed, and maybe even entertained when you're not riding.

Once a uranium mining boomtown, Moab is booming again thanks mostly to tourism. With its sights and recreational opportunities, it draws huge crowds on some weekends, especially in spring and fall, when it's relatively cool. It's especially favored by off-roaders, mountain bikers (it's home to the world-famous

Steve: If you're riding from the north via US 6 and US 191, use caution and stay alert: This road can be dangerous in either direction. It's a major truck route, with traffic bunching up behind all manner of large vehicles (including semi-trailers, RVs, and pickups hauling ATVs). When there is an opening to pass, several vehicles go at once. The road is in good shape but constantly under construction in one place or another. When I ride or drive it, I like to get myself out of traffic "wolf packs" and ride independently or with other bikes. ●

Swasey's Beach is a short ride north from downtown Green River and a soothing way to end a long, hot day on the bike.

Slickrock Trail), and hikers, but you will also see plenty of motorcycles on Main Street.

Moab also has some of the best restaurants in southern Utah, which is a nice bonus. With all that to offer, it can become crowded, which can make finding last-minute lodgings difficult. You should be able to find an inexpensive room in Green River if Moab is booked.

Green River is a biker-friendly and welcoming, if less-refined, alternative to Moab. It's central to southern Utah climbing, rafting, hiking, and geode hunting and is surrounded by ATV and SUV trails as well as miles of paved and gravel roads. Hook up with the Green River Motorcycle Club or at least consider grabbing a copy of the *San Rafael Motorized Route* map, which covers everything from paved roads to dirt-bike trails. (Unpaved roads tend to get sandy quickly, making them impassable for anything but all-out dirt bikes.)

Green River is also home to a number of locally owned businesses, including biker-friendly Ray's Tavern—which serves some of the best burgers in the state—and the Green River Coffee Company (good for breakfast), whose owners also ride. Don't miss the Green River Melon Days festival in September. The John Wesley Powell River History Museum, in the middle of town on the main drag, offers exhibitions and information about this area.

From Green River, you can head southwest on UT 24 toward Hanksville and the Bicentennial Highway (see ride 9), but we go southeast on US 191 to Moab. US 191 is one of those roads you get to know well if you do any touring in this area, since it cuts through eastern Utah and keeps going all the way through Arizona to the Mexican border, passing through landscapes both arid and mountainous.

To get to Utah's southeastern corner, jog east on I-70 at Green River and pick up US 191 at Crescent Junction. Riding the gently curving descent into Moab, you get an idea why it's renowned for its scenery: Even without leaving the road, you get an eyeful. Even better sights are close by.

Entrances for Arches and Canyonlands national parks are just north of Moab, so you may want to stop before you hit town. That might not be wise if you're hoping for a hotel room and don't have a reservation. You may want to check in and possibly put on some comfortable shoes, then retrace US 191 a short distance to the parks.

Arches is hard to beat in the sights-per-mile category, and the ease with which you can see its best attractions makes it a must in this area (entrance fee for motorcycles is $5, a bargain). The undulating two-lane desert roads through the park total about 20 miles or so, with some of the park's famous rock formations visible from

Tourists flock to Delicate Arch to get a shot of its brilliant red rock right at dusk.

the road. Closer looks are often just short, easy walks from pull-outs or parking lots.

The park contains an astonishing 2,000 natural stone arches, including Delicate Arch, which is featured on Utah license plates. Getting to the arch itself requires a fairly steep 3-mile hike. If you want to see it up close, bring good shoes and lots of water. Natural arches are scattered all over the Southwest, but nowhere in the world are they as plentiful as they are here.

Now, on to Canyonlands National Park, a huge swath of undeveloped, government-owned land left in something close to its natural state. Paved roads only touch on the edges but the views from the road give you an idea of what's beyond.

The Colorado River and its tributaries divide Canyonlands into its three main districts: Island in the Sky, the Needles, and the Maze. Two main entrances take you to different parts of the park. The most easily accessible of these is the Island in the Sky, north of Arches. Here, you have to get off the bike, walk a bit to

---

A deep salt bed called the Paradox Formation, originally deposited over 300 million years ago when the region was covered with water that eventually evaporated, lies under this area. Over the ensuing centuries, floods and wind laid sand and debris on top of the salt, eventually hardening and compressing into a thick layer of rock.

The unstable salt bed began to move under the weight of the overlying stone. That, in turn, shifted the surface rock, thrusting it up into domes or dropping it into crevasses, where it landed vertically. Erosion stripped away some of the rock, leaving upright fins, then chunks broke off the rocks and sometimes created openings in them.

It took millions of years to create these formations and the process is still going on. In 2008 one of the park's larger arches, Wall Arch, collapsed suddenly in the middle of the night. ●

The Colorado River winds and grinds its way through Canyonlands National Park.

the overlooks, and gaze out over the edge to get an idea what makes the place special. As the name suggests, Canyonlands is full of, well, canyons, as rivers running through the Colorado Plateau drain into the Colorado River, creating seemingly endless red-rock panoramas.

Although not part of Canyonlands, Dead Horse Point State Park might as well be. It's a short and rewarding ride branching off from the Canyonlands entrance road (UT 313) that takes you to yet another grand vista, this time from the top of a mesa surrounded on three sides by sheer cliffs. The Colorado River flows 2,000 feet below. (The story behind the name is that someone fenced off a group of horses on top of the mesa, where, unable to escape to find food or water, they died.) If you plan it right, Island in the Sky and Dead Horse Point State Park are great in the early morning or late in the evening, when shadows make the canyons here even more dramatic.

Before introducing you to the south entrance of Canyonlands, we'd like to suggest another couple rides in the Moab area. For an alternative route into or out of Moab, try UT 128, an official

This roadside distraction a few miles south of Moab is a 5,000 square foot home carved out of a huge rock.

scenic byway that follows the Colorado River before rejoining I-70. This is the only place where a road runs alongside the river as it cuts through the Colorado Plateau. If you're planning to move on to Colorado, it's a great way to escape the interstate, see some lovely scenery, and ride a refreshing road that bends itself into sweeping curves at the base of red-rock cliffs. And, at only 44 miles long, it won't cost you time if you're already headed east.

Stop off at Fisher Towers, about 30 miles from Moab and at the end of a well-maintained mile-long dirt road. These vertical rock formations are so red, almost purple, that they stand out even in a land of brightly colored rock. The highway leaves the river and heads into wide-open desert, ending at Cisco (a ghost town with no services) and the junction with I-70.

UT 128 can also be part of a longer loop incorporating the La Sal Scenic Mountain Loop. This road hugs the flanks of the 12,000-foot-plus La Sal Mountains, which rise incongruously out of the red rock. This is an especially good ride if you've just spent a few days in hot desert and want a change of scenery and temperature. The turnoffs can be a little hard to find. From UT 128, take Castle Valley Road, 18 miles from Moab. From the south, the turnoff from UT 191 is six miles south of Moab. Either way, follow signs for FR 062.

The La Sal loop carries you up from desert floor onto alpine slopes covered in evergreens and aspens. The road is paved all the way but the surface is occasionally rough, with some serious switchbacks, so maintain speed accordingly.

Back to Canyonlands National Park. If you're planning to head south from Moab anyway, you might want to take the south entrance to Canyonlands as a detour on that ride rather than have to backtrack to Moab. On the way, you'll see Hole N" The Rock (with its inexplicable punctuation) carved out of a rock wall near Wilson Arch, which is conveniently located right off the side of UT 191. About 32 miles south of Moab, you will also pass the Needles Overlook Road, a paved road, 16 miles each way, to a vista looking out over the southern section of the park.

The south Canyonlands entrance, which takes you into the park's Needles District, is at the end of a 34-mile road (UT 211) that leaves UT 191 about 50 miles south of Moab. The road, which divides and ends at a couple viewpoints looking up at canyon walls rather than down into them, is an official scenic byway and well worth doing, although the view at the end is not quite as spectacular as those in the northern section. The gently curving road runs through meadows and valleys bordered by imposing cliffs. One of those cliffs is the site of Newspaper Rock, just off the road. The 50-foot-high rock face covered in ancient art is one of the most visited and photographed panels in the region.

Steve: On a ride from Park City to Cortez, I was headed south on UT 191 just south of Moab one early morning when I was well rested and alert. It was a gorgeous morning, with the sun relatively low in the sky. I had the sudden realization that this stretch of UT 191 is perhaps one of the great motorcycle roads in this part of the Utah, if not the region, with red rock that creeps all the way to the edge of the road and big winding turns that rise and fall with the terrain it cuts through. I saw incredible views of tall mountains lounging in the distance; slickrock of all shapes and sizes; and huge, wide-open desert vistas around any given turn. It is a road I have traveled many times, but until this particular day on this particular ride I hadn't really appreciated the beauty of the surroundings. It was eye- and mind-opening, reminding me to look at things with fresh eyes and an open mind. I think it may have influenced everything else on the rest of that trip. ●

RIDE

8

Zion and Environs

Directions:
north on I-15 from St. George to UT 9
east on UT 9 to Mount Carmel Junction
south on US 89 from Mount Carmel Junction to Kanab
west on AZ 389 and UT 59

Distance:
about 175 miles

Time:
half a day or more, depending on how long you take to see
the sights

Services:
St. George, Hurricane, Springdale, Kanab, Colorado City,
and Hildale

Best Time of Year:
early spring to late fall; summer in the lower elevations can
be hot

Highlights:
wide-open red-rock territory, Zion National Park's cliffs and
canyons, one-of-a-kind small towns

We'll do this ride as a loop from St. George, just one of many options for ways to see this region. You could also get here via US 89 northbound from Arizona (see ride 19) or leave this ride heading north toward Bryce Canyon or Capitol Reef national parks (see rides 5 and 6).

St. George is a booming little city most people either retire to or pass through on the way to Las Vegas. In the summertime, it feels like an oven, with temperatures regularly above the 100-degree mark, and there's not much to do in town unless you're Mormon or want to see church historical sites. It's also not a great place to get a gourmet meal or a drink. Some prefer to stay in Mesquite, an hour south just across the Nevada border along

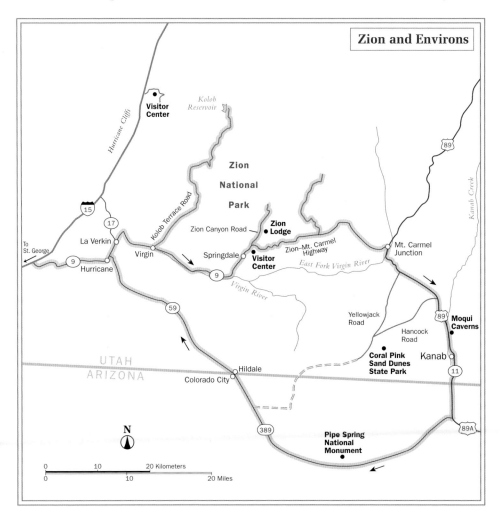

Zion and Environs

I-15. Like West Wendover to the north, Mesquite exists only to provide the people of Utah with a chance to do some gambling and buy cheap booze. The highway between St. George and Mesquite is remote, fast, and twisty.

Zion National Park is about 40 miles from St. George. There are actually three entrances to the park. The northernmost is just off I-15 north of St. George and takes you to the Kolob Canyons section of the park, which is not connected by road to the rest of Zion. If you're on I-15 anyway, take exit 40 to the north entrance, an in-and-back 5 miles each way offering great views—especially in the evening, when diagonal sunlight hits the red-rock cliffs.

The second entrance takes you to another fairly quiet section of the park via Kolob Terrace Road, which branches off to the north from UT 9 at the town of Virgin, about 10 miles west of the main entrance. This is a narrow two-lane road, with a few twisty sections, that tops out on a plateau high above the park. From several pullouts along the road, you can see a top-down view of the canyons most people see from the bottom up. The road eventually switches to gravel at Kolob Reservoir. On a good day it's possible to follow that gravel road all the way to Cedar City and UT 14 (see ride 5) through aspen trees and meadows along the top of a high plateau, but only if the road is in good condition all the way. If you're really serious, ask at a ranger station before you go.

Steve: We bought our Buell Ulysses in St. George from the Harley-Davidson. The day I picked up the bike was the weekend of the big Laughlin River Run rally, so the highway was full of bikes, lots of them stopping in at the dealership. It's a very nice, friendly place—it even has a barbecue every Saturday during the summer. This was the end of April and the place was packed with people. It's a big store, as is its sister store in Las Vegas two hours to the southwest. The Vegas location also offers bikes for rent. ●

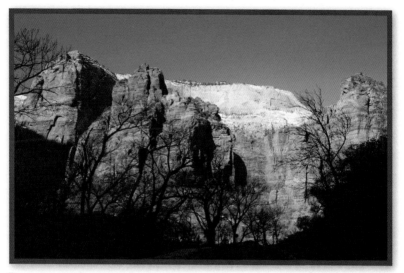

The road through Zion National Park hugs the base of its famous multihued cliffs.

Most people enter the park via the main (west) entrance, just past the artsy small town of Springdale—a good place for a meal or coffee, or to refuel your bike if you haven't yet. Before you get there, you'll pass through small towns with funny names—Hurricane (pronounced "HUR-i-kin"), LaVerkin, and Virgin before beginning the ascent into the hills surrounding Zion. It's a beautiful ride, and it feels great to climb out of the valley and the heat. There are some shifts in the road, as is common on mountain roads, so take note. Be careful of drivers coming the other way, since they cut corners. If you tend to ride close to the line, move over to the right a bit, especially on the last couple of miles of switchbacks that climb to the park's west entrance.

There's a $12 entrance fee for bikes (it's $25 for cars), making this one of the more expensive parks. Still, it's worth it. Zion's scenery is beautiful, dramatic, stunning, and awe-inspiring. You must stop and take in some of the short walks. If you can, stay in the park at least one night (or in Springdale if park lodgings are booked—you have to make reservations for park lodgings months in advance by calling 888-297-2757 or going to www.xanterra.com). During the summer (April to November), the park deals with huge crowds by making tourists park at the entrance and take shuttles along Zion Canyon Scenic Drive to the most popular attractions. It's pretty painless and allows you to avoid fighting traffic.

Hiking and sightseeing options range from very short and paved to long and potentially life threatening. Stop in at the very informative visitor center and ask which ones are right for your time frame and abilities. The paved Emerald Pool and Weeping Rock trails are easy and essential.

After you've done some looking around, tackle the Zion-Mount Carmel Highway, which will take you out the other side of the park and on to your next adventure. Even if you're planning to head back the way you came, at least take a tour to the east side of the park. Switchbacks up the side of a cliff carry you ever higher and give you more and more impressive views of cliffs on the other side of the canyon. Watch out for rubbernecking drivers.

The road goes through a tunnel more than a mile long blasted out of the rock face. When you get to the entrance, take your sunglasses off and try to be at the back of the line of traffic to navigate more easily. Besides, if you don't have people right behind you, it's easier to sneak a peek out the rock windows to the valley below.

After the tunnel, there are a few interesting sights (including Checkerboard Mesa, with crossing striations in the rock), and then the road flattens out on a juniper-dotted plateau to Mount Carmel Junction. From this junction with US 89, you can either go north toward Bryce Canyon and Capitol Reef, or south toward the Grand Canyon.

If you go north on US 89 from Mount Carmel Junction, you will pass through a series of small towns, each with its own place in the history of Utah and the West. Mount Carmel was home to renowned Western painter Maynard Dixon, who was married to Depression-era photographer Dorothea Lange. It's now the headquarters of the Thunderbird Foundation, dedicated to Dixon's work and the Maynard Dixon Country gathering each August.

Towns along this stretch of US 89, with names like New Harmony and Orderville, were founded as utopian communities by Mormons sent from the Salt Lake valley by Brigham Young.

Christy: Towns settled by the Mormons have the same basic characteristics, including streets neatly laid out in a grid pattern. But a few went even further and organized into communal settlements where people were supposed to share their wealth and work for each other's benefit. This kind of utopian experiment had already been set up by other religious groups back East and they were already failing by the time these towns were founded in the middle to late nineteenth century. Maybe these people figured that here, in the kind of remote area where people had to depend on each other to survive anyway, it might work. Like the others before them, though, these eventually dissolved into more typical small-town Utah societies. ●

We go south on US 89. About 4 miles south of Mount Carmel Junction, you'll see a paved turnoff for Coral Pink Sand Dunes State Park. Although the recreational opportunities are limited to hiking, camping, and sand-loving vehicles, all those mounds of pink sand are pretty spectacular. All 18 miles of road into and out of the park are paved (you can either go in and come out the same way or enter at one entrance and leave through the other). The dunes are the result of a notch between two nearby mountains that funnels blowing sand from miles around into this one 3,000-acre area. When you get to the dunes themselves, feel free to take off your boots and wander around a bit (just don't get hit by a dirt bike tearing through). The loop continues out the other end of the park and that road could serve as a shortcut to points south and westward, but parts are unpaved and can be sandy.

After the park, distant cliffs come closer and the road enters a canyon, with sculpted rock encroaching on the road at most of the curves. About 6 miles north of Kanab, you'll pass Moqui Caverns. Built into the cliff, the place is sort of half museum (exhibits include dinosaur tracks and Indian artifacts) and half gift shop. Since it's just off the main road, it's an easy stop if you're into

Pipe Spring National Monument is a former Mormon fort built around a spring.

that sort of thing; the owner also likes to chat with bikers about nearby rides.

Kanab has all amenities, including a number of motels. It can be a little tricky to find lodging in Kanab when things are busy. The most reasonably priced motels are at the intersection of US 89A and US 89. There are a couple of small motels right at the stop light and just a block or two to the east. The realm of the chain hotels/motels is north of the intersection. They have more amenities but prices are considerably higher and they fill up first.

Your options here are to go east and make a loop through Page, taking either US 89 or US 89A (see ride 19 for a description of those highways), or to return to the St. George area. We go back to St. George, since trying to get from St. George to Zion to our next destination, the Grand Canyon, would be a little too much for one day.

Besides, going back via AZ 389 gives us a chance to see Colorado City and Hildale, two little towns on the Utah/Arizona border that are not only surrounded by spectacular red-cliff scenery but also populated by polygamists. If one of your objectives is to see an alternative lifestyle in action, you should take this route. It also goes past Pipe Spring National Monument, a former Mormon fort built around—you guessed it—a spring.

RIDE 9

Red-Rock Paradise

Directions:
south on US 191 and US 163 from Blanding or Bluff to
Monument Valley Tribal Park
north on UT 261
west on UT 276
north on UT 95 to Hanksville

Distance:
from Blanding to Mexican Hat: 49 miles
from Bluff to Mexican Hat: 23 miles
from Mexican Hat to Monument Valley Tribal Park: 24 miles
from Mexican Hat to Hanksville: 121 miles

Time:
half to most of a day, unless you spend significant time
seeing sights

Services:
Bluff, Mexican Hat, Blanding, and Hanksville

Best Time of Year:
early spring until late fall, though summer can be uncomfortably hot

Highlights:
desert landscape of Monument Valley and Valley of the
Gods; the hairpin turn climb to the top of the Moki over-

look, with rewarding views at the top; short hikes and tall rock bridges at Natural Bridges National Monument; relaxing and invigorating tour through the middle of nowhere on the Bicentennial Highway

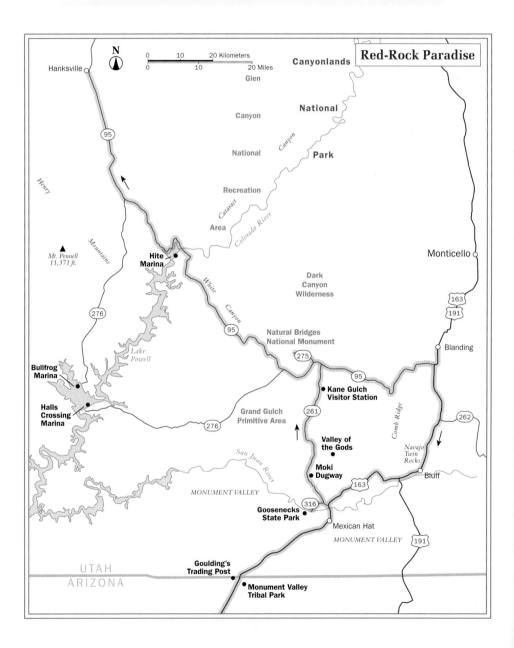

This ride takes you through one of the most famous landscapes of the entire Southwest, Monument Valley, with its red-rock spires rising out of a dusty desert floor. From there, we go north, across a plateau and colorful canyons and formations. You could also continue from Monument Valley southward into Arizona, through the massive Navajo Indian Reservation.

We'll start in Bluff, a funky little hamlet in far southeastern Utah. You may be starting out from one of the surrounding towns in the area, some of which (such as Monticello

It's easy to miss the sombrero-shaped rock for which the town of Mexican Hat is named.

and Blanding) have more amenities. But the Twin Rocks Café and Gift Shop in Bluff, where the cuisine includes Navajo dishes, is a good place to find a decent breakfast. Look for the twin rocks the shop is named for as you pull into town.

Either way, you'll end up going through Mexican Hat on your way to Monument Valley. As you approach the town (named for a sombrero-shaped rock formation just off the highway), you'll see hillsides covered with wavy stripes of white, yellow, and red.

Wherever you're going from here, you'll want to refuel at Mexican Hat, your outpost of civilization amid a number of long roads branching off in all directions. You really don't want to run out of gas in this desolate country. This might be a good time to check your tire pressure and oil, too, and maybe stock up on some water and snacks for the road. If you want a full meal, check out the Swinging Steak restaurant (with hotel), where you'll find some of the best steak you've had in a while in a place where you're likely to meet up with friendly fellow travelers.

Heading south from Mexican Hat on US 163, you'll be dwarfed by the spires and cliffs of Monument Valley, one of the American West's quintessential vistas. You really shouldn't miss it. Much of the best scenery is right near the Utah/Arizona border and contained in Monument Valley Tribal Park, run by the Navajo (their name for themselves is Diné, pronounced "dee-nay"). At least ride into it until you get to the tribal park headquarters just across the border. This area is very much a sacred homeland to the Navajo and every rock formation has a name and identity.

The visitor center offers a few amenities, plus jewelry and kitschy souvenirs made in China or Mexico (only the beautiful rugs are handmade by locals). You will find the same inexpensive trinkets, plus fresh-baked Navajo tacos, for sale at shacks along the road.

The visitor center is also the place to arrange for a tour of the reservation's scenic sights (guides will often take you out in their own vehicles, relieving you of any struggle with the sandy dirt roads through here, many of which are not open to unescorted tourists anyway).

This was once a prime filming area for Western movies, and guides will happily take you to a few locations you might recognize. Also, stop in at Goulding's Museum & Trading Post, just off US 163 near the border, which celebrates its moviemaking history with displays and a gift shop along with a motel. You can also arrange tours of Monument Valley here.

Your options are to continue south into Arizona, eventually linking to rides there, or backtrack along US 163 northward. We'll do the latter.

From US 163, head north on UT 261. Make sure to stop off for a view of Goosenecks State Park, where the San Juan River winds like a green snake through a twisty-turny desert canyon. The overlook, 1,000 feet above the canyon, is at the end of a short, paved spur off the main road.

You'll also pass a turnoff for the 14-mile dirt road that winds through the Valley of the Gods, a smaller version of Monument Valley. Parts are bound to be sandy or otherwise impassable,

Christy: Although (or maybe because) there's very little in the way of civilization between Bluff and, well, anywhere, people tend to be happy to meet fellow travelers—especially if they're on bikes. We struck up a conversation at the Mexican Hat gas station with Sven and Leon from Kansas, who were taking their Ducati and Triumph Speed Triple on a long tour. Then there's Lance, a machinist from Minnesota. By the time we met him in September 2007, he had been on his new bike since May 2006. He said he was headed to the nearest Harley dealership for new tires and the 50,000-mile tune-up—having covered that 50,000 miles in a year and a quarter. Sometimes it's nice to share some tales of the road and connect with another person every now and then, especially when the long miles are piling up. ●

Sven and Leon from Kansas were touring on a Ducati and Triumph Speed Triple when we met them in Mexican Hat.

The towering spires of Monument Valley are what many people picture when they hear the word *Southwest.*

especially after a rain. Besides, the best view of Valley of the Gods will come in just a few minutes, from the top of the Moki Dugway Scenic Backway overlook.

Increasingly ominous signs count down the miles as you approach the Moki switchbacks, a wonder you should try if you're up for it. The short climb is generally well-maintained gravel that's pretty heavily washboarded in places. People do it on all kinds of vehicles, including Harleys. As with any unpaved road, don't try it when it's wet or if you're not sure of your skills on gravel. In this case, don't try it if you're afraid of heights, either. We don't recommend trying it downhill, so tackle it from the south.

Carved into the side of a cliff face, the road gets you about 1,000 feet in elevation gain. A 5-mile-per-hour speed limit tries to prevent idiots from flying off the edge (there are no guardrails). Hopefully, this will also keep them from barreling downhill and running you over. Still, keep your eyes open. The road takes you up through one steep curve after another, each with a view more stunning than the last. On the sharpest curves, pavement appears just in time to help you negotiate before returning you to gravel.

Once you do get to the top, you're in for a treat: stunning views for miles on end, looking out over the desert floor and the spikes and spires of Valley of the Gods and Monument Valley. In the springtime plant life makes for a bright contrast of green against the red rock, itself juxtaposed against a bright blue sky.

From here, you can make a loop back to Blanding on UT 95 or continue northwest on UT 95, the Bicentennial Highway, as it cuts through some of the most remote territory in the Lower 48. Between here and Blanding, the road's biggest attractions are some easily accessible views of ancient ruins and the red and yellow cliffs of Recapture Fold, where millions of years of geologic change are on display where uplift caused several layers of rock to push up vertically from the valley floor. It's also a fun road to ride.

To the west from the Moki turnoff, the road starts off across high undulating plateaus covered in healthy juniper forests. Not far from the junction, Natural Bridges National Monument is a great little side trip. Because of its remoteness, it's almost never crowded and you'll often feel you have it mostly to yourself. That lonely outpost sense is also one of the reasons this place was named the nation's first official "dark sky park," which means light pollution is kept to a minimum—a bonus for stargazing campers. You can get information at the visitor center, but it's low on other amenities. Do be sure to grab extra water here if you aren't topped off. There won't be more for a while.

The loop through the park is well worth taking, as are most of the short hikes to see the bridges themselves. Some also lead to views of ancient Puebloan architecture on cliff walls; ask at the visitor center which hikes give the most bang for your buck (we did at least parts of all of them, which is a nice option). You could make this detour and just return to Blanding on UT 95 eastward, or you can continue on UT 95. Either way, you're surrounded by wilderness areas where hikers can explore for days without seeing another human being.

The Bicentennial Highway (so named because it was built during America's bicentennial in 1976) winds its way across the high desert flats and past a couple Indian ruins before joining White Canyon, which it will follow through here. You'll pass a turnoff to UT 276; there's another one past the Hite Marina. These are probably not worth taking unless you want a very long, dry loop of desert riding with a ferry ride in the middle

As you take in the views from the top of Moki Dugway, give yourself a pat on the back for a job well done.

The bridges at the Natural Bridges National Monument are massive; their scale is evident when you see how small Christy looks underneath one.

from one marina to the other (it also joins the Burr Trail, discussed in ride 5).

UT 95 hugs the base of red-rock cliffs that jut out at regular intervals and rise to form mesas, making for an undulating road with fantastic views. To the east, you can sometimes look off into the deep white-walled canyon through which the river flows. It's an all-out ride where you'll see almost nobody along the way. Since it's a well-maintained surface with little traffic, you can keep your speed on most of these curves.

You'll cross Lake Powell at Hite Marina, where UT 95 used to provide a shortcut for boaters coming from the north and east. A decade of drought dropped the level of the lake enough to make that impossible, so this is now mostly a ghost town. But it's worth a stop to take a look down the river toward the lake. Lake Powell comprises almost 2,000 miles of shoreline—more than the coastlines of California, Oregon, and Washington combined.

From here, the road climbs again into serious desert territory. It can get very hot here in the summer, and there's little water, so it's not a great midafternoon ride.

To the east, you'll see the craggy peaks of the Henry Mountains, the last in the Lower 48 to be explored by white people (it's still remote enough to contain its own buffalo herd). Mining interests drove exploration, and the Henrys are full of old mine sites. Sadly, unless you have a very tough, high-profile four-wheel-drive vehicle, you won't get any closer than UT 95.

The Bicentennial Highway ends in Hanksville, which has gas and assorted other amenities. There are a couple relatively cheap hotels here but not a lot of action. If you still have light to spare, grab some fuel (perhaps from the odd gas station carved out of a cliff just at the end of UT 95) and head west to Torrey, with its better dining and lodging options and Capitol Reef National Park, which we explore in ride 6.

COLORADO

Better known for the Rocky Mountains that dominate the state (and make for great skiing), Colorado is home to some of the country's most beautiful red rock as well as great vacation towns like Durango and a lot of wild history. And did we mention the riding? This is a favorite touring destination and not just because it serves as the gateway to the rest of the Southwest (although it does). Here, explore the majestic San Juan Mountains along the famous Million Dollar Highway or the ruins at Mesa Verde.

The history here starts at least 65 million years ago, when two of Earth's plates collided, pushing up layers of rock that were subsequently eroded into cliffs and valleys by wind and water. To the west, the Colorado Plateau drops off from high-elevation mountains into a comparatively level layer with rivers carving into it. The Rockies and plateau country join right here in what is now southwestern Colorado.

But this place is about more than ancient history. It's also got diverse and satisfying modern amenities. When you're done with your ride or being a tourist, you can relax with good beer, good food, and good company in some of the best recreational towns in the country. We like Durango, but Cortez is also not bad. Nor is Telluride, with its bounty of entertainment and scenery. Overall, southwestern Colorado is probably the most "urban" part of the Southwest (which isn't saying much). It has the most towns and the most amenities the shortest distance apart, although parts of the state can be as wide-open as anywhere.

Be warned: This is home to some of the most high-elevation riding you will ever encounter in the Lower 48, so be prepared for all kinds of weather on any day in any month. High elevation means chilly temperatures pretty much anytime, even when it's hot in the valleys. This is one of the world's most fun and spectacular places to ride a motorcycle, and we wholeheartedly recommend you do.

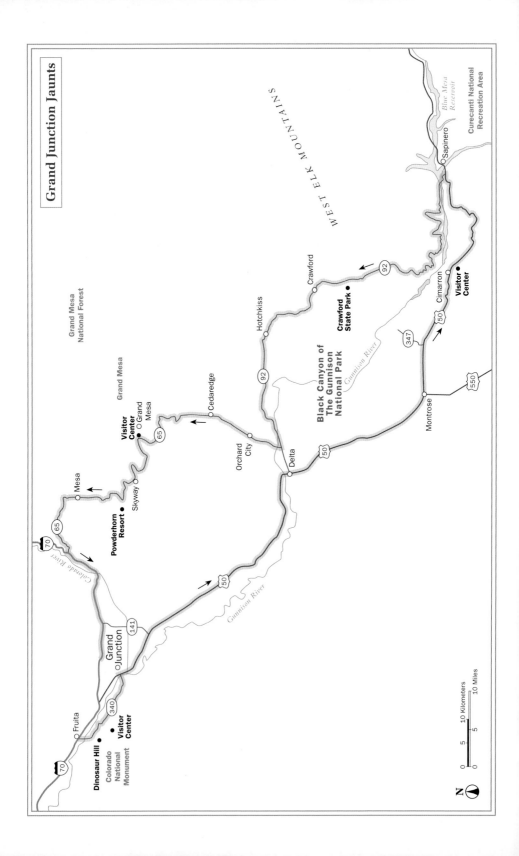

Grand Junction Jaunts

RIDE
10

Grand Junction Jaunts

Directions:
south on US 50 from Grand Junction to Black Canyon of
the Gunnison National Park
north on CO 92 to junction with CO 65
north on CO 65 to junction with I-70
west on I-70 back to Grand Junction

Distance:
about 150 miles

Time:
a few hours to a full day, depending on stops

Services:
at Grand Junction, Delta, Montrose, Crawford, Orchard City,
and Cedaredge

Best Time of Year:
anytime except winter, when Black Canyon of the Gunnison
is closed and high-elevation roads may be snowy

Highlights:
Black Canyon of the Gunnison National Park; Colorado
National Monument; ups and downs through cliffs, mesas,
and valleys

These routes, which could take one day or several, cover some of the great riding around Grand Junction. Its centerpiece is the deep and mysterious Black Canyon of the Gunnison.

Grand Junction has grown a lot in the last ten years, partly due to its location in the middle of some great recreation territory (it also conveniently appears when travelers coming in from the west are really tired of I-70, which runs through town). You'll see folks on bikes of every description—especially the human-powered variety, since this is home base for some major mountain-bike routes. The outskirts are still pretty rural and it's not a big city, but downtown is pretty hip and happening, with nice restaurants, bars, and cafes, plus a lot of sidewalk sculpture to keep you entertained. Outside downtown, there isn't much besides the usual suburban strip malls and fast food.

For today's main ride from Grand Junction, take the turnoff and ride south on US 50, a divided four-lane highway. The road is good and fast across sun-baked grassy badlands, farms, and mesas.

Montrose is an attractive town in the shadow of the mountains. With an old-fashioned Main Street, it's a good place to stop for supplies and a meal. Check out the Ute Indian Museum in town if you're intrigued by the history of the tribe that long dominated this region.

Hang a left at the junction of US 50 and US 550 and ride east to the Black Canyon of the Gunnison National Park (go south

Steve: Southwestern Colorado holds a special place in my heart both as a destination to ride and as a place that feels like home. It provides spectacular scenery of all kinds in any direction. Its people are some of the warmest and welcoming anywhere in the Southwest. Since it is somewhat isolated and difficult to reach from the major urban centers, I think they appreciate visitors who enjoy visiting as much as they enjoy living there. ●

UT 139, a scenic byway that runs through the western edge of Colorado, is an alternative to taking highways US 6 and US 191 through eastern Utah if you're going north from here or coming south from there anyway (it's not worth a special trip). From northeastern Utah, take US 40 into Dinosaur, just on the Colorado side of the border, and pick up UT 64 south toward Rangely. This is the "real West," as evidenced by ranch lands

UT 139, the Dinosaur Diamond Prehistoric Highway, brings you to the intersection of Brontosaurus and Stegosaurus Streets in Dinosaur, Colorado.

and, of course, lots of oil and natural gas rigs.

Pick up UT 139 in Rangely, the beginning of the Dinosaur Diamond Prehistoric Highway (does "prehistoric highway" mean dinosaurs once used this very road?). This official scenic byway stretches 73 miles to the intersection with I-70 near Grand Junction. After the extra-dry desert of the Dinosaur National Monument area along the Utah/Colorado border, the ascent into high-elevation forests is a welcome change. All through here, Fremont Indians decorated entrances to side canyons with eerie pictures typical of the period and people. •

on US 550 to begin the Million Dollar Highway, which we cover in ride 11). Unlike the surrounding mountains, this spectacle doesn't rise into the sky. Instead, it's a deep crevasse that will have you looking 2,000 feet below where you started, all the way down to "basement rocks" that are 1.7 billion years old—yeah, that's billion with a *B*.

Overlooks allow you to peer into the dark recesses of the Black Canyon of the Gunnison.

CO 347 (it's impossible to miss) enters the park and becomes a winding, occasionally steep road along the edge of the canyon. While you're moseying along the top of the cliff, stop and walk the short distance to some of the many overlooks (the best are Gunnison Point, Chasm View, Painted Wall, and Sunset View). From the rim of the canyon, you can gaze down into the dark, yawning rocky chasm below you and contemplate millions of years of history made visible. The park road is closed during the winter. If you're not sure whether it's open, check ahead with the rangers in Montrose.

From the canyon, you can either return to Montrose or go east past Blue Mesa Reservoir and south on CO 149 toward

Christy: There are not many ways to get to the bottom of the canyon—or at least, to get there slowly. A few suicidal or stupid souls, including some on bikes, have taken the fast way over the edge (rangers might be willing to tell you where exactly, if you ask). If you'd like to look up at the canyon walls instead of down, call ahead to book a boat tour that leaves twice a day from the river's edge east of the main entrance (take the Pine Creek Trailhead road)—that's *if* you're ready to make the steep hour-long hike to the bottom and out again. ●

Pagosa Springs if you're not planning to get back to this area any-time soon. The Grand Mesa National Scenic and Historic Byway is a good round-trip option to Grand Junction and a great taste of all this area has to offer.

To get started—and for even more dizzying views of the black canyon—take CO 92 across Blue Mesa Dam. You'll have to go around the canyon for a while before you can cross it—an indication of just how big and deep it is. CO 92 meanders along the canyon's northern edge, then cuts westward toward Delta. (To get to official overlooks along the north rim, take the gravel road from the east end of Crawford State Park. It should be in good shape in the summer, but check at the visitor center at the state park.)

Continue on CO 92 past Hotchkiss and go north on CO 65, which takes you to the top of a mesa dotted with small lakes (and attendant recreation areas), then back down again. The beginning and end of the ride are classic ranching territory, while the middle crosses Grand Mesa and passes the alpine Land O'Lakes area, Powderhorn ski resort, and a visitor center with restrooms and answers to any questions you might have about the region. The Land's End Observatory road is a spur that takes you out to the edge of the mesa for views across hundreds of miles west into Utah and south to the Black Canyon of the Gunnison National Park. An interpretive display tells you what you're seeing.

A number of short, scenic drives are easy to reach via I-70 out of Grand Junction. Colorado National Monument is an easy side trip out of Grand Junction, whether you want to do it as an out-and-back or the beginning or end of a longer day trip. It's an interesting place from a geological perspective as Rim Rock Drive climbs past monoliths and gives a nice view of the valley. The road is steep, with very tight curves and low speed limits. On busy days, it's packed with cyclists and cars driving 5 to 10 miles below the posted limit in both directions, which can easily drive you nuts. Since the best times to see it are early morning and late afternoon just before sunset, it might be worth trying to beat the crowds and go when others aren't likely to be there.

Take in the Coke Ovens formations from the Coke Oven Overlook in Colorado National Monument.

For other side trips, you could head east to check out Rifle Falls State Park, with its three successive 80-foot waterfalls, or farther east into the high Rockies. Another option, just off CO 340 to the south, is Dinosaur Hill, where a 1-mile walking trail takes you through a former dinosaur dig. More dinosaurs are being dug up today at the Rabbit Valley Paleontological Area, within a recreation area just across the Utah border. Look for the .75-mile Trail Through Time walk. Since this is a popular off-roading spot, you'll probably run across some dirt bikes on less ancient trails here.

RIDE
11

Million Dollar Highway

Directions:
south on US 550 from Ridgway to Durango
west on US 160 to Cortez
north on CO 145 to junction with CO 62

Distance:
about 250 miles, including a visit to Telluride
from Ridgway to Durango: 84 miles
from Durango to Telluride: 112 miles
from Telluride to Ridgway: 34 miles

Time:
a full day or more

Services:
at Ouray, Silverton, and Durango

Best Time of Year:
late May through September

Highlights:
dramatic mountain landscape, a classic motorcycle road,
cool and welcoming Southwest towns

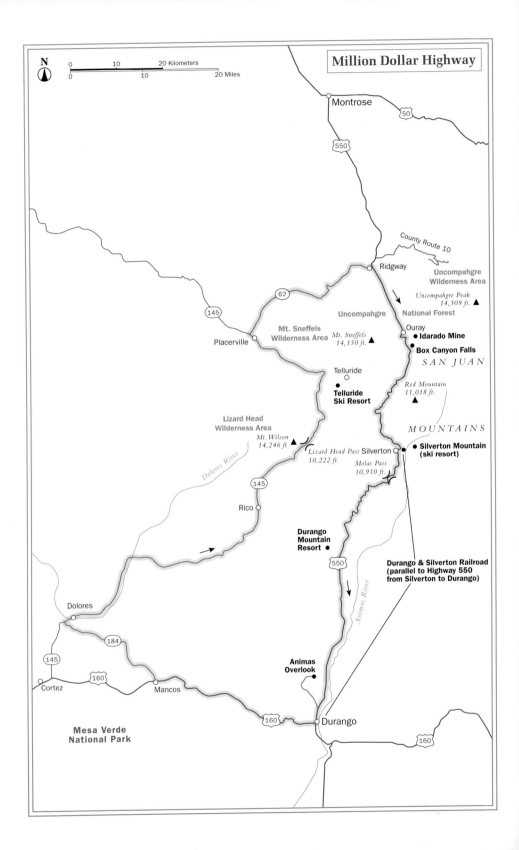

Million Dollar Highway

N

0   10   20 Kilometers
0   10   20 Miles

Montrose

50

550

County Route 10

Ridgway

Uncompahgre
Wilderness Area

62

Uncompahgre Peak
14,309 ft. ▲

145

Uncompahgre   National Forest

Mt. Sneffels
Wilderness Area

Mt. Sneffels
14,150 ft. ▲

Ouray
● Idarado Mine
● Box Canyon Falls

Placerville

SAN JUAN

Telluride
○

Red Mountain
11,018 ft.
▲

● Telluride
Ski Resort

Lizard Head
Wilderness Area

MOUNTAINS

Mt. Wilson
14,246 ft. ▲

Silverton   ● Silverton Mountain
(ski resort)

Lizard Head Pass
10,222 ft.

Molas Pass
10,910 ft.

145

Rico

Durango
Mountain
Resort ●

Dolores River

Durango & Silverton Railroad
(parallel to Highway 550
from Silverton to Durango)

550

Animas River

Dolores

184

145

Animas
Overlook ●

Cortez   160   Mancos

160   Durango

160

Mesa Verde
National Park

The Ouray-Durango-Telluride-Ridgway (or vice-versa) loop is one of the Southwest's most popular day rides, although it can easily take two or more days if you stop to look around—and you may want to. We thought about trying to do it in a day but didn't want to bypass any appealing stops, so we took two days, starting from the north and staying overnight in Durango. This is prime motorcycling territory full of things to see, side trips, and biker-friendly towns that are a pleasure to visit.

US 550 offers some of the highest-elevation driving you will encounter anywhere in the United States. The road climbs to an elevation of 11,750 feet in the San Juan mountain range, which encompasses more land above 10,000 feet in elevation than any other section of America. Earthquakes, volcanoes, and glaciers created these distinctive and often colorful pyramid-shaped peaks. The good news is that makes this a lush, green oasis that comes alive with wildflowers in midsummer.

Don't get caught in such rugged conditions without gear for temperatures ranging from high 80s at low altitude to below freezing up top. You may encounter rain, sleet, wind, and cold—and possibly even snow. We rode in summer heat in Ouray, then shivered through the natural chill of high elevation as well as heavy rain, hail, sleet, and wind—all in the same day. So be prepared with layers of clothing and the knowledge that you might have to pull over or turn around due to, say, a snowstorm in July.

We start this ride, a must-do for anyone traveling through the region, in Ridgway, the last bucolic farm town before the mountains (as signs will tell you, this is "right to farm" country, which theoretically makes it harder for encroaching interests to put farmers out of business). The road quickly gains elevation from about 7,000 feet through juniper forests and into mountains rising out of river valleys, then starts to zigzag up the slopes. For the adventurous, there's a decent hard-packed dirt road, CR 10, that branches off about 2 miles north of Ridgway (follow signs for Owl Creek Pass) and runs through the high meadows of Uncompahgre Wilderness, with views of 14,000-foot peaks.

Ouray, a picturesque yet rugged old mining town, is tucked into a canyon nestled into mountains amid cliffs and waterfalls. Stop in at the helpful visitor center just off the highway for information about the many recreational opportunities here as well as advice on the best places to eat or do pretty much anything else in the region. This is a great place to spend a few hours or a day, since the area features lots of hikes, hot springs (check these out if you're into the spa thing, whether it's the luxurious type or the do-it-yourself kind—sometimes they're right off the side of the road), gold panning, and waterfalls (short trails take you right to the two most famous, Cascade and Box Spring).

US 550 climbs sharply around Ouray with plenty of tight switchbacks. On busy weekends, there can be a lot of traffic (not to mention tourists rubbernecking at the scenery) along this route, so be careful passing. As the hillsides turn into cliffs, little waterfalls cut crevices into canyon walls.

You won't find many passing lanes, so it might be hard to take those corners as fast as you'd like if you're behind a slowpoke. Some riders will take the risk and pass across the double yellow. We'll leave that decision up to you, but we suggest against it.

Be sure you're prepared for this next portion of US 550—amenities are scarce and altitudes vary for the next stretch. A number of side trips branch off from here, mostly dirt roads

As you're taking in the scenery, you might notice the lack of guardrails where the road drops off precipitously to the side. That's because this place gets so much snow in the winter, plows would have no place to push the white stuff if rails blocked their way. Rumor has it that the job of snowplow driver is a much-coveted position in these parts (it's steady work for a good portion of the year) despite the alleged loss of at least one plow and driver per year! Although this may be a scary sight, the roads are well maintained and the riding is more exciting than difficult. ●

leading to ghost towns. Check in town about conditions if you're interested.

This is major mining country and has been continuously since the 1860s. That and the fact that US 550 was originally a very expensive toll road give this stretch its nickname, the Million Dollar Highway. You will see all sorts of old mining remnants and evidence of mines that are still pulling ore out of the mountain. Look for the distinctive flat tops of old slag piles, now planted over, and boarded-up shafts drilled into the mountainsides.

The road's other name is the San Juan Skyway and that's also for good reason. The San Juans are the biggest single mountain range in the country (Vermont could fit inside it) and from just about any vantage point, they look as awesome as they are.

Many of the mountaintops that rise above tree line all through this region are colored various shades of red, indicating the iron oxide they contain. Just south of Ouray, the Red Mountain area was a mining hotbed where miners extracted thousands of ounces of gold, silver, lead, and copper from mines famous for the quality of their ore. The information panels at the Idarado Mine site turnoff, about 6 miles south of Ouray, tell more about the area's history and there's a nice view to boot.

The road climbs steadily for about 25 miles between Ouray and Silverton, offering spectacular high alpine vistas with seemingly endless ridgelines. Silverton, nestled at 9,320 feet and surrounded on all sides by high peaks, is named for the metal that made this a busy town by the 1870s, even though it was cold and isolated for much of the year. The old town center still has the look and the charm of its heyday, but few of the bars and none of the whorehouses.

In addition to museums and many well-preserved old buildings, the town has all services, so you should be able to refuel here if you need to. Silverton is also the final stop for the Durango & Silverton Narrow Gauge Railroad, built in 1882 as a spur from Durango and used to haul freight (mostly mining related, including silver and gold ore) and passengers. Although it fell into disuse as a freight train, it was used for filming movies (including

Bikers roar up and down Main Avenue in Durango, showing off various accessories and the volume of their engines.

Butch Cassidy and the Sundance Kid) and converted to a tourist attraction in the 1980s, which means it's pretty much been in continuous operation since it was first built—and still uses some of the original equipment.

US 550 from Silverton continues to climb, reaching Molas Pass about 6.5 miles from Silverton, at an elevation of about 11,000 feet. The road continues to wind and weave its way through the mountains south of Silverton with sweeping, high-mountain curves, gradually descending to Durango at an elevation of a little more than 6,500 feet.

The road brings you into Durango from the north and becomes Main Avenue, a hotel/motel row. If you're looking for lodging, this is one of the best places in town to find it. If you're headed for downtown, stay in the middle or left lanes and go straight at West 17th and Main and cross over the Animas River. If you're headed for US 160, stay in the right-hand lanes and hang a soft right onto West Park Avenue. You will be skirting downtown, with the Animas River on your left. Head east on US 160 for Pagosa Springs

Depending on conditions, you might want to take a short side trip from Silverton toward Eureka and Animas Forks. Silver was discovered in Animas Forks in 1875, and it was once called the "Largest City in the World (at this elevation)." Take the right fork from Main Street. While it's only paved for a while, you may be able to continue on toward the Animas Forks site for another stretch, depending on conditions (ask at the visitor center in Silverton). Photogenic mining-town remnants sit rusting on the steep hillsides. The road goes along an old railroad bed, which means grades gentle enough that trains could get up the hill, but only slowly. ●

and west for Mancos, Mesa Verde, Cortez, and the Four Corners area, as well as the second half of this ride.

Adventurous types flock to Durango to raft rivers, ride mountain bikes, hike up peaks, and, of course, tour via motorcycle. It's no wonder Durango is a favorite of outdoor enthusiasts and bikers alike, with its combination of interesting territory, sights, history, good food, and watering holes. It's got innumerable hotels, restaurants, bars, stores, and repair shops. All that, plus a general motorcycle-friendly vibe, makes it a great base camp for exploring this area. Hotels fill up on summer weekends, especially during rallies or other special events—and they seem to happen often.

Many of the best restaurants line the historic Main Avenue (which often sports a number of bikes parked in beautiful formation along the curb), including Francisco's Restaurante Y Cantina (Mexican), Durango Diner (good for breakfast), and Ken and Sue's (steaks). Carver's Restaurant and Brewery is good for breakfast in the morning and beer in the evening. The best beer, though, is at Steamworks Brewing Co. on Second Avenue.

If you prefer something smaller, or if you've already spent some time in Durango and want to explore other places, Cortez is also a good base.

Christy loved the sequined helmets Nancy and Amy from Denver were wearing when we met them in Telluride.

From Dolores, just north of Cortez, CO 145 heads north and back into the mountains. The next town, Rico, is tucked into a tight valley and appears rugged, even haggard. Given the relative prosperity of Cortez and Dolores to the south and Telluride to the north, Rico inexplicably looks like a town left to slowly decay. Services are scarce and the one gas station doesn't have premium.

CO 145 will wind down to the valley below, past the Telluride Mountain Village turn-off. It's steep and tight so watch speed in the turns, especially during inclement weather. At the T intersection, taking a right will lead you 4 miles or so to picturesque downtown Telluride.

Although Telluride itself bumps up against the canyon cliffs, roads do connect it directly with Ouray and Silverton (not far from here, as the crow flies). But those are steep and unpaved. Continue on CO 145, which clings to the wall of the canyon as it descends through the tiny towns of Sawbuck and Placerville, old gold mining towns that are now more suburbs of Telluride. Just after Placerville, you can go east on CO 62 toward Ridgway or west on CO 145—which would connect you to ride 12, which continues on CO 145 past Telluride instead of completing the loop through Ridgway.

RIDE

12

Around the Plateau

Directions:
north on CO 145 from Cortez to Gateway
northeast on CO 141 to US 50 to Grand Junction

Distance:
233 miles, give or take a few miles if you stop in Telluride
from Cortez to Telluride: 74 miles
from Telluride to Placerville: 17 miles
from Placerville to Naturita: 37 miles
from Naturita to Gateway: 52 miles
from Gateway to Grand Junction: 53 miles

Time:
four to five hours or more, depending on stops

Services:
at Cortez, Dolores, Telluride, Norwood, Naturita, and Grand
Junction

Highlights:
the heights of Lizard Head Pass; mining history including
the engineering marvel of the Hanging Flume; the spectacular scenery of the Unaweep/Tabeguache Scenic and
Historic Byway

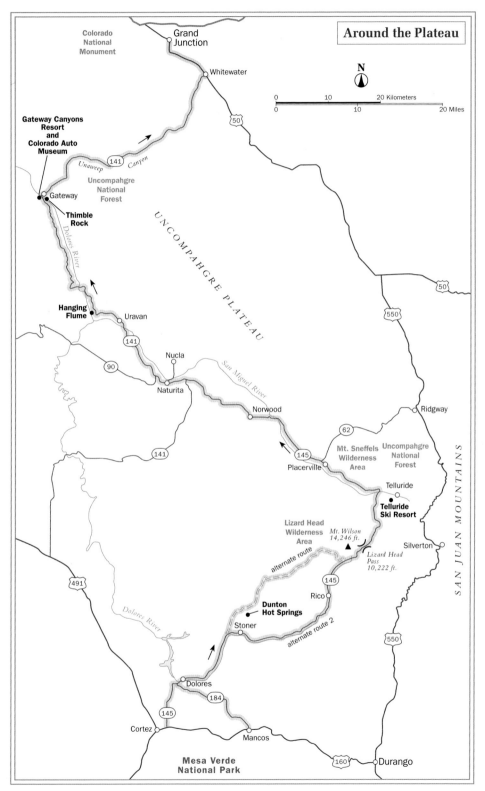

Around the Plateau

N

| 0 | 10 | 20 Kilometers |
| 0 | 10 | 20 Miles |

Colorado National Monument

Grand Junction

Whitewater

50

Gateway Canyons Resort and Colorado Auto Museum

Unaweep Canyon

141

Uncompahgre National Forest

U N C O M P A H G R E   P L A T E A U

Gateway

Thimble Rock

Dolores River

Hanging Flume

Uravan

141

90

Nucla

Naturita

San Miguel River

Norwood

141

Ridgway

62

145

Mt. Sneffels Wilderness Area

Uncompahgre National Forest

Placerville

Telluride

Telluride Ski Resort

Lizard Head Wilderness Area

Mt. Wilson 14,246 ft.

Silverton

alternate route

Lizard Head Pass 10,222 ft.

145

Rico

Dunton Hot Springs

alternate route 2

Stoner

550

Dolores River

491

Dolores

184

145

Cortez

Mancos

Mesa Verde National Park

160

Durango

S A N   J U A N   M O U N T A I N S

50

550

This route is one of the most unexpected pleasures of touring the Southwest and a fantastic alternative to US 50 and US 550 north or south. It's little known except by locals, who will either tell you what a great ride this is or try to keep it a secret for themselves. It offers some diverse and invigorating riding as it skirts the geologically and historically fascinating Uncompahgre Plateau.

You can access it in a few different ways; we pick it up in Cortez, although you could also come from Ridgway and join it at the junction of CO 145 and CO 62 near Placerville. If you are riding south from the Grand Junction area, you can still pick up US 550 to Ouray by doing this ride in reverse and taking CO 62 from Placerville to Ridgway.

We start in Cortez, one of several good bases in this area. Mancos (which, like many Four Corner towns, hosts a rally over Labor Day weekend) has a couple cool cafes and lots of friendly people, although not many hotels. Dolores is a base for river-rafting tours that last anywhere from a few hours to a few days.

The ride north on CO 145 from Cortez to Telluride and Placerville is also the second leg of the Million Dollar Highway loop. If you don't mind some fairly extensive riding on gravel, the whole region is full of unpaved roads that are well maintained and offer spectacular views. We took Dunton Road, which splits off CO 145 just before the unfortunately named town of Stoner and goes past Dunton Hot Springs, once a ghost town and now an exclusive spa retreat, before rejoining CO 145 just past Rico. The road starts out paved and you can just turn around when the pavement ends. But most of the fun comes after that, as the road winds its way through beautiful mountain meadows. Other roads can take you all the way to the west side of the mountains. Ask about conditions in Mancos, Dolores, or Cortez.

CO 145 climbs steadily through the heart of the Lizard Head Wilderness Area (with peaks towering more than 14,000 feet), following deep red-rock canyons carved by the Dolores River over eons. You'll eventually top out at Lizard Head Pass south and west of Telluride, at an elevation of 10,222 feet.

Spectacular views of the surrounding peaks greet you if you make it to the top of Dunton Road.

Founded as a mining town but now a quintessential tourism destination, Telluride is nestled in one of the most picturesque settings imaginable. Things can be slow in the off-season (early spring and late fall), which is just as well, since when it's crowded, it can be really crowded.

Even hordes of tourists can't detract from the stunning cliffs rising up in dramatic vertical walls on three sides of the canyon. It's a great place to stop for lunch, dinner, or a beer, with restaurant

Telluride has worked hard to make itself a destination for festivals and concert series throughout the summer, with one event or another going on pretty much all the time. There's a bluegrass festival, a wine festival, a jazz celebration in June, a tech festival in August, the film festival over Labor Day weekend, and a blues and brews festival in September. They got so burned out on all the activity, some residents created the Telluride Nothing Festival in July—officially described as "Nothing, nothing . . . followed by nothing." •

Two-wheeled vehicles of all types are popular in Telluride.

choices ranging from fancy (Cosmopolitan Restaurant) to low-brow (Last Dollar Saloon). We had a classic health-food lunch—consisting of a great burger, Tater Tots, beer, and a chocolate-chip cookie—at the laid-back Cornerhouse Grille on Fir Street.

Part of Telluride's charm lies in its remoteness; it's 366 miles from Salt Lake City and 363 miles from Denver. If you want to get here, you pretty much have to drive. If you plan to spend any amount of time, it's worth getting a room in advance.

Like most of the towns around here, Placerville was built on mining. Its claim to fame is that by about 1920 it was producing 30 percent of the world's vanadium (a metal used to harden steel). Also like other towns, it later switched over to uranium. From here, CO 145 follows the San Miguel River with nice, sweeping S turns and some blind hairpins as the road and the river carve through the canyon. The cliffs encroaching on the road begin to open up. You are about to leave the confines of the canyon when you encounter a sharp left-hand turn that crosses the river where the road immediately begins to climb.

You'll be ascending Norwood Hill to the town of Norwood. Every time we've been to Norwood, the entire town seemed to be closed. (There is a gas station where you can pay at the pump 24/7.) This sleepy little town has a colorful past. The largest rancher in the area during the 1880s was one Harry B. Adsit. One of Harry's cowboys was none other than "Bud" Leroy Parker—aka Butch Cassidy. Legend has it that in 1889 Butch rode the same trail you just did. However, he rode it to rob a bank in Telluride—the first of many heists.

Farther north on CO 145, you come across the towns of Nucla, Naturita, and Uravan. Just past Naturita, you will pick up CO 141 heading north toward Grand Junction.

Each of the surrounding towns in the area has its own unique history. Nucla was a short-lived experiment in communal living and agriculture by the Colorado Cooperative Company in 1894. Naturita has long been a base for those wanting to explore the plateau and now has a cafe, a gas station, a few motels, and a grocery store, along with a visitor center. On CO 90 just south of town, the Bedrock Store has been a setting for movies such as *Thelma and Louise.* Uravan (uranium plus vanadium) was a company town formed in 1936 when U.S. Vanadium Corporation located a processing plant there to extract uranium and vanadium from ore. Processing left behind "mildly radioactive" tailings that are in the process of being stabilized and covered.

Just north of Uravan is the Hanging Flume, the remnant of a 13-mile-long wooden aqueduct, the last 5 miles of which were attached to the canyon walls. The flume, built over three years in the 1880s, carried water to a nearby mining site and used gravity to create the hydraulic pressure necessary to separate gold from gravel. According to the historical marker at a parking area overlooking the flume, more than twenty-three million gallons of water were delivered to the mine site in a twenty-four-hour period. The mine and the flume were abandoned after three years of dismal yields. It's amazing that the structure still exists after more than one hundred years.

Remnants of the Hanging Flume are visible from the overlook several miles north of Uravan.

Steve: I was riding the Buell and stopped at the Hanging Flume. A man riding a Suzuki stopped shortly after I did. I had been taking photos of the flume and was just getting ready to roll as he drove up. We talked for a few minutes and found we were both headed in the same direction, toward Grand Junction. He saw the Buell and revealed that his grandmother on his mother's side was distantly related to the Buell family, even more distantly to the Harleys and the Davidsons—names we all know well, names I grew up with in the Milwaukee area.

He seemed a little off, a little twitchy, in the way a homeless guy in the park of a big city seems twitchy. He spoke of some episode he had recently had to deal with and how being on the road cleared his head. He seemed to be just barely hanging on to the conversation and perhaps his sense of reality. As I was packing up my cameras he said he might "catch up with you later." Good reason in my mind to hit the road and pull back the throttle. If he was teetering on the edge, I didn't want to be around when he went over. ●

The crumbling remains of Driggs Mansion sit near the base of Thimble Rock just north of Gateway, Colorado.

The next stretch of CO 141, from the Hanging Flume to Gateway, is perhaps one of the most beautiful yet little-known roads we've ever been on. The Dolores River has carved magnificent canyons out of the deep purple rock. Views of huge buttes and mesas sculpted from the rock stretch out for miles. Officially known as the Unaweep/Tabeguache Scenic and Historic Byway, the road is essentially a series of uninterrupted giant, sweeping curves rolling through the canyon from left to right and vice versa. This is one of those roads where you need to use caution because the curves can come up faster than you expect them to when you find yourself peering into the distance or looking to the left or right to view the cliffs and mesas.

Gateway is a tiny town that time seems to have forgotten. Its main attractions, aside from its location on the scenic drive, are the Gateway Canyons Resort and the Colorado Automobile Museum, which includes a 1954 Oldsmobile F-88 Concept Car.

Just outside town, the rubble of the Driggs Mansion sits at the base of Thimble Rock. Lawrence Driggs hired Italian masons in 1914 to build his house out of stone hewn from nearby cliffs; the house eventually fell into disrepair.

Pass north out of Gateway and enter Unaweep Canyon. The canyon lies where the Gunnison River used to flow. During the gradual uplift of the Uncompahgre Plateau over millions of years, the river slowly cut through the rock, creating the canyon. Now, a stream splits at Unaweep Divide (unaweep means "out of two mouths") on top of the plateau and flows down through Unaweep Canyon to either side of the plateau as East Creek and West Creek, through cliffs originally carved out by the path of the ancient river.

As you pass through Gateway, the landscape on the north side will change dramatically. The canyon changes from broad and wide to more of a narrow gorge. The surrounding rock formations appear strikingly similar to those of Yosemite National Park in California. The canyon continues to narrow as it climbs toward Grand Junction.

About 14 miles south of Grand Junction, you hit some pretty tight curves on a steep descent into the town of Whitewater. A section of road passes through an area that looks as if the surface of the earth was ripped open, then tipped forward, resulting in boulders of all sizes and shapes spilling out.

Heading north on US 50, the surrounding landscape is dramatically different from any you've passed through for hours and is an abrupt ending to a spectacular ride. It's wide-open four lanes surrounded by barren hillsides until you reach Grand Junction.

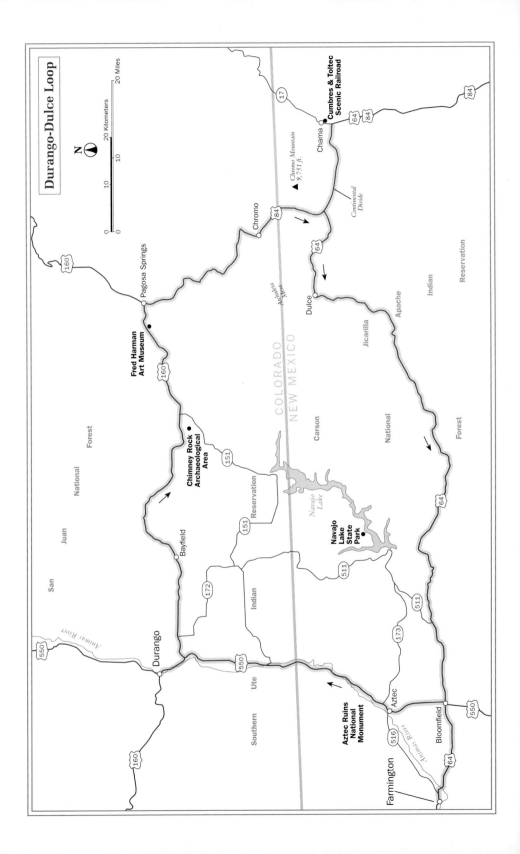

Durango-Dulce Loop

N

20 Miles
20 Kilometers

Cumbres & Toltec
Scenic Railroad

17

84

64 84

Chama

Chromo Mountain
9,751 ft.

Continental Divide

160

Chromo

84

Pagosa Springs

64

Fred Harman
Art Museum

Dulce

160

Jicarilla   Apache   Indian   Reservation

Archuleta Mesa

COLORADO
NEW MEXICO

Chimney Rock
Archaeological
Area

151

Carson

National

Forest

64

National   Forest

San   Juan

151

Reservation

Bayfield

511

Navajo
Lake

Navajo
Lake
State
Park

Animas River

172   Indian   511

550

Durango

Southern   Ute

550   173

511

550

Aztec Ruins
National
Monument

Aztec

Bloomfield

516   Animas River

550

160

Farmington

64

RIDE

13

Durango-Dulce Loop

Directions:
east on US 160 from Durango to Pagosa Springs
south on US 84
west on US 64
north on US 550 back to Durango

Distance:
225 miles

Time:
at least a half day

Services:
Pagosa Springs, Dulce, and Bloomfield

Best Time of Year:
late spring to fall

Highlights:
historic and relaxing Pagosa Springs; looking for little green men in Dulce; a great high-alpine ride that takes you across many, many mountains

Durango is an ideal hub for touring in this part of the country and this is one of several loops you can do using it as a home base. This is about getting to know the landscape you might otherwise just pass by on your way to somewhere else.

Depending on when you hit the road, things can be pretty slow leaving Durango. There's a fair amount of congestion, made all the worse by lots of businesses and merging roads along US 160, but passing lanes emerge right where they should. Soon, though, the highway becomes essentially a rural road, two lanes much of the way and pretty straight without a lot of elevation change. You're skirting the base of huge mountains to the north.

This is one of those roads where you have to slow down every time you pass through another little town. If you need a break or want to make some new friends, stop in at one of several bike-friendly establishments like the Harley-loving Billy Goat Saloon in Bayfield.

The road rises a bit into pretty pine-forested hills as you hit about 7,000 feet—some of the surrounding peaks tower in excess of 14,000 feet, so 7,000 seems like nothing. As with any area that looks this way, watch out for deer and moose. You'll pass Chimney Rock Archaeological Area, named for a distinctive rock formation that has long been a sacred site for Native American tribes (it is now surrounded by the Southern Ute Indian Reservation). You can take a 2½-hour guided tour of this site's ancient ruins May 15 to September 30; the visitor center is a half mile from CO 151.

As you get close to Pagosa Springs, you'll find lots of opportunities to buy things, from wood carvings to jerky to a ranchette. Pagosa Springs is a nice alpine town surrounded by imposing mountain peaks. It feels a little less upscale than Durango, but it has plenty of amenities, including gift shops, liquor stores, and lots of motels and restaurants—including the infamous Boss Hogg's Restaurant and Saloon. You could also try Kips Grill & Cantina or JJ's Riverwalk Restaurant and Pub (restaurants named after people seem popular here). If you happen to need pastries, try the Pagosa Baking Company.

US 160 goes right through the center of town, and its main drag features lots of thriving small businesses. It also means a single pedestrian can stop a whole freeway of traffic. The town is also famous for the Fred Harman Art Museum, which is as much a voyage into Americana as it is a tribute to the cartoonist

> **Steve:** I would choose Cortez over Pagosa Springs as an alternative to Durango any day. Cortez seems a little more rugged and has more of a small-town feel to it. For me, Pagosa Springs is a contrived and superficial wide spot in the road. But I guess if you just put your wife or girlfriend through 500 miles of wind, rain or 100-degree heat, you might be able to use one of the spas in Pagosa Springs to mend some fences.
>
> **Christy:** I agree that Cortez has its charms, but Pagosa Springs has the feel of a mountain town plus cute shops, good food, and yes, spas. All this might mean visiting the area more than once to see which you prefer. ●

who created the *Red Ryder and Little Beaver* comic strip in the 1930s.

As the name implies, there are hot springs here, right in the middle of town, and that's one reason this has been a tourist hotspot for a good long time. All this makes Pagosa Springs a good base for the many alpine and desert rides around here.

Follow signs for US 84, which turns southward a couple miles east of town (continuing east is not an option, and you'll see why if you note the barrier of giant peaks ahead). More second-home developments are spread out on the south side of town, offering people who can afford it a more permanent connection to the recreation and beauty around here. The road is mostly in good condition, with occasional damage. There's sometimes not much of a shoulder and an occasional bump might surprise you. You might also run into some slow traffic, including trailers and RVs. There aren't many passing lanes, but you'll find quite a few dashed-line sections where you could accelerate past slowpokes.

After a while, civilization fades away, replaced by beautiful, wide-open views around every turn: valleys, cliffs, mountains, trees, and lots of small farms. There's not much at Chromo besides forested mesas. A little farther down the road and you're in New

Steve was surprised to find he was crossing the Continental Divide on US 84 south of Pagosa Springs.

Mexico. About 6 miles south of the Colorado/New Mexico border you'll come to the intersection of US 84 and US 64. If you're headed farther south in New Mexico, stay on 84 to Chama. For this ride, we pick up US 64 and head west toward Dulce.

If you use US 84 to get from one area to another, or if you want a nice side trip, check out Chama, which is just east of here on US 84. One popular ride goes through Chama onto CO 17 all the way to Antonito, Colorado, south on US 285, then back on the beautiful section of US 64, reconnecting with US 84 at Tierra Amarilla.

Nestled in a valley and surrounded by mountains, Chama is a cute little town and a great place to stop if you need a bite to eat and to refuel. Restaurants like the High Country Lounge and Restaurant are abundant. You may also notice G-Force Chopper, a motorcycle shop where the main road meets Harley Drive. Yes, this is biker country.

Chama has long been another kind of hub. It's the start of the narrow-gauge Cumbres & Toltec Scenic Railroad, which winds along the southern slopes of the Rockies from here to Antonito. Built in 1880, the rail line served as a spur linking silver mines throughout the region to the rest of the world until silver prices crashed. In the 1970s, historical preservationists bought it and it has hauled

The Cumbres & Toltec Scenic Railroad departs from this old-fashioned station and winds through the Rockies from Chama, New Mexico, to Antonito, Colorado.

tourists ever since. You can either catch a ride on the train or ride alongside it for a few miles as it follows the highest and longest length of narrow-gauge track in America. The railroad crosses CO 17 a couple times, giving you a rare chance to see a steam engine in action, before they diverge just after Cumbres Pass.

Steve: On my way south to Taos, I got turned around as I was leaving Chama and accidentally took CO 17, which passes right through the center of town. The road climbs up and across a wide alpine valley into the surrounding mountains. I was greeted with huge, wide-open sweepers just begging for me to push the posted speed limits. I was having so much fun that I didn't realize I had gone off in the wrong direction until I saw a sign telling me I was entering "Colorful Colorado." I did a quick U-turn and rode back down the valley. A word of warning if you take CO 17: The railroad crossings are marked but not gated. From the signs warning you to be alert for trains crossing the road, I gathered that trains have the right of way. ●

US 64 goes through a patchwork of public and private land. When this landowner says "Keep Out!" he definitely means it.

Dulce lies on the northeastern corner of the Jicarilla Apache Indian Reservation. It appears to be a quiet little town with little reason to spend much time there. You'll be able to fuel up and grab a snack if you want.

For those who enjoy a conspiracy theory, Dulce has a secret second life; some might call it a crazy underground scene. This seemingly innocuous little town is at the center of a bizarre subterranean alien-government experiment and animal-mutilation conspiracy theory. Some believe that aliens, with the help of the U.S. government, conduct secret experiments on humans and animals under nearby Archuleta Mesa. Apparently, a former security guard at the facility escaped with the "Dulce Papers" documenting horrific experiments, including cloning and aliens perfecting their abilities to take human form. Given that Roswell and Area 51 (not to mention actual, established government testing sites at Los Alamos and Alamogordo) are not too far away, anything's possible.

Hang around and look for aliens or spacecraft or men in black if you want to (we just hope they're sympathetic to earthlings in leathers); we're headed west on US 64. The road cuts through beautiful sandstone canyons and climbs over and around cliffs and mesas of various sizes with incredible wide-open views of classic northern New Mexico canyon country.

US 64 is the main east-west artery through this part of the state, but you'd never know that with such an absence of traffic. It makes sense, given that this is a lightly populated part of a lightly populated state. The area can be prone to summer monsoons, which in some spots can carry a considerable amount of debris across the highway. The road undulates through numerous low-lying washes, so be alert after storms. Despite the possibility of detritus, US 64 is mostly just you and the scenery, so get out and ride it.

Take US 64 all the way into Bloomfield where you'll pick up US 550/NM 544 North. Before you get to Bloomfield, you will pass the turnoff for NM 539 and Navajo Lake State Park, which we discuss in ride 16 and which could make an alternative route back to Durango if you have time. Otherwise, it's an out-and-back 33 miles that aren't particularly interesting unless you like to fish.

Steve: One thing you might find more of than traffic along here is debris—mostly sand, gravel, brush, and branches—across the road. You'll see signs warning of the possibility. A pretty severe thunderstorm came through here the night before I did, sending a boulder tumbling down the side of a cliff and breaking a chunk out of a concrete barrier. So consider yourself warned. This doesn't occur just in low-lying areas: There were a couple of high curves where the road was banked just right to allow sand and gravel to flow across the road at long angles. In a couple of the turns, if I hadn't had enough visibility to allow me to slow down and get the bike a little more upright, I could have hit the stuff at full lean.

You'll want to be alert to the possibility of heavy equipment as well. I came around one big, sweeping turn to find a huge front-end loader blocking my lane. The operator was clearing a wash of sand that was about 6 inches deep and about 30 feet wide. Good thing they got an early start.

The scenery isn't great on US 550, but the road is wide, quick, and efficient, and it will take you right back to Durango where you started. ●

FOUR CORNERS

Certain things come to mind when you think of the American Southwest: towering cliffs and rock spires; rivers flowing through deep canyons; a history of people who lived long before Columbus ever thought about setting sail anywhere; and baking sun blazing in a blue sky. It's all here in the Four Corners region, one of the most famous yet uncrowded places in America, a place unlike anywhere else. You'll find—all within a few hours of riding—an interconnected history made up of ancient cultures' intact remains mixed with the relatively modern towns of the present.

Nowhere else in America do the corners of four states come together at one spot, but that fact both defines this as a region and seems arbitrary given its history. Riding through ruins and the clearly delineated landscape, you can envision what this area was like 1,000 years ago, when many related groups of people lived, traveled, and traded with each other among the mesas and valleys in a system of governments that look nothing like the state boundaries dividing it into four states today. If you travel enough, you'll notice the ways the landscape changes, sometimes in subtle aspects like the condition and quality of the roads at state borders. And if you spend even a few days riding in this region, you will go from classic Southwest desert to some of the highest alpine roads in the country.

You'll find ranching, irrigated agriculture, mining, and modern and abandoned towns right next to each other. You will also find some of the best rides we've ever encountered clustered in relatively close proximity. Depending on your tastes and budget, no matter where you choose to make home base, you are only a half a day in any direction from whatever kind of riding you might desire. When you ride here, remind yourself that people come from all over the world to ride these roads. We are lucky for the invention of the asphalt that enables us to ride this region. If you live anywhere near here, you're even luckier, because all you have to do is get on your bike and ride to get back here soon.

RIDE

14

Four Corners Trail

Directions to Hovenweep National Monument:
south on US 491 from Utah border to Cortez
west on Montezuma County Road G

Directions to Four Corners:
south on US 491 from Cortez to junction with US 160
west on US 160 to Four Corners and Teec Nos Pos
east on US 64 to Shiprock, with a jog south on US 491 to
Shiprock Pinnacle
north on US 491 back to Cortez

Distance:
from Cortez to Hovenweep National Monument and to Four
Corners (both rides combined): 204 miles
from Cortez to Hovenweep and back: 90 miles
from Cortez to US 160: 20 miles
from junction of US 491/US 160 to Teec Nos Pos: 24
miles
from Teec Nos Pos to Shiprock: 27 miles
from Shiprock to Cortez: 43 miles

Time:
most of a day to a full day if you do both loops

Services:
at Pleasant View and Cortez in Colorado, Shiprock in New
Mexico, Blanding and Monticello in Utah

Best Time of Year:
spring and fall

Highlights:
the unique chance to visit four states at the same time,
wide-open scenery and stately volcanic remnants

If Monument Valley to the west of here is knock-your-socks-off Southwestern desert, this ride presents its quieter, more complex cousin. But it's no less classic Southwest. You can do this ride from a number of different starting points, including southeastern Utah, Cortez in Colorado, or Farmington in New Mexico. It makes a nice day trip from any of them in conjunction with Hovenweep National Monument. Between the small towns out here is a whole lot of nothing, so be sure to bring plenty of water and snacks and don't get caught in the desert without fuel or supplies.

Hovenweep National Monument is pretty much out in the middle of nowhere, but it's worth the trip—a quick loop or in-and-back. Hovenweep National Monument visitor center is located down 24 miles of paved road from Pleasant View, Colorado, on CR 88 and CR 10. You can also enter the monument from the west (head south on US 191 to UT 262), in which case the visitor center is about 45 miles from Blanding or 35 miles from Bluff via US 191 to UT 262.

From Cortez, head south for 3 or 4 miles on US 160/US 491, looking for County Road G. Watch for signs to the airport; if you go past the airport, you've gone too far. The two-lane road will take you into McElmo Canyon and parallel McElmo Creek through a rich river valley that is a mix of agricultural and residential land. The posted speed limit is 40 or 45 miles an hour, and no one seems to be in a hurry. The roads are narrow with tall vegetation and encroaching cottonwood trees that create a few blind curves, especially in the narrower parts of the valley. The terrain will eventually open up, so be patient.

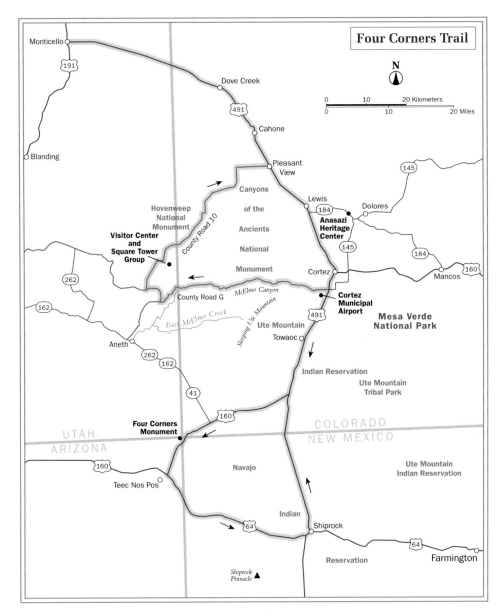

After about 20 or so miles on CR G, watch for signs for Hovenweep National Monument. You will have to make three right-hand turns to get to the entrance to the visitor center and the first one, to IR 5068, is easy to miss. Go a little more than 4 miles on IR

5068 and turn right onto Reservation Road. With each right turn, the condition of the road gets progressively worse but at least the signage here is a little more visible. Go about 1.5 miles and turn right onto Hovenweep Road. From here go about a mile to the Hovenweep visitor center entrance.

Admission is $3 for motorcycles and $6 per vehicle. Amenities are fairly scarce here. There is a thirty-site campground near the visitor center. But there are no hook-ups, no dump stations, and no gas.

Hovenweep is a Ute word that means "deserted valley," and it must have felt that way for many generations who discovered it anew, just as we are now. This place has been inhabited for at least 10,000 years. At first, nomadic peoples hunted here but by A.D. 900, they began to settle into agricultural communities. The monument encompasses the ruins of six Ancestral Puebloan villages, some with amazing architecture. Close to Mesa Verde National Park, this is part of what used to be a sprawling, inter-connected group of civilizations that populated this region.

The entrance roads pass through Canyons of the Ancients National Monument, which occupies much of this corner of Colorado and is administered by the Bureau of Land Management. Besides Hovenweep, its 164,000 acres contain building sites, art, and artifacts, many of which haven't yet been cataloged. Canyons of the Ancients is full of unpaved roads snaking up into its multitude of branching canyons, many of them rarely maintained and with few on-site resources for travelers. For information, go to the Anasazi Heritage Center 10 miles north of Cortez, at the intersection of CO 184 and CO 145.

Hovenweep is divided into four separate sections. There are several quick hikes from the visitor center, including a steep 1.5-mile loop that goes past many of the ruins. We hiked in riding gear and leather boots to Tower Point, an easy hike and well worth it. Hovenweep is best known for its towers, which stand like sentinels looking out across an expanse of rolling desert to mountains in the distance. The main attraction near the visitor center—and the only one on a paved road—is the Square Tower community,

The towers at Little Ruin Canyon are an easy walk from the visitor center at Hovenweep National Monument.

a collection of buildings, stone towers, and stone dwellings clustered around and below the rim of Little Ruin Canyon. The group is located atop the Cajon Mesa, a 500-square-mile raised block of land in the heart of the Four Corners region.

Hovenweep Castle is built right on the edge of the cliff. Across from the Square Tower are Twin Towers, one with an oval foundation and one shaped like a horseshoe. The Square Tower community is not the only significant ruin in the area. About 700 years ago, a system of settlements and communities flourished here. Most of the structures at Hovenweep were built between 1200 and 1300. The Ancestral Puebloans who lived here built in a variety of shapes and sizes, including square and circular towers, D-shaped buildings, and many round ceremonial kivas. Hovenweep is known for its skillfully executed masonry, which exceeds that of better-known Mesa Verde in its quality. Even though they were often built on rocky surfaces, these buildings were engineered well enough to remain standing more than 700 years later.

Their beauty and diversity have evoked speculation among the generations who have continued to rediscover them since. Were the towers built to observe the skies? Were they defenses against invaders? Were they used for storage? Or were they centers of government for the region? The many kivas suggest they served an important religious function. It is strange now to think of this lonesome, isolated settlement as the middle of a thriving civilization, but its location in the middle of this once well-populated area makes us wonder what went on here back then.

When you leave, you can head back the way you came in or make a loop, winding through Canyons of the Ancients National Monument. We left through the entrance near Pleasant View, which is surrounded by irrigated cropland. The sight of vast farms and huge circles of green crops is a bit of a shock after spending time, both physically and mentally, in a place that is and feels so ancient.

The second part of this ride is a trip to Four Corners, which many consider a must-do in the Southwest—if only to say you've been there. In Cortez, US 491 merges with US 160; follow the highway south out of town. If you're in southern Utah, you could take US 191 south through Blanding and Bluff, then choose to continue south on either US 191 or UT 262, either of which eventually connect with US 160. From the visitor center in Hovenweep, head almost due south to Aneth and pick up UT 262 to US 160.

You can feel and see the road descending relatively quickly into classic desert terrain as you head toward Four Corners. Cortez is about 6,200 feet above sea level, and you will eventually

Christy: This stretch of US 491 from the southeastern corner of Utah into southwestern Colorado and northern New Mexico used to be part of the infamous US 666, nicknamed the Devil's Highway because of that number's supposed occult connection. After getting a few complaints from people who didn't like that notion, or the notoriety—and after having to replace a whole lot of stolen road signs—state officials changed it in 2003. Like some who complained at the time, we kind of wish they had kept the old designation. On the other hand, highway fatalities have apparently gone down since the change. But that could also have something to do with the improvements in the road that happened at about the same time. We'll let you decide what you think. ●

drop to 5,000 feet. It feels like more than a 1,200-foot drop (and 5,000 feet is considered low elevation in this part of the world). About 20 miles south of Cortez, turn west on US 160. Follow the signs for Four Corners and you can't miss it—there aren't exactly a lot of roads out here competing for your attention.

Four Corners is the only place in the United States where four states meet at one point. The spot, officially known as Four Corners Monument, is in the Navajo Nation (the northeastern section is on Ute land) and is managed by the Navajo Parks and Recreation Department. It is little more than a wide spot in the road—just a simple turn off US 160. Admission is $3.

The site, which is open year-round, includes a large parking area flanked by a long line of Native American vendors selling jewelry and an array of arts and crafts, plus a commemorative metal plate set into a stone patio on the exact spot where the states come together. There are also vendors selling Navajo fry bread and bottled water, a small visitor center, and a gift shop. Spend a little time near the patio to get a chuckle out of watching visitors from all over the world stretch and contort them-

Visitors to the Four Corners Monument try to get themselves in all four states at one time.

selves to get one body part in each of the four states at the same time.

The nearest town is Teec Nos Pos, 6 miles past the monument. Here, pick up US 64 eastbound (you could also get to Monument Valley or Hovenweep from here by continuing west on US 160). Teec Nos Pos offers minimal services, which is fine. Shiprock, only about 27 miles farther down the road, has plenty of gas stations, convenience stores, and fast-food restaurants.

An excellent view of Shiprock Pinnacle is about 10 miles down US 491 south of the town. The rock itself is what geologists call a diatreme, or the remnant of an ancient volcano's core. Once you know what to look for (a shaft of vertical rock rising out of the valley floor), you'll start to see them all over this area. At a height of 1,700 feet, Shiprock is the biggest and most famous. About 27 million years ago, an explosion sent molten rock mixture up from 10,000 feet below the surface through a volcanic conduit. When it cooled, the rock grew harder than the earth surrounding it. Erosion gradually wore that softer soil away, leaving the volcanic rock standing. The Navajo call it *Tsé Bit'A'í,* or "rock with wings."

You can get a good view of Shiprock Pinnacle from the road about 10 miles south of Shiprock, New Mexico.

Steve: I was watching my odometer and was pretty sure I was looking at Shiprock Pinnacle but I was also looking for a turnout with a historical marker. I passed the turn-out, came back around, parked the bike, and realized the marker had been destroyed; two beat up-posts were all that survived. It must be a popular spot to hang out as the desert behind where the marker once stood was strewn with broken bottles of every variety. If you care to wiggle your way through a hole in the barbed-wire fence, are will-ing to walk about 100 yards, and have a long enough lens on your camera, you can eliminate the power lines from your photo of Shiprock Pinnacle. ●

Head north on US 491, through Shiprock and back to Cortez. It's a pretty straight shot and the roads are in good shape, but none of these are truly great motorcycle roads. The surrounding terrain is interesting if you like desert scenery. The ride from Shiprock to Cortez was made more interesting by fast-moving storm clouds rising above the cliffs to the north and east—a common sight in the summer monsoon season.

RIDE 15

Mesa Verde National Park

Directions:
US 160 from Cortez or Durango to park entrance

Distance:
Park entrance is 10 miles from Cortez, 8 miles from Durango. Visitor center is 15 miles from entrance.

Time:
at least half a day, more to really see everything

Services:
at Cortez, Mancos, and Durango. Limited services in the park.

Best Time of Year:
March through October; summer is hot but doable; expect thunderstorms late July through August

Highlights:
Up-close looks at ancient cliffside architecture, refreshing short hikes, easily accessible views from the top of a magnificent mesa

The most famous Ancestral Puebloan site is Mesa Verde National Park, the only national park in the country created to preserve man-made rather than natural structures. The park's features

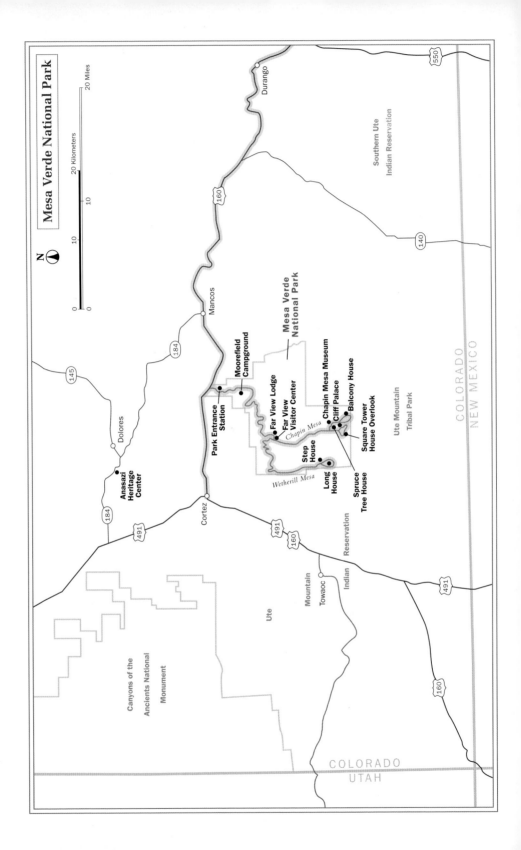

Mesa Verde National Park

N

20 Miles

20 Kilometers

Durango

550

140

Southern Ute
Indian Reservation

160

Mancos

Mesa Verde
National Park

184

Moorefield
Campground

Far View Lodge
Far View
Visitor Center

Chapin Mesa Museum
Balcony House
Cliff Palace

Park Entrance
Station

Chapin Mesa

Square Tower
House Overlook

Step
House

Ute Mountain
Tribal Park

145

Dolores

Anasazi
Heritage
Center

Wetherill Mesa

Long
House

Spruce
Tree House

COLORADO
NEW MEXICO

184

Cortez

491

160
491

Reservation

Indian

Mountain

Towaoc

Ute

491

Canyons of the
Ancients National

Monument

160

COLORADO
UTAH

Rangers give tours of Spruce Tree House, one of Mesa Verde's accessible complexes.

include many short walks and hikes, both paved and unpaved and for all ability levels, to breathtaking overlooks on the mesa and in the canyons carved out of it. During summer, you might want to plan to be somewhere besides the mesa top in the afternoon, since you're now well out of the mountains and into the desert heat of the Colorado Plateau.

This ride could start anywhere in the Four Corners region, all once part of the Ancestral Puebloan network. Although their homeland now crosses borders of four different states, the inhabitants who lived here a thousand years ago had their own governments and boundaries, now lost in time.

Cortez and Durango are your last towns of any size before Mesa Verde National Park and both are good for fueling up before you hit the meandering entrance road to the park.

Signs point the way to the park, which lies just off US 160; the motorcycle entrance fee is $8. If you're into archaeology and history, you might want to stay in or near the park, since the many accessible ruins can keep you occupied for a full day or more.

Unlike, say, Yellowstone, there's not much in the way of lodges or other amenities—at least, not built in the last 700 years. The park does have Far View Lodge, with motel-style accommodations, and a few places to get some cafeteria-quality food.

The rides into and out of the park will take at least forty-five minutes each, plus another twenty minutes or so to get to the main sites, so plan accordingly. Although it's surrounded by desert, the entrance is at 7,000 feet and the road climbs steadily from there through the piñon forests that gave the mesa its name (fires in the summers of 2000 through 2003 burned out a lot of the trees). You'll soon be skirting the side of the mountain on switchbacks with few places to stop (the steep cliffs create avalanche and rockfall danger), so take advantage of the designated ones. There are great views off to mountains and valleys in the distance, thousands of feet below. The road is narrow, so be careful passing (the NO TOWED VEHICLES signs at the entrance give you an idea of what's ahead), but it's definitely more fun for a bike than a car. The road is mostly in excellent condition.

Mesa Verde was named by Spanish explorers who passed through here in the 1760s and 1770s, but it remained relatively unexplored until ranchers started populating the area. The site was extensively damaged and looted before archaeologists truly began to realize its importance and the need to protect it. Theodore Roosevelt designated it a national park in 1906.

The park preserves at least 4,000 remnants of human activity, each with its own history. The most spectacular part of the park, and the aspect that draws thousands of visitors every year, is the cliff dwellings (there were once 600 or so here), some of which have been restored to give you an idea of what they looked like in their heyday.

Make a beeline to the visitor center, especially if you don't have much time. The park closes at dusk and the visitor center is only open 9 a.m. to 5 p.m. More important, some of the most significant attractions—Cliff Palace, Balcony House, and Long House—can only be seen by making an appointment to join a guided tour. While you can join one the same day, they fill up

Now, as in the past, a visit to Mesa Verde's Balcony House requires climbing ladders up the cliff face, which means the tour isn't for anyone with a fear of heights.

fast, and you might have to wander the park for a couple hours or more before your tour time. This isn't a problem as long as you plan ahead a little. So stop in at the visitor center and talk to a ranger before you head off to farther-off points. Rangers are happy to help you plan your trip based on how much time you have,

Waiting out the rain under the eaves of a popular convenience store in Cortez.

Steve: The clouds massing to the north and east as I was headed north toward Cortez on US 491 went from interesting to black. I had time to put on another layer of gear and make it to a convenience store on the outskirts of Cortez, where I was the fourth biker to take shelter under the eaves. I waited out the rain for a little more than an hour, sipping coffee and watching a steady stream of locals buying coffee, smokes, and pizza.

The three riders there when I arrived were donning full rain gear, everything from rubberized nylon to waterproof-breathable Harley suits. The rain settled down a bit while they were getting ready, but about ten minutes after they took off, the skies opened up with a torrent. I was glad I decided to stay put a while longer.

The rain was moving quickly from west to east. I was headed east to Durango and knew either it would chase me down from the west or I would ride into it heading east. I followed US 160 into Durango, riding in the rain pretty much the entire 50 miles, happy I called ahead to secure a room and had a place to wring everything out. ●

although visitors rarely give themselves enough time to get to everything they want to see.

Once you've gotten your bearings and booked a tour, you have a lot to discover. Chapin Mesa Archaeological Museum, 5 miles south of the visitor center, has exhibitions about Ancestral Puebloan culture.

Much of what makes this park famous is easily accessible from the road via short walks. Whether you have a little time or a lot, the Mesa Top Loop is a great option via bike, since it leads to many of the park's best overlooks, all of which are just a short distance from pullouts. Be sure to stop at the Square

Square Tower House, visible from a paved overlook trail, is named for its distinctive main feature.

Tower House and Cliff Palace overlooks, which are especially nice in late afternoon. Paved trails lead to structures dating as far back as the 600s. The main road also offers expansive views; being on the mesa provides you with a great viewpoint in many directions, with mountain ranges and mesas all around, plus valleys covered in a patchwork of farm and ranch land.

Wetherill Mesa, the farthest from the visitor center, is at the end of another winding 12-mile road atop a branch of the mesa. It's much less crowded than the rest of the park.

Ute Mountain Tribal Park, just south of Mesa Verde on US 491, also contains a number of Ancestral Puebloan sites, although tours of this area have to be arranged in advance and must be accompanied by a guide (they take either half or a full day and are on gravel roads). You cannot enter without a guide. Go to www.ute mountainute.com for more information.

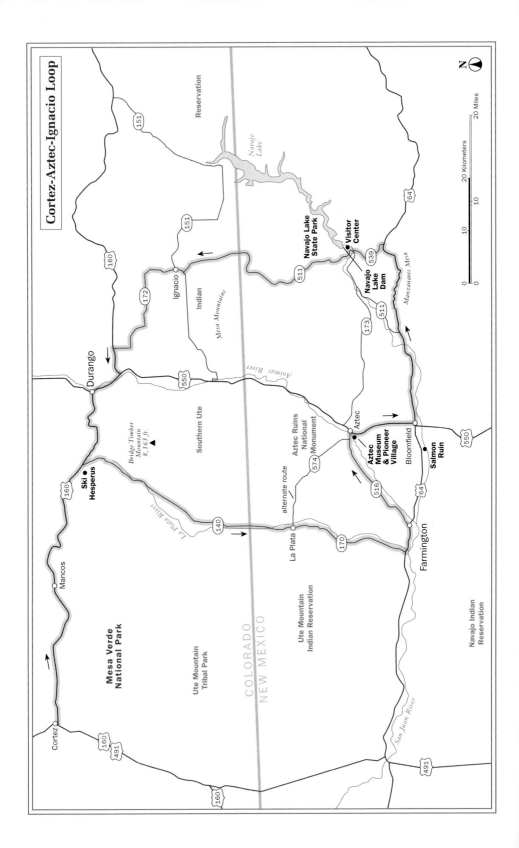

Cortez-Aztec-Ignacio Loop

RIDE 16

Cortez-Aztec-Ignacio Loop

Directions:

east on US 160 from Cortez to Hesperus

south on CO 140, which becomes NM 170

east on US 64 toward Farmington

east on NM 516 toward Aztec

south on US 550 to US 64

east on US 64, then north on NM 539 to Navajo Lake

west on US 64 back to NM 511

north on NM 511 to CO 172

north on CO 172 to US 160 back to Cortez

Distance:

210 miles

Time:

four to six hours or more, depending on stops

Services:

in almost every town except Hesperus

Best Time of Year:

early spring through late fall

Highlights:

a wide-open road with little traffic, the ruins of Aztec National Monument, the funky little town of Ignacio, and some weird road signs

Here we explore a few short rides, some of which are out-and-back or place-to-place and others that can be combined into loops. We use Cortez as a home base for convenience and partly because Durango was full up the weekend we did this ride (it was Labor Day weekend and the annual Four Corners Biker Rally was in full swing). Besides, the more time we spend in this rugged little cowboy town, the more we like it. Not as developed or "finished" as Durango, it's a little rough around the edges and a little less refined—and we like that.

Cortez is a cowboy town. This becomes even more evident as you head south on CO 140. For one thing, when you pass through Hesperus, Colorado, make a mental note of the Four Corners Test Facility. The test facility is where the Four Corners bull tests are conducted. Yep, bull testing. Nothing says cowboy country like bull testing.

As you continue south, the rich vegetation and ranching give way to a much more agricultural feel. CO 140 becomes NM 170 at the Colorado/New Mexico border. You'll want to continue south toward Farmington.

As an alternative, you could pick up NM 574 (also called North Light Plant Road or Old State Highway 173) about 5 miles south of the border. A word of warning: This is a decent shortcut to Aztec, but the road was in pretty tough shape when we rode it, with lots of potholes and blind curves. It was rutted with a nasty hump in the middle of the road and it runs through some fairly low-lying areas. There was a lot of mud from vehicles entering

Cortez, along with Durango and Mancos, is one of the sites of the annual Four Corners Biker Rally, held over Labor Day weekend—one of many activities in the Four Corners area over the long weekend. Any time of the year, stop in at a number of biker-friendly establishments in Cortez, including Blondies Pub and Grub (yes, you will find a number of welcoming blondes). ●

Take the self-guided walking tour through the ruins and kivas at Aztec Ruins National Monument.

from the mostly unpaved side roads. In short, stay on NM 170 unless you need the shortcut or the roads department gets around to resurfacing NM 574.

If you take CO 140/NM 170 into Farmington, you will pick up US 64 eastbound to West Broadway (it should be signed for US 64) to East Main Street, which becomes NM 516 into Aztec. Farmington is, as its name suggests, a center for a lot of farming activity in this area—and increasingly for recreation of all kinds in the Four Corners area. With a population of about 42,500, it's also one of the biggest cities in the area.

When you get to Aztec, find a local business or the Aztec Chamber of Commerce (at 201 West Chaco St.) and grab a copy of the *Official Aztec Visitor's and Relocation Guide*. It has loads of information about the town, the nearby ruins, and the surrounding area. NM 516 crosses the Animas River downtown and intersects with US 550. Turn onto Ruins Road, which parallels the river and then heads straight into a small, tidy residential neighborhood.

Aztec Ruins National Monument is about two-thirds of a mile off NM 516 and is worthy of a visit. Established in 1923, it was called Aztec Ruins by newcomers who wrongly assumed the Aztecs built these structures. Even if you have a copy of the official visitors guide, do yourself a huge favor and purchase *The Trail Guide to Aztec Ruins,* available at the monument visitor center for $1.50. Aztec Ruins National Monument is a historical link to ancient cultures that existed here but it is also a bridge between the past and the present. This site remains a sacred, spiritual place for Native American tribes with a long history in the Four Corners region.

If you have the time, take the 700-yard-long self-guided tour with twenty-two stops through the ruins. The guide provides interesting facts about the history of the ruins and their restoration. There are several displays of artifacts discovered at the site and the guide points out interesting architectural features that you wouldn't notice or appreciate without it. Included in the guide are writings by Gregory A. Cajete from the Santa Clara Pueblo, a community of people whose ancestors were among the people who built stone villages throughout the region.

Upon leaving the monument, head back to NM 516. You can take a hard left toward downtown or a soft left across NM 516,

---

Steve: Once you're back on US 64 and heading east out of Bloomfield, stop at the Carson National Forest Ranger Station on the eastern edge of town. From a sun-faded brochure posted outside the entrance, I learned that about a hundred wild horses roam the northern half of the Jicarilla Ranger District in small bands. The best time to see them is early in the day or late afternoon and early evening. According to the brochure, the best places to see them are in some of the more remote canyons southeast of Navajo Lake. Be advised that the area is a maze of dirt and gravel roads, so unless you have a bike that can handle that type of terrain, I'd suggest renting a four-wheeled vehicle of some sort. The creatures are elusive and skittish, so your odds of seeing them are slim. ●

leading to US 550 across the Animas. Take a right on US 550 and head south. Watch your speed south of town; we saw lots of cops with flashing lights and vehicles pulled over. US 550 heads straight south to Bloomfield, where it intersects with US 64. You'll be taking a left on US 64 and heading east.

If you're a history buff and want to see more ruins, take a right on US 64 in Bloomfield and continue about 3 miles west to the Salmon Ruin. Salmon Ruin boasts the oldest Chacoan great house in the San Juan Valley. The ruin is named for George Salmon, who homesteaded the property in the late 1800s. For more than ninety years, he and his descendants protected the ruin from vandals and treasure hunters. The on-site museum displays prehistoric pottery and other artifacts. Visit www.salmonruins.com for more information.

At the intersection of US 64 and CR 527, the road begins to ascend and the vegetation changes to juniper and piñon. CR 527 is an access road to Navajo Lake State Park, a long and twisting reservoir (sometimes referred to as a miniature Lake Powell) that straddles the Colorado/New Mexico border. Recreation junkies flock here to water-ski, camp, fish, swim, or spend some time on a houseboat. If you carry a fishing pole on your bike, you're in luck: The reservoir is stocked with fish, including record-breaking smallmouth bass and kokanee salmon. The San Juan River is one of the world's most famous trout fisheries in the world.

It's about a 33-mile round-trip to the lakeshore. Unless you are at the end of your ride and plan on camping at the park, there's no overwhelming reason to spend the time or the gas to check it out. There is a shortcut from here to the dam, our next destination, but it's unpaved.

Back on US 64, continue until you can take a right on NM 511 toward Turley and the Navajo Lake Dam. The feel of the road changes immediately as you turn onto NM 511, and you know this is going to be fun. The road narrows, rolling and rising, diving and twisting. Big sandstone cliffs flank your right side, with the San Juan River on your left. The road curves, dips, dives, and climbs its way to one side of the Navajo Lake Dam and rises

The marina at Navajo Lake is just past the Navajo Lake Dam on NM 511.

diagonally at about a 45-degree angle to the top at the other. It feels a little weird to be riding across the face of a dam. It's even stranger if you look up and see cars and trucks driving across the top of it above you.

The odd feeling of cutting across the dam passes after you reach the top and take the first of many hills and curves that

Steve: There is nothing spectacular about the road or the scenery at Navajo Lake State Park. There are some interesting road signs if you appreciate those things. One sign read RESIDENTIAL AREA. OBSERVE SPEED LIMIT. For me this begs me to question whether I must observe the speed limit anywhere else. The other sign I found strange was on one of the curves as I was getting close to the park. It said, LAKE AHEAD. SLOW DOWN. I wondered if this was merely a casual warning or perhaps a response to incidents of people driving too fast and finding themselves and their vehicles in the lake. ●

surround Navajo Lake and the dam. Continue north on NM 511. Within a few miles, the road opens to the sort of rural agricultural area that is very common in northern New Mexico. By now you've probably gotten used to the less-than-perfect road conditions that are also common here. Before long, you cross back into Colorado, NM 511 becomes CO 172. The surface changes virtually at the state line: Gone is the reasonably decent, somewhat rutted, a little beat-up and seemingly forgotten asphalt; you are greeted by an almost tarmac-smooth, apparently brand-new ribbon of pavement that slices through the ranching country of southwestern Colorado.

A killer paint job on one of hundreds of bikes lining the streets of Ignacio during the Four Corners Biker Rally.

Follow CO 172 and you will drop into the town of Ignacio, the tribal capital of the Southern Ute Indian Tribe and longtime site of the Ignacio Bike Week, which happens in conjunction with events all over the Four Corners area over Labor Day weekend.

Wrap up the ride by following CO 172 north to US 160 just east of Durango, then go west on US 160 back to Cortez.

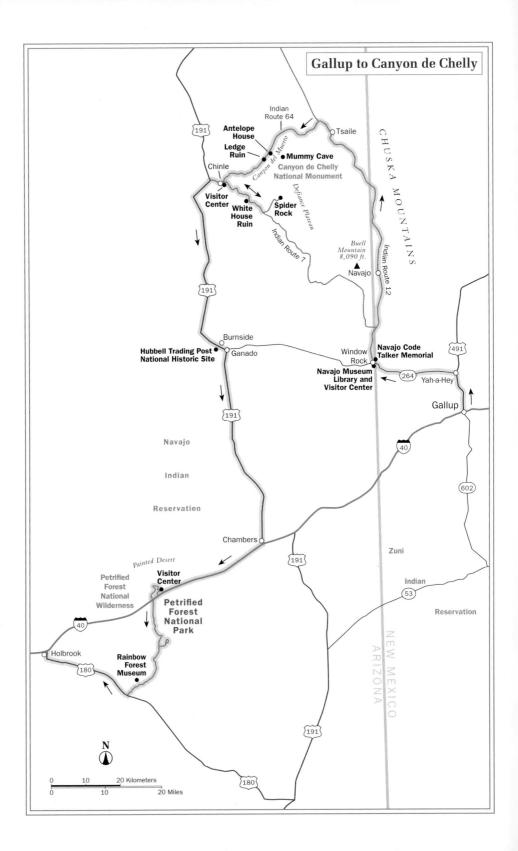

Gallup to Canyon de Chelly

Indian Route 64

CHUSKA MOUNTAINS

Antelope House
Tsaile

Ledge Ruin

Canyon del Muerto

Mummy Cave

Chinle

Canyon de Chelly National Monument

Visitor Center

White House Ruin

Defiance Plateau

Spider Rock

Indian Route 7

Buell Mountain 8,090 ft.

Indian Route 12

Navajo

191

Burnside

Window Rock

Navajo Code Talker Memorial

491

Hubbell Trading Post National Historic Site

Ganado

Navajo Museum Library and Visitor Center

264

Yah-a-Hey

Gallup

191

40

Navajo

Indian

Reservation

602

Chambers

Zuni

191

Indian

53

Reservation

Painted Desert

Visitor Center

Petrified Forest National Wilderness

Petrified Forest National Park

40

Holbrook

180

Rainbow Forest Museum

NEW MEXICO

ARIZONA

N

191

0   10   20 Kilometers
0   10   20 Miles

180

RIDE
17

Gallup to Canyon de Chelly

Directions:
US 491 north from Gallup
SR 264 west to Window Rock
IR 12 north to IR 64 in Canyon de Chelly National
Monument
IR 7 out and back along the south rim of the canyon
US 191 in Chinle south to SR 264
SR 264 to US 191 to I-40 at Chambers
west on I-40 to Petrified Forest National Park

Distance:
210 to 240 miles, depending on how much riding in Canyon
de Chelly National Monument and Petrified Forest National
Park
from Gallup to Window Rock: 26 miles
from Window Rock to Canyon de Chelly: 75 miles
from Canyon de Chelly to Chambers: 82 miles
from Chambers to Petrified Forest: 22 miles

Time:
one long day depending on time spent in Canyon de Chelly
National Monument

Services:
at Gallup, Window Rock, and Ganado

Best Time of Year:
spring and fall

Highlights:
ruins at Canyon de Chelly National Monument, Petrified Forest National Park, the Painted Desert

This ride allows you to explore some of the Navajo Indian Reservation, the largest in the country, and to get to know its people—and, of course, get some good riding in. Starting from Gallup, New Mexico, this route takes US 491 and SR 264 into Arizona, but they are fairly unremarkable desert driving. The ride doesn't really start until you get to Window Rock, Arizona.

Window Rock, the administrative capital and center of the 300,000-member Navajo Nation, gets its name from the hole in the 200-foot-high sandstone hill located just behind the Navajo Nation administrative buildings. The town is also home to the Navajo Code Talker Memorial, honoring the Navajos who helped the Allies win World War II by baffling the Axis powers with their complicated unwritten language, which the Allies used as a code

> **Steve:** Road signage in this area seems a little less complete than in other parts of the country. I entered Window Rock from the east on SR 264. I had trouble finding signs for IR 12 northbound; perhaps they were lost in the overwhelming mix of streetlights and signs for strip malls, gas stations, and fast-food restaurants. I completely missed the turn and had to do a U-turn and pass the intersection again before I located the signs for Window Rock. It wasn't until I saw those signs that I realized I had just turned onto IR 12 northbound. As I sometimes find when I'm traveling, I was accidentally right where I needed to be. ●

The Navajo Code Talker Memorial in Window Rock honors Navajo veterans of World War II.

to communicate. It's worth a stop, since it's only a half a mile or so off IR 12.

Back on IR 12, relax and enjoy the ride and the scenery. Shortly after leaving Window Rock, the road weaves and winds its way north, hugging a beautiful series of red-rock cliffs on your right. The terrain begins to open up, with ancient volcanic formations in the distance. You don't even realize it, but as IR 12 makes its way north, it crosses the Arizona/New Mexico border several times as it climbs toward the Chuska Mountains. You will steadily gain elevation; depending on the time of the year, this could be very welcome as higher elevations allow you to leave the heat of the desert behind, making the ride pleasant. The road eventually levels out and you will feel as if you are back in the mountains. You are, but not for long.

At that point, perhaps 10 miles south of the junction with IR 64, you will be entering an area that is slightly more inhabited than what you've just come through. Take IR 64 West at Tsaile. You are now on the road that will take you to the north rim of Canyon de Chelly (pronounced "de-SHAY"). You leave the cooler air behind and if it's summer, the heat of the desert quickly intrudes.

It's not long before you enter Canyon de Chelly National Monument, which is surrounded on all sides by reservation land. The labyrinth that is Canyon de Chelly is really several canyons, including Canyon de Chelly and Canyon del Muerto, plus numerous side canyons. The rock walls at the mouth of the canyon are only 20 or 30 feet high. But deeper into the canyons, especially

Steve: A few things to remember while riding here: Much of the Southwest is a patchwork of Indian reservations. Most of this ride takes you through parts of the Navajo Nation, which has its own laws (and police force). Speeds vary, but the maximum on the open road here is 55 miles per hour. If you're like me, the inclination is to push it a little since the roads are in good shape and you are out in the "middle of nowhere." Police on reservations take speed limit enforcement very seriously. This area can also be hit by summer monsoons, usually in late July and August. Be aware of low-lying areas and washes across the road. When I rode through, there was quite a bit of sand and gravel in some of the lower areas—no surprise since most of the region had been getting rain.

Also, domestic animals and livestock seem to roam freely on reservations. Keep a sharp lookout for horses and goats on or near the road. Just south of Tsaile, at the intersection of IR 12 and IR 64, I passed a horse lying dead in the ditch; by the smell, it must have been dead for several days. A little farther down the road, I slowed when I passed a big gray stallion. As I went by him, he bolted, running along the side of the road in the direction I was traveling. When I looked in my rearview mirror, he was running down the middle of the road. He eventually stopped and stood sideways across the center line. If other riders or vehicles of any type had been right behind me, there would have been trouble. ●

Visitors can view Spider Rock from the Spider Rock Overlook at the end of the paved section of South Rim Drive in Canyon de Chelly National Monument.

to the east, the walls can reach more than 1,000 feet above the floor. There is evidence to suggest that Ancestral Pueblo people from the Mesa Verde area may have moved to Canyon de Chelly sometime around A.D. 1280. As at Mesa Verde, they built brick structures, now long abandoned, that still cling to the sides of canyons.

The White House Ruin Overlook provides great views if you aren't up for the hike down to the ruin and back.

If you want to know more about the Navajo people and their history, the Canyon de Chelly visitor center is a good place to start. Unlike most national monuments, no hikes lead from the visitor center to the canyon, and only White House Ruin is open to the public without a guide. Free ranger-led hikes are limited to ten people; check with the visitor center for times and locations. The best way to see the canyon is from within. If you have your own four-wheel-drive vehicle, you can hire a Navajo guide. Check with the visitor center for more information. If you don't have your own vehicle, you can sign on to a Navajo-led tour from Thunderbird Lodge.

If you aren't planning on taking a guided tour, you are limited to viewing the canyon from either the north or south rim. Entering from the east on the north rim, you'll be following the edge of Canyon del Muerto. One of the first overlooks you come to is for Mummy Cave. Two well-preserved mummies were discovered during an archaeological expedition in 1880, hence the name (the traditional Navajo name is "House Under the Rock"). This site may have been occupied for nearly 1,000 years, making it perhaps the longest occupied in the canyon. Continuing on the north rim, you will come to Antelope House and Ledge Ruin Overlook. The road to Ledge Ruin Overlook was closed as of 2008 and may be closed permanently. Ask a ranger for an update.

South Rim Drive (or SR 7) also branches off from the visitor center. If you are pressed for time, zip out to the Spider Rock Overlook at the end of the paved road. Amid 1,000-foot canyon walls, Spider Rock is an impressive 800-foot sandstone spire at the confluence of Canyon de Chelly and Monument Canyon. According to ancient Navajo lore, Spider Woman chose the top of the rock for her home and it was she who long ago taught Diné (Navajo) ancestors the art of weaving on a loom.

Working your way back along the south rim, the next stop is White House Overlook, with great views of picturesque White House Ruin. It's named for a long wall in the upper part of the dwelling that is covered with white plaster. White House Ruin is the only place in the monument that's open to the unaccompanied public. From the overlook, you can hike down to 1,000-year-old structures on the floor of the canyon. It's about 2.5 miles round-trip and takes about two hours if you're in reasonably good shape. Get an early start in summer and carry plenty of water any time.

After Canyon de Chelly, it's a hot ride south on US 191. From here, we headed for Petrified Forest National Park, so at the intersection of US 191 and SR 264 (toward Burnside) we took a left, headed east for about 6 miles and picked up US 191 again in Ganado. Burnside is a crossroads with the basic amenities, while Ganado is more of a full town. At Ganado, the Hubbell Trading Post National Historic Site is the place where John Lorenzo Hubbell started trading with the Navajos in 1878. The Hubbell family operated this trading post until 1965, when the National Park Service bought it. The store is now run by the nonprofit Western National Parks Association, which sells authentic Indian goods and other items.

South of Ganado, the terrain changes again and climbs back onto juniper-covered hillsides. The road climbs and dives with the underlying terrain providing a giant roller-coaster feel almost all the way to I-40.

The multicolored hues of the Painted Desert are best viewed in the soft light of early evening.

The entrance and visitor center for the Petrified Forest National Park is 22 miles to the west on I-40. There is a 28-mile road running north to south within the park. Overlooks are close to the road, providing easy access to the rich array of colors that is the Painted Desert, as well as trails in Petrified Forest that allow you to walk among the remains of ancient trees that stood as dinosaurs walked among them.

In addition to having one of the world's largest collections of petrified wood, the park contains historic structures, archaeological sites, and fossils. Be sure to stop at the visitor center just off I-40, Kachina Point in the Painted Desert, and the Rainbow Forest Museum at the south end of the Petrified Forest Drive. Don't take a piece of petrified wood for a souvenir. Federal law prohibits the removal of petrified wood (or any natural, archaeological, or historical object) from its setting.

If you drive the entire length of the park from north to south, you can exit from the south end. The town of Holbrook is 47 miles to the west. Take US 180 west and enter Holbrook from the southeast. Holbrook looks like just the kind of town that would have been fun to explore more if we hadn't been moving on.

NEVADA

For the most part, Nevada is a large state with vast distances between meager services. There are places in Nevada that fall into the "if this isn't the middle of nowhere, you can see it from here" category. There are stretches of road that are so straight for so long that they fall off with the curvature of the earth. Vehicles coming from the opposite direction pop up above the horizon line and eventually pass, and then you each drop below the other's horizon line shortly thereafter. It is a place where wind gusts come out of nowhere and can move you and your machine into the other lane in a matter of seconds. We are willing to accept an invitation to tour Nevada from the back of a bike from someone who knows the state well, but until then, we see it mostly as a place to pass through as quickly as possible.

There are a few notable exceptions. For those who like to play tables or slots or otherwise have a good time with a little sin mixed in, then Las Vegas is the place. It's also a common start to a journey through the Southwest for visitors from far and near. There's another kind of escape here, on the other end of the adventure spectrum: the vast open deserts sprinkled with impressive geological formations. Great Basin National Park falls into this category.

The immense stretches of Great Basin desert and Sierra Nevadas that make up much of Nevada are beyond our scope, so we only introduce the corner of it that most would consider part of the Southwest.

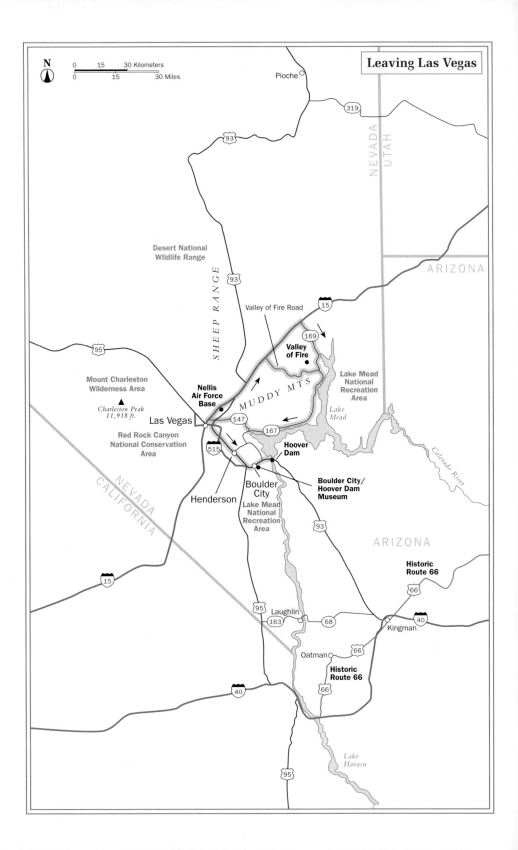

N

0   15   30 Kilometers
0   15   30 Miles

Leaving Las Vegas

Pioche

319

NEVADA   UTAH

93

Desert National
Wildlife Range

ARIZONA

93

Valley of Fire Road

15

169

Valley
of Fire

Lake Mead
National
Recreation
Area

95

MUDDY MTS

SHEEP RANGE

Mount Charleston
Wilderness Area

Charleston Peak
11,918 ft.

Nellis
Air Force
Base

Lake
Mead

Las Vegas

147

Red Rock Canyon
National Conservation
Area

167

Colorado River

515

Hoover
Dam

Boulder City/
Hoover Dam
Museum

Henderson

Boulder
City

Lake Mead
National
Recreation
Area

93

ARIZONA

NEVADA
CALIFORNIA

Historic
Route 66

66

15

95   Laughlin

163   68   40   Kingman

66

Oatman

66

Historic
Route 66

40

66

95

Lake
Havasu

Leaving Las Vegas

Directions:
to Valley of Fire: northeast on I-15 to SR 169
to Hoover Dam: south on US 95/US 93, follow US 93 to
Hoover Dam

Distance:
to Valley of Fire: about 100 to 150 miles, depending on route
to Hoover Dam: 60 miles round-trip

Time:
about three hours for each ride, more if you want to check
out attractions along the way

Services:
in most places

Best Time of Year:
anytime, although it gets very hot in summer

Highlights:
the wild and wooly Las Vegas scene, a taste of red rock
and history at Valley of Fire, Hoover Dam

Las Vegas is a world-famous destination in itself, and we'd have to write a whole book to cover everything going on there (and others have already done that). We'll let you decide which of the

The fountain outside the Paris Hotel and Casino is one of many odd and interesting features you'll see on the Vegas strip.

Las Vegas means "the meadows," which seems a misnomer unless you know that the city was built on top of an underground aquifer whose water rose to the surface in springs. Those are now under casinos on the famous Las Vegas strip. The first white permanent residents were Mormons (remnants of their original fort are enclosed in Old Vegas State Historic Park, at the intersection of Las Vegas Boulevard and Washington Avenue), but Nevada, like the rest of the West, has always been fond of gambling. Although it was illegal for twenty-five years or so at the beginning of the twentieth century, it flourished underground and was officially legalized again in 1935, the same year Hoover Dam was finished. Gambling, the addition of Nellis Air Force Base, and the city's status as a transportation crossroads led to increases in population, but it wasn't until the 1950s that it really took off. ●

guilty pleasures you want to partake in. (If you plan to stay in Vegas, call ahead and make reservations, especially if it's a popular weekend.) We're more concerned with the unique pleasures of the open road.

Many bikers use Las Vegas as a starting or ending point for tours of the Southwest, which means you'll have plenty of company. Your biggest question will be where to start, and it's a big question indeed. Here, we go through some of your options in the Las Vegas area.

The Las Vegas cityscape is an ever-changing whirl of neon, construction cranes, and hotel and apartment towers, with more on the way. Check out the sights and attractions; there is plenty here of interest to bikers. For one thing, Vegas offers a bounty of dealerships and smaller shops and rental places. The Harley dealership is one of the best in the West; it offers rentals as well as advice, service, and gear.

A lot of the territory surrounding Las Vegas isn't exactly an indication of how beautiful the Southwest can be. It's exceedingly dry, sparsely vegetated, and mostly lacking the colorful stone you see in places like the Grand Canyon and Monument Valley to the east of here. Still, there are some nice sights not too far away.

One option, if you're heading into town on I-15 from the north (or just want a quick couple-hour trip), is the Valley of Fire Loop, which takes you to the shores of Lake Mead. The loop, about 50 miles long including a short stretch of I-15, takes you through red sandstone formations and even some petrified forest. Turn off I-15 onto SR 169, which takes you to the 11-mile Valley of Fire Road.

The two-lane road is in good condition and doesn't take on a lot of elevation, although it dips and rises past rugged mountains and open valleys and occasionally goes through washes (they will almost always be dry; this region gets about 4 inches of rain a year, most of it in a few torrential summer showers). Short hikes take you right up to the strangely shaped rock formations, petrified wood, and rock art created by the Basket Maker and Ancestral Pueblo people who lived here from about 300 B.C. to A.D. 1100. You will have to pay a $6 entrance fee at the visitor center, which also has displays and lots more information.

On the park's far side, the highway joins with SR 167, called Northshore Drive because it flanks the northern side of Lake

Lake Mead National Recreation Area is popular year-round for outdoor enthusiasts such as boaters, hikers, swimmers, and photographers.

Mead, following the curves of the lake until the road rejoins US 93 south of Las Vegas. Lake Mead is the largest man-made lake in the United States, but its shores don't have any of the vegetation you'd expect from a giant freshwater body: It's hot and arid and this water gets pretty warm. That makes it a very popular recreation area for locals. The road is narrower and the condition is not as good, but it's a more scenic (and less busy) alternative to I-15.

Another option starting from Las Vegas is US 93 northbound toward Great Basin National Park (see ride 4). At nearly 500 miles there and back, a trip to the park would work best as at least a couple-day escape from the heat of the desert. Don't pass up chances to refuel, especially if you need high octane and see a place that offers it. If you like hiking, bring suitable shoes—recreation opportunities are plentiful. Because elevation climbs to 6,000 feet on US 93 and more than 10,000 in the national park, cool-weather gear is a good idea.

US 93 branches off northward from I-15, 22 miles east of Las Vegas and heads straight across a desert floor whose emptiness is enough to balance Las Vegas's hype. This is an official national scenic byway, but you may be wondering how they define scenic—unless you love wide-open desert, in which case, you'll feel right at home.

The road rises into mountains, and you'll pass several state parks, recreational areas, and wildlife refuges taking advantage of the landscape. After so much desolation, Pioche is a welcome combination of modern amenities (including restaurants and lodging) and well-preserved history. If you want to explore, pick up the informative Lincoln County walking and driving tour guide from a local business.

From Pioche, Great Basin National Park is another long, lonesome ride. If you've already seen the park, make a loop back to Vegas through Utah. Go east on SR 319 from Panaca into Utah's Dixie National Forest. You can turn south again and get back to I-15 via UT 18, a scenic mountain and desert byway.

Now, for the attractions south of Las Vegas. US 93 is a starting point for tours heading south and east into Arizona. It connects with Kingman and the famed US 66 as well as I-40 toward Flagstaff.

Christy: Because of its colorful history, Pioche is one of my favorite Western towns. Although some of its original residents were Mormons, it was famous for a level of mayhem only possible this far from the law. Mining here began in the 1860s and Pioche became a central site for ore processing for surrounding mines for hundreds of miles. By 1872 Pioche had 6,000 residents served by seventy-two saloons and dozens of houses of ill repute. The town has survived outlaws, booms, busts, floods, and fires—one of which lit 300 pounds of blasting powder stored under a mercantile, setting off an explosion that killed a handful of people and leveled a section of town. A lot of the nineteenth-century buildings are still standing, including the Million Dollar Courthouse, which went way over budget when it was built in 1871 and wasn't paid off until the 1930s. ●

Hoover Dam was named one of America's Seven Modern Civil Engineering Wonders in 1955 and designated as a National Historic Landmark in 1984. The bypass bridge, visible in the background, is due to be completed in 2010.

US 95 and US 93 split south of Las Vegas, with US 95 heading southbound toward Laughlin and Bullhead City. US 93 jogs eastward through Boulder City, passing several museums, including the Boulder City/Hoover Dam Museum, which could be a good introduction to the majestic dam. Be advised: Boulder City is one of the few places in Nevada that does not allow gambling.

When Hoover Dam was finished in 1935, it was the world's largest concrete structure and the largest electric power generating station. This marvel of engineering helped prepare the area for the growth that would follow and gained must-see status as a tourist attraction.

The road itself is one of the most dramatic short stretches you'll ever see, as it winds down via a multitude of switchbacks across the face of the colorful canyon and across the top of the dam. A million people take the dam tour each year and if you want to be one of them, you might want to plan ahead. Tickets for dam tours are available on a first-come, first-served basis. If

For a long time, Hoover Dam served as the only crossing point for miles along the Colorado River. Because US 93 is not only a major tourist route but also a heavily used truck route through here and into Mexico, the two-lane section crossing the dam has been prone to clogs for years. It wasn't unusual to see traffic snaking up the switchbacks on both sides as pedestrians crossed the road. Authorities finally decided the traffic congestion was significant enough to make building a new bridge across the canyon worth the trouble. The Hoover Bypass, a 3.5-mile corridor, breaks off from US 93 north of the dam, crosses the Colorado River about 1,500 feet downstream, and rejoins US 93 in Arizona. ●

you want to avoid waiting for your assigned start time or missing out entirely, you might want to arrive in time for the first one, at 9:15 a.m., which is usually the slowest time of day. Tickets to tour the entire dam are $30 and admission to just the visitor center is $8. Those are fairly steep prices, but the inner workings of this enormous structure are fascinating, especially once you get deep inside it.

From here, you can explore the shores of Lake Mead via several short roads that branch off US 93 and US 95, enjoy inexpensive gambling and buffets at Laughlin, or head back into town. Laughlin is also home to Laughlin River Run, billed as the "West Coast's Largest Motorcycle Event on the Banks of the Colorado River" and held every April. Of course, for a lot of people, this is just the start of a much longer tour into southern Utah and northern Arizona. Whether you go via US 93 or US 95 (which continues south until it hits I-40 near Lake Havasu), the road is pretty flat and dull desert until you get to the mountains and ghost towns of the Kingman/Oatman area and historic US 66.

NORTHERN ARIZONA

When most people think of Arizona, they think of desert: the red rocks of Sedona and the striated walls of the Grand Canyon. And it's true; all of that is here for the exploring. But much of northern Arizona is mountainous and alpine, and no matter how hot the valleys get in the summertime, those who travel and live here know they are never far from a cool mountain escape.

One of the best things about this part of the country is that the Wild West lives on in towns such as Flagstaff. True, many of the old-time cowboys are now riding two-wheeled horses, but the spirit of rugged independence is still all over the place. There's also a sense of live and let live, which means other people are pretty willing to leave you alone if you want them to.

The riding here is some of the most accessible and spectacular in the Southwest. Aside from obvious draws like the Grand Canyon—a must-see, of course—there are lots of winding roads throughout the mountains and deserts. Northeastern Arizona is part of the Colorado Plateau, which drops off dramatically at the Mogollon Rim in the middle of the state. There, forested highlands give way to colorful cliffs and the desert below.

The west side of the state's northern half is more typical desert. Unlike much of central Arizona, cities are few and far between here, resulting in the long stretches of open road that made US 66 famous.

The entire northeastern quarter of Arizona is Navajo and Hopi land. Some facts:

- At 27,000 square miles, the Navajo Nation is the largest swath of Native American–owned land within the United States.
- In 1863 and 1864, as part of the Indian Removal Act of 1830, the U.S. Army forced about 8,500 Navajos (along with some of their neighbors, the Apache) to march to a million-acre reservation known as the Bosque Redondo Indian Reservation at what is now Fort Sumner, New Mexico. Starved into submission, forced to march hundreds of miles in what the Navajo call the Long Walk, and suffering from poor conditions during incarceration, nearly one-third of them died. After six years, the reservation was deemed a failure and the Native Americans were allowed to go home.
- Despite challenges, the Navajo have retained a sense of community and identity. They are known throughout the Southwest for their artistry in metalwork, which they started doing in the 1850s. By about 1900, they were known for a flourishing silver jewelry business, and they continue to offer their wares for sale throughout the region today.
- The Navajo and Apache languages are similar, but they are unlike any other Native American tongue in the Southwest. Their closest linguistic relatives, called the Athabascans, are in western Canada and Alaska. ●

RIDE
19

Highway 89's Better Half

Directions:
south on US 89 from Kanab, Utah, to Fredonia, Arizona
east on US 89A to intersection with US 89
south on US 89 to Flagstaff

Distance:
from Kanab to Flagstaff: 201 miles
from Kanab to Grand Canyon North Rim to Flagstaff: 291
miles

Time:
most of a day to a full day if you choose to stop at the
North Rim of the Grand Canyon

Services:
Kanab, Fredonia, Page, Cameron, and Flagstaff

Best Time of Year:
March through October, but check in advance for the possibility of snow; the road to the Grand Canyon's North Rim
is open from at least mid-May to mid-October, longer if the
weather is mild

Highlights:
true John Wayne territory; wide-open red-rock scenery,
including the Vermilion Cliffs; a peek at the Grand Canyon
from the less-busy North Rim

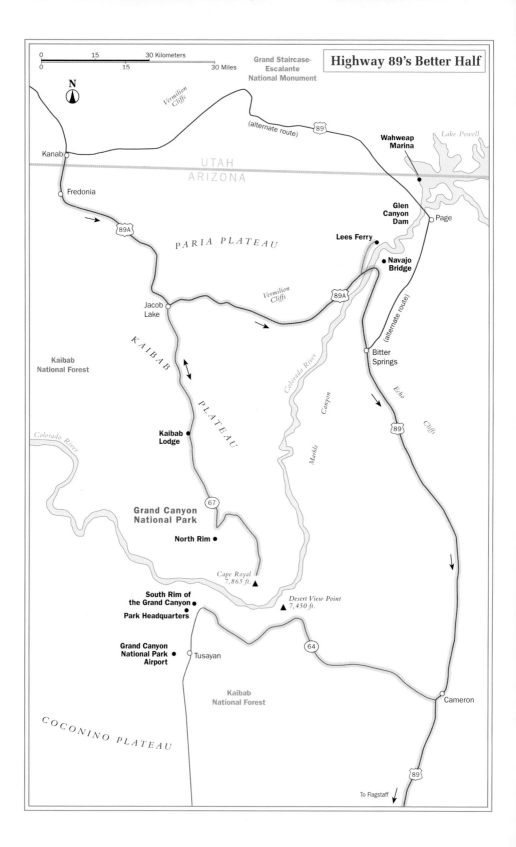

This ride starts at Kanab, which most people reach via US 89. From here, many continue through Page on US 89 toward Lake Powell and Arizona, a quick ride over rolling sagebrush plains. The route bisects the southern corner of the enormous Grand Staircase-Escalante National Monument, with its rolling red dirt and sagebrush vistas. If you do go that way and want to know more, stop by at the visitor center along the road between Kanab and Page.

US 89A, a designated scenic byway that branches off to the south, is a much more beautiful and interesting ride. With views across the Grand Canyon and possible California condor sightings on the agenda, this is a good time for binoculars if you have them.

Either highway will meet up with US 89 southbound in Arizona, which intersects with AZ 64, the road to the South Rim of the Grand Canyon. Although the north and south rims are not far apart as the crow flies, getting from one to the other takes hours by road.

Kanab has plenty of amenities, although a thriving nightlife is not one of them (if you want that, Fredonia, over the Arizona

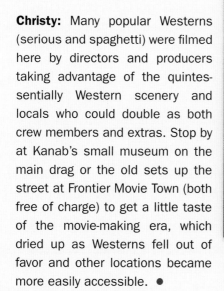

Christy: Many popular Westerns (serious and spaghetti) were filmed here by directors and producers taking advantage of the quintessentially Western scenery and locals who could double as both crew members and extras. Stop by at Kanab's small museum on the main drag or the old sets up the street at Frontier Movie Town (both free of charge) to get a little taste of the movie-making era, which dried up as Westerns fell out of favor and other locations became more easily accessible. ●

Don't shoot! This is just a cutout silhouette on one of the Old West movie sets in Kanab.

border to the south, is a slightly better bet). Back in the 1940s and 1950s, Kanab was a major filmmaking center, as was Monument Valley to the east.

Fredonia is the last town of any size on US 89A until Page. The rest of this ride (except for the North Rim of the Grand Canyon, which offers all the typical amenities of a national park) is pretty remote, so make sure you're fueled up and have plenty of water before you embark. US 89A crosses the Kaibab Plateau and skirts the Paria Plateau, reaching elevations of almost 8,000 feet, so if there's any question about road conditions, check before you go.

The road runs to the southeast until it begins to climb onto the Kaibab Plateau. It's from the height of this plateau that the Grand Canyon descends, creating dramatic drops from top to bottom. To get to the canyon's North Rim, take SR 67, which leaves US 89A on top of the plateau at Jacob Lake (whose lodges and recreational activities cater to Grand Canyon–bound tourists spring through fall). From the turnoff, it's another 45 miles through thick pine forest to the visitor center.

The views may not be quite as dramatic as those from the South Rim, but they are spectacular, and some Grand Canyon lovers prefer the North Rim for its forested surroundings and relative peace. While you'll encounter plenty of tourists in summertime, it's nothing like the zoo the South Rim can be when it's crowded. And the higher elevation on this side makes it cooler in the hottest parts of summer.

Several short roads branch off from the visitor center, taking you to various outcroppings from which you can see across to the other side.

Back on US 89A, the road descends again off the plateau and toward the Vermilion Cliffs (there's a viewpoint as you leave the plateau, if you want a good look from a distance). True to their name, the cliffs—at the southern edge of the Paria Plateau—are a brilliant red. The road skirts their edge, with lots of chances to step off the bike and admire them.

Just before the two US 89s converge, a short in-and-back of about 6 miles each way will take you to Lees Ferry, the only place

The rich red color of the Vermilion Cliffs continues to get more beautiful as the sun drops lower in the western sky.

Christy: Vermilion Cliffs National Monument is famous for more than its scenery. Conservationists chose this remote area to release California condors to the wild as part of a breeding program that brought them back from the brink of extinction. In 1987 only twenty-two of these birds remained in the world. They were captured and bred in captivity in California, then successfully reintroduced there. In 1996 a few were released here. The wingspans of these magnificent, if homely, birds can measure 6 feet. If you're lucky, you might catch a glimpse of some (they usually travel in small groups) here or around the Grand Canyon. ●

in 700 miles of the Grand Canyon area where visitors can drive to the Colorado River. It's now the point where rafting companies put their boats in for the long adventure through the Grand Canyon on the Colorado River. From 1872 to 1928, it was the site of a ferry crossing, which you can find out more about at the historical site. You will cross the Colorado River on Navajo Bridge, a double span over Marble Canyon. The original bridge, built in 1929, now serves as a pedestrian crossing next to its modern replacement. If not for this bridge (and the ferry in the past), travelers would

Glen Canyon Dam holds back the Colorado River; it and the red-rock cliffs that support it create Lake Powell.

have to go 800 miles to get from one bank of the Colorado River to the other.

Page is a few miles north of the intersection with US 89 and has all amenities, plus great views of Lake Powell. For dinner, try Fiesta Mexicana or, for something fancier, the Rainbow Room on the shore of Lake Powell.

From here, you could go back west on US 89A or south toward the intersection with SR 64 and the South Rim. Be forewarned that services are sparse between the US 89/US 89A intersection south of Page and the turnoff for the South Rim—or any other place to the south, for that matter. Cameron, at the junction of US 89 and SR 64, has a convenience store; from there, it's 50 miles to the South Rim and another 65 miles to Flagstaff.

US 89 from Page to Flagstaff is a necessary evil. In most places it is a two-lane road, and traffic can get backed up during high tourist season with a line of RVs and motor homes, so stay attentive. Motorists will attempt to pass these monsters of the open road at risky times, to the potential peril of both them and you. Flagstaff serves as a great home base for the many good rides throughout northern Arizona.

RIDE

20

Grand Canyon

Directions:

north on US 180 from Flagstaff to the junction with SR 64

north, then east, on SR 64

north on US 89 to Page (or back to Flagstaff)

Distance:

from Flagstaff to Page via the Grand Canyon South Rim: about 140 miles

from Flagstaff to the South Rim to Kanab: 206 miles

Time:

at least half a day up to several days, depending on time in the park

Services:

at Flagstaff, the intersection of SR 64 and US 89 at Cameron, and Page (the park has food but not fuel)

Best Time of Year:

spring and fall

Highlights:

the hospitable and laid-back town of Flagstaff, plateau and mountain riding in the heart of the desert, the Grand Canyon

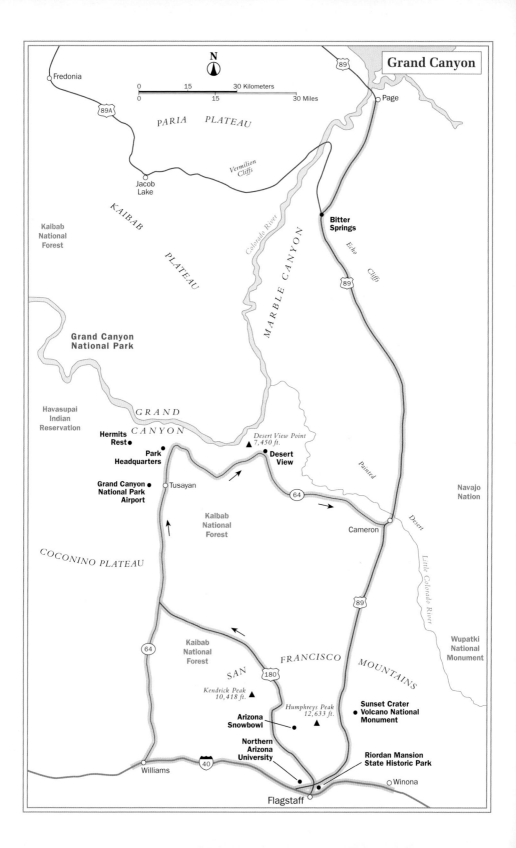

If there's one place everyone associates with the Southwest, it's the Grand Canyon, and you (literally) can't miss it if you're in this part of the world.

Flagstaff is the closest town of any size to the Grand Canyon's South Rim, and it makes a great base for rides around here. It's a college town (Northern Arizona University is here), but it also preserves some of the character of its logging and ranching-oriented past and present. The old Route 66 winds through here, parallel to US 40, if you want to take a spin along memory lane. Check out the old towns made famous by this road and the cowboy, mail, and train routes before it.

Flagstaff has a plethora of motels and restaurants. Some local favorites: Busters, just off US 89 on Milton Road, is known for a variety of entrees—from chicken to pork chops to oysters on the half shell—friendly atmosphere, and desserts including Bananas Firecracker. Drink a hundred beers there and you get your name on the wall. The town also boasts a lot of good breakfast options— and, if your gut is rebelling from all the road food, there are a number of laid-back yet health-conscious restaurants offering fresh ethnic and American cuisines.

While you're here, Flagstaff also offers a lot of touristy things to see, including Riordan Mansion State Historic Park, which showcases the 13,000-square-foot arts-and-crafts style log house built in 1904 by two brothers who made their fortunes in the booming timber industry. Sunset Crater Volcano National Monument, to the north off US 89, allows you to check out the debris from an eruption that happened as recently as A.D. 1100—you can only imagine its effect on the people living here at the time. The Museum of Northern Arizona has displays on everything from dinosaurs to art. Flagstaff is also home to the Lowell Observatory, which offers daily tours.

But, of course, the main attraction on this ride is the Grand Canyon, one of America's most famous landmarks. Bring comfy shoes and a jacket—at 7,000 feet or so, the rim of the Grand Canyon is often breezy and can be chilly.

From Flagstaff, take US 180 north. The road goes through a bit of suburbia before setting out as a scenic byway that takes you past the volcanic San Francisco peaks and past the Arizona Snowbowl ski area. (If you've been spending a lot of time in the deserts around here, the ski resort might seem a surprise, but the hills are actually pretty steep. Those who like the cross-country variety swoosh through the pines at the Flagstaff Nordic Center.) You'll pass through national forests filled with stands of ponderosa pine and quaking aspens interspersed with meadows.

The road curves a bit around Humphreys Peak, Arizona's highest at 12,562 feet. Not surprisingly, this area gets a lot of snow in winter and early spring. Check before you go if you're worried about conditions. You could always jog west to Williams and north on SR 64, which sticks to a lower elevation but isn't as scenic. Perhaps because of wintertime damage, the surface is a bit rough at times, so watch for those patches.

After rounding the mountain, the road flattens out but remains at fairly high elevation all the way to the Grand Canyon. This means it can be windy and even cool almost any time of year. You know you're getting close when you see the trappings that crop up outside any major national park. In this case, that means the cheesy theme park, Flintstone Bedrock City, near the junction of US 180 and SR 64, as well as gas stations and some motels. After the junction, the road becomes flat and fast with plenty of passing lanes to accommodate all the traffic heading into the park.

The Grand Canyon is, of course, all it's cracked up to be. As you might expect, the park itself can be something of a zoo, with huge crowds much of the time. Watch out for hordes of tourists, RVs, and out-of-town visitors wandering aimlessly about.

To get to the visitor center, park in one of the designated lots around the park and hop onto a free shuttle bus (one of the great things about being on a bike is that it's much easier to find parking). The buses are convenient, and in certain parts of the park they're your only option most of the year. In winter when it's less busy, things loosen up a bit. If you want to stay here, make reservations well in advance, especially if you plan to be here

This photo doesn't do it justice. The Grand Canyon is even more spectacular when seen in person.

during busy times (summer and holiday weekends); call (888) 297-2757.

As the map you'll get at the entrance will show you, there are several information centers throughout the park. Since this is *the* Grand Canyon, after all, you'll want to check out many, if not most, of the overlooks just off the main road. Depending on how much time you want to spend here, you could choose from a number of activities. Rangers hold mini-tours and informational workshops. Hikes vary from flat (along the rim) to very steep and even death defying. Outfits just outside the park will be happy to take you on an airplane ride over the canyon.

The canyon's famous multicolored hues are best seen early in the morning, when light is clearest. The worst time is the middle of the day, when bright, direct sunlight flattens the grandeur. From most of the viewpoints, you can see for miles to the east and west, as well as up to 4,600 feet down from the rim to the Colorado River below. The canyon is 8 to 16 miles across. The different colors of rock, seen as horizontal stripes, represent eras of time; the "basement rocks" at the bottom are up to 1.8 billion years old.

At the park entrance, the friendly ranger who greeted us said a California condor was spotted a few days earlier feeding on the corpse of a poor unfortunate visitor who fell off a cliff. The scavengers eat large dead animals, usually deer in this part of the world. We thought becoming condor fodder would be a cool alternative to burial or cremation—helping feed an endangered species and all—but the ranger informed us that human bodies are considered hazardous waste, since people ingest so many toxic substances. We agreed that our bodies undoubtedly would fit in that category.

That same summer, a friend of a friend almost died after getting lost while trying one of the canyon's multiday hikes. She and her boyfriend thought they were prepared with plenty of food and water, and they did manage to keep their wits about them and survive. But take warnings seriously: Dying in the Grand Canyon would be a major vacation spoiler. By the way, this ranger, like many at the Grand Canyon, also rides and was happy to give us tips about touring the region. ●

California condors like this one are sometimes seen soaring on the thermals above the Grand Canyon. Do your best not to feed them with your remains.

From the west side of the park, you have several options: go back to Flagstaff, take SR 64 eastward and join US 89 northbound, or head west and explore one of the access points on the western side of the canyon. Those western roads are unpaved and rough except for IR 18, which branches north for 68 lonely miles from US 66 near Peach Springs. There are no services on that road north of US 66.

We took SR 64 out through the park's east entrance toward US 89. The road is in good condition as it runs across the juniper-dotted plateau, then drops into a desert valley. A few miles after leaving the park, you'll start to see smoke shops

Late afternoon sun hits the Desert View Watchtower at the east end of the Grand Canyon's South Rim.

and Navajo trading posts, signaling you've entered the enormous Navajo Indian Reservation. North of the road, the Little Colorado runs through its own steep-walled gorge that is very nice, although it pales in comparison to what you've just seen.

From here, we went north on US 89 (you might want to buy gas at Cameron, at the junction of SR 64 and US 89) to Page, a decent-size town that serves as a base for massive Lake Powell and Glen Canyon National Recreation Area. Page connects with highways US 89 and US 89A along the Utah/Arizona border (see ride 19) which take you to the north or west.

RIDE 21

Flagstaff/Sedona/Prescott

Directions:

south on I-17 from Flagstaff

south on US 89A toward Sedona (exit 337)

west on US 89A to Cottonwood, Tuzigoot National Monument, and Prescott (89A becomes Pioneer Parkway outside Prescott)

left on Williamson Valley Highway to Iron Springs Road

right on Iron Springs Road, which becomes CR 10 through Skull Valley to Kirkland

left on CR 15 to Kirkland Junction (short cutoff), then left onto SR 89

north on SR 89 to Prescott

south on SR 69 to SR 169

east on SR 169 to I-17 back to Flagstaff

Distance:

243 miles for the entire loop, a few more if you take any additional side trips.

from Flagstaff to Sedona: 30 miles

from Sedona to Jerome: 26 miles

from Jerome to Prescott: 34 miles

from Prescott to Skull Valley: 17 miles

from Skull Valley to Kirkland: 7 miles

from Kirkland to Kirkland Junction: 5 miles

from Kirkland to Prescott: 22 miles

from Prescott to I-17: 40 miles

from I-17 to Flagstaff: 55 miles

Time:
better part of a day, depending on how many stops you
make

Services:
at Flagstaff, Sedona, Cottonwood, Jerome, and Prescott,
plus more limited options at many small towns

Best Time of Year:
March through October

Highlights:
Twisty Oak Creek Canyon, ancient ruins at Tuzigoot National
Monument, the mountain mining history of Jerome

Our home base for this ride is Flagstaff, a funky mountain, college, and tourist town with a tidy little downtown. Pick up I-17 south toward Phoenix. About 4 miles later, leave I-17 behind, take the exit for SR 89A to Sedona (also signed for Flagstaff Pulliam Airport) and head south into Oak Creek Canyon. With Flagstaff at an elevation of about 7,000 feet and Sedona at about 4,400 feet, Oak Creek Canyon is a fairly steep and beautiful 25 miles of hairpins and curves and tight twisties cut into the red rock for which this part of Arizona is famous.

You leave the tall open pine forest behind and wind your way down and through the canyon. A word of warning: Some of the curves are poorly banked, so it's best to observe suggested speeds. Besides, the road seems to get a lot of local traffic even on weekdays. The curves come quickly, one after another, leaving little opportunity to pass the slowpokes—and even if you do, there is sure to be another little pack of them not too far ahead. Relax, enjoy the slow pace, and view the surroundings.

About 6 miles north of Sedona, you'll find Slide Rock State Park, a 43-acre apple farm in the canyon. A hundred years ago,

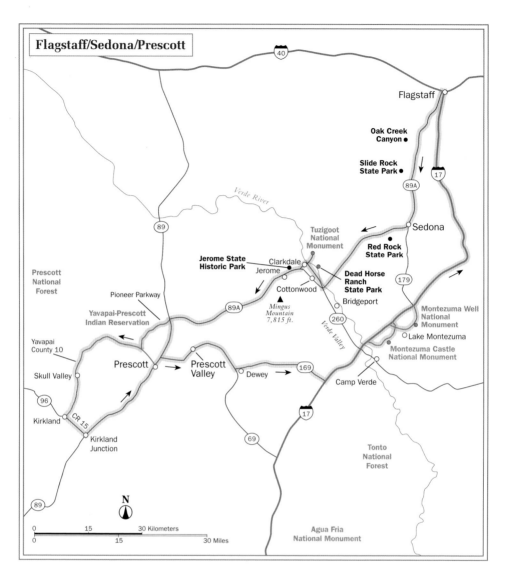

Frank L. Pendley established an irrigation system to plant his first apple orchard here. The park has done a good job of preserving the historic buildings and the orchards from the original homestead and still celebrates an Apple Festival each September. On an early weekday visit during late summer, the parking lot was already more than half full. Summer days can be very busy.

Slide Rock is an 80-foot natural waterslide near the homestead. Visitors can slither down the chute or just wade or sun themselves along the creek. More daring types jump off a cliff

Kids jump from a rock into a deep green pool at Slide Rock State Park.

into a deep blue-green pool of water. The park has some services, namely the Slide Rock Market, which is open year-round. A little farther south down the road, a set of roadside stands near the Dairy Queen offers a selection of jewelry made by Native American craftspeople.

Ever since the 1970s, when it was first identified as the center of a spiritual vortex, Sedona has been a magnet for people looking for . . . something. A lot of things. Now, its population is a combination of old-time cowboy types (rapidly disappearing these days), outdoors enthusiasts, artists, tourists, and New Agers seeking a spiritual haven—and a slew of people hoping to make money off the influx. Depending on your perspective, it can be a nightmare or a delight. It's got all the amenities, beautiful scenery, and some nice restaurants and spas, which makes it worth visiting, if even for a few hours. But we're more interested in the rides nearby.

SR 89A continues southwest through Bridgeport, where it curves and merges with SR 260 toward Cottonwood. The towns in this part of Arizona can easily blend together, so be alert. The highway curves left and becomes North Main Street in Cottonwood. Do your best to stay on SR 89A/SR 260 as it winds through town (we got a little turned around and had to retrace our steps). When you see signs for Dead Horse Ranch State Park, you know you're headed in the right direction. You may see the occasional sign for Historic or Old 89A, which means you are right where you should be.

The turn for Tuzigoot National Monument will be on your right. It's about a mile to the visitor center. You are now in the Verde Valley of central Arizona. The valley, which runs north-

---

Steve: On a ride at the end of July, from my vantage point, Sedona appeared to be mostly under construction. At an elevation of about 4,400 feet (significantly lower than the surrounding hills), it was *hot*. Especially sitting in the traffic caused by the construction. I'm not much of a shopper. I don't really buy into the whole vortex thing, and I had a lot of ground to cover, so I passed on through without stopping. I was headed for Tuzigoot National Monument. With a name like Tuzigoot, it had to be interesting. ●

west to southeast, was home to the Southern Sinagua culture (*Tuzigoot* is an Apache word meaning "crooked water" and *Sinagua* is Spanish for "without water"). As you ride in and around this part of Arizona, you'll notice how lush this valley is compared to its somewhat parched surroundings. The visible dwellings at Tuzigoot are built on a ridge 120 feet above the valley below. This ancient village consisted of 110 rooms and two- and three-story structures dating back to about A.D. 1000. The Sinagua people were farmers who traded widely and used irrigation to grow crops. The last inhabitants of Tuzigoot left the area in the early 1400s.

Tuzigoot National Monument is an easy ride from Flagstaff, Prescott, or Phoenix.

Montezuma Castle is at the southeast end of the Verde Valley. The southern Sinagua began building this impressive five-story dwelling in the early 1100s. It's nestled in a cliff recess about 100 feet above the valley. As with a lot of ruins in this region, early settlers assumed it was of Aztec origin, thus the name Montezuma Castle.

Take a right out of Tuzigoot National Monument and follow the road into Clarkdale, take a left on Main Street, go a couple blocks, and make another left onto Old Hwy. 89A, then a soft right as you merge back on to SR 89A.

The road climbs 2,000 feet in about 5 miles to the top of Cleopatra Hill and the town of Jerome. Jerome is named for Eugene Murray Jerome, a New York attorney who was one of the principal backers in the purchase of the claim that started it all. When it was the fourth-largest city in the Arizona Territory,

Say "so long" to Jerome before the last uphill curve takes you out the back side of town.

almost 15,000 people lived in the "Wickedest Town in the West," where they hoped to capitalize on the riches of the town's mines. The mines fell silent in 1953 and in the 1960s, artists and hippies found it an inexpensive place to set up shop. Visit the museum at Jerome State Historic Park for more about the area's colorful history.

Leaving Jerome out the top and back of town, the road continues to twist and climb its way up and over Mingus Mountain. It's a fun road, with lots of tight curves and switchbacks, that eventually drops you northwest of Prescott Valley, almost due north of Prescott.

If you want something of a firsthand account of what it was like in the early days, stop by Ghost Town Gear at 415 Hull Ave. and chat with Noel Knapp, father of Morgan Knapp, the owner of the store. Noel and his wife moved to Jerome in the late 1970s and scraped together enough money to buy the building that houses both Ghost Town Gear and the art gallery above it. To get to the gallery where Noel's wife, an artist, shows her work, you have to go around the block to what should be the back side of the second floor of the building. The hills in Jerome are so steep, you'll end up on Main Street facing what appears to be the front side of an entirely new set of buildings. ●

From here you are headed on a loop that takes you into Skull Valley and around the back side of Sierra Prieta. Depending on what you read and who you believe, Skull Valley gets it name from mounds of bleached skulls found by early settlers, the result of a clash or clashes between local Indian tribes or from a clash between local Apaches and an army detachment from the Whipple Barracks. The bones served as a warning to other marauding tribes to think twice before attacking.

From the intersection of SR 89A and SR 89, SR 89A becomes Pioneer Parkway. Stay on Pioneer Parkway, since there is no reason to venture farther into Prescott from this direction unless you need to. When SR 89A/Pioneer Parkway intersects Williamson Valley Highway, take a left and head south. Go about 2 miles and take a right on Iron Springs Road. You will quickly leave the suburbs of Prescott behind as Iron Springs Road becomes CR 10. The road opens up as you leave the hills behind you and descend into Skull Valley and the northern reaches of the Sonoran Desert.

Continue on CR 10 to Kirkland, then take a left onto CR 15 to Kirkland Junction and a left back onto SR 89. Be alert, because the towns here are pretty much just wide spots in the road and the turns are not always well marked.

As soon as you get on SR 89, there's a 5- or 6-mile stretch of pavement that is so straight and with such excellent visibility that the road invites you to pull the throttle back and open it up, just to see what your machine is capable of—not that I'm suggesting you exceed the posted speed limits. If the bike had wings, you could probably take flight. That stretch is short-lived and you'd better get ready to work a little. You've got about 20 miles of 20- to 35-mile-per-hour curves and switchbacks to prove your skill. Some will be banked and some flat, and a few blind curves will test your nerves. It's a little bit of work, but this kind of work makes you smile. If it's hot—and it very often is in this part of Arizona—you'll probably work up a sweat. That's OK; as the turns begin to loosen, you'll have a little shade in which to cool off as you roll back into the forests that border Prescott to the south.

Stay on SR 89 through downtown Prescott. Pick up SR 69 south to SR169 east back to I-17. If you're in the mood for more curves, get off I-17 at SR 179 north, head back toward Sedona, and reverse your track back up Oak Creek Canyon.

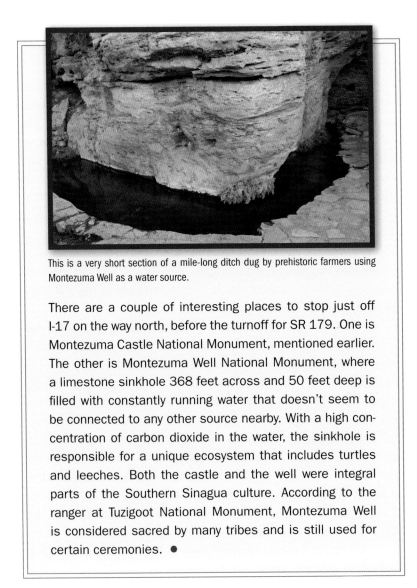

This is a very short section of a mile-long ditch dug by prehistoric farmers using Montezuma Well as a water source.

There are a couple of interesting places to stop just off I-17 on the way north, before the turnoff for SR 179. One is Montezuma Castle National Monument, mentioned earlier. The other is Montezuma Well National Monument, where a limestone sinkhole 368 feet across and 50 feet deep is filled with constantly running water that doesn't seem to be connected to any other source nearby. With a high concentration of carbon dioxide in the water, the sinkhole is responsible for a unique ecosystem that includes turtles and leeches. Both the castle and the well were integral parts of the Southern Sinagua culture. According to the ranger at Tuzigoot National Monument, Montezuma Well is considered sacred by many tribes and is still used for certain ceremonies. ●

RIDE
22

Flagstaff/Camp Verde Loop

Directions:
south on SR 179 or I-17 from Flagstaff to Camp Verde
north on SR 260 to SR 87
SR 87 north to Clints Well
north on FR 3/SR 487 through Mormon Lake, past Lake
Mary
north on I-17 to I-40
east on I-40 to Walnut Canyon National Monument, then
back to Flagstaff

Distance:
186 miles for the entire loop, including Oak Creek Canyon

Time:
about a half day, depending on stops

Services:
at Camp Verde, Long Valley, and Mormon Lake

Best Time of Year:
summer and fall

Highlights:
good alpine riding a short distance from Flagstaff and
Sedona

If you've already done ride 21, you have a couple of options with this one. If you're in a hurry, getting a late start, prefer the speed of the interstate, or simply don't want to ride the same road twice, you can head south on I-17 (Black Canyon Highway) to the Camp Verde/SR 260 exit. If you prefer the slower pace of back roads, take Oak Creek Canyon to Sedona where you will pick up SR 179, a nice 15-mile jaunt through the heart of the Arizona red-rock country. From Sedona SR 179 will cut almost due south and intersect with I-17. You'll take I-17 south about 12 miles and get off at the Camp Verde/SR 260 exit. Given the

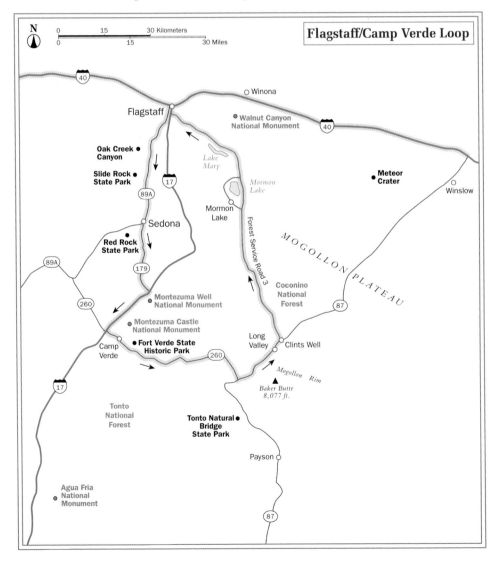

choice, we'd take the slow curves and scenery over the roar of an interstate any day!

In town, Fort Verde State Historic Park is the best-preserved example of an Indian wars–era fort in Arizona. The fort was a base used by U.S. Army scouts, soldiers, officers, and doctors from the 1860s until 1891. Soldiers helped the U.S. government move members of numerous Indian bands onto nearby reservations in the 1870s and kept the peace after that. You can tour the museum-ified original buildings and, if you time it right, check out one of the frequent historical reenactments.

Camp Verde/SR 260 has every service you might need, so gas up and get a snack or coffee or anything else you deem necessary. It's not that far to Long Valley and Clints Well, but since the amenities are available, you might as well use them.

If you've done ride 21, you might recognize the east end of the Verde Valley, an area with a significant Native American history. South of here on I-17, Agua Fria National Monument preserves a stretch of the Agua Fria River, an area of abundant wildlife as well as many signs of ancient cultures. It's only accessible by dirt road. To the east on SR 260, a lovely alpine ride with great views of the Mogollon Rim connects this area to Payson. Tonto Natural Bridge State Park is the site of a natural travertine bridge over a creek. The story goes that in 1877, a Scotsman discovered the place while hiding from Apaches. He was so taken by the spot that he moved his whole family there.

With Camp Verde at approximately 3,150 feet above sea level, you've descended almost 4,000 feet from Flagstaff. Camp Verde doesn't appear to be near any relief from the heat, but SR 260 begins to climb to the top of the Mogollon Plateau within a few miles and continues to steadily for the next 25 to 30 miles. Before long, you'll notice the terrain changing from dry desert to rich ranch lands that in spring and summer can parade both a variety of colorful wildflowers and desert plants in full bloom.

You'll leave the ranch lands behind and return to the forest. For the next hour or so, there will be no services and no scenic overlooks, just good higher-elevation riding on good roads and big, wide

You can tell the Mustang is the place to stop around here by all the bikes and pickups pulling campers out front.

Steve: The Mustang in Long Valley is the only place around here with services. You'll find a gas station with a little cafe tucked back against the trees off to the right. I rode right past it thinking that Clints Well, being at the intersection of SR 87 and SR 487, would have more to offer. I got to the turn about three-quarters of a mile down the road to find nothing but the intersection. I made a U-turn and went back to the Mustang. I should have known that this was the place to stop, given the number of bikes in the parking lot. ●

turns through the forest. So settle in, pull back the throttle, and enjoy the 34 miles or so to the intersection of SR 260 and SR 87.

In this kind of terrain, it's easy to relax and roll through the hills and curves. Don't relax too much: The intersection of SR 260 and SR 87 comes up quickly, and if you're not paying attention to your speed, you could easily miss the stop sign and blow through it. Traffic on SR 87 doesn't stop, so that could be a potentially devastating mistake.

Take a left at the intersection. SR 87 climbs to 7,450 feet, then slowly descends toward Long Valley and Clints Well. Once again, it was hard to remember that this was central Arizona in August. Shortly after the turn onto SR 87, the forest gets noticeably richer, greener, and more lush. This just doesn't jibe with preconceived notions of Arizona.

If you continue on SR 87 for another 50 miles or so as it heads northeast from Long Valley, you'll end up in Winslow, Arizona. A few miles south of I-40 near Winslow is the Meteor Crater National Landmark, where a meteor impact created an explosion equivalent to 150 atomic bomb explosions. The shock waves dug out a 4,000-foot-wide crater that is clearly visible from above. The site is still privately owned by the descendants of Daniel Barringer, who bought the land there in 1903 hoping to mine the iron

---

Steve: As I looked at the map and contemplated the loop I was riding, I couldn't help but think of the lyrics from the song "Take It Easy" by the Eagles:

Well, I'm a standing on a corner in Winslow Arizona
And such a fine sight to see
It's a girl, my Lord, in a flatbed
Ford slowin' down to take a look at me.
Come on, baby, don't say maybe
I gotta know if your sweet love is
gonna save me
We may lose and we may win though
we will never be here again
so open up, I'm climbin' in,
take it easy.

I used to listen to that song and dream about hitchhiking cross-country and being picked up by a girl in a flatbed Ford—or any vehicle, for that matter. I'm older now, but it's still fun to dream. ●

---

he thought the meteor would have left (there was less than he thought and mining operations closed down in 1929). There is a $15 fee to visit.

Look for the turn at Clints Well about three-quarters of a mile down the road from the Mustang. Clints Well is the start of a couple of popular unpaved byways along the Mogollon Rim; the gravel surfaces are generally in good condition in the summer but they are fairly long. Check in with a ranger at the Blue Ridge ranger station a few miles north on SR 87 if you want to check them out.

Maps show SR 487 angling northwest toward Mormon Lake and Lake Mary, then eventually back to I-17 and Flagstaff. The sign marking the turn reads FOREST ROAD 3.

The road is mostly a nice ride. It's not in as good a shape as SR 87, so watch for some significant potholes and chunks of missing pavement. It is a road less traveled, and given its close proximity

---

Steve: Just before I got to Mormon Lake, I noticed a couple of forest rangers installing a new road sign. I stopped and approached them to clear up the confusion I was feeling about SR 487 and FR 3. I explained that I was writing a motorcycle-touring book and wanted to make sure my information was accurate. The ranger I spoke with had been working for the U.S. Forest Service for about thirteen years, and in those thirteen years, SR 487 (as it was listed on my map) had always been "Forest Road 3" or "FS3 Road." Online maps had it listed as both SR 487 and FS3 Road.

We talked for a few minutes and I learned that the road, SR 487 or FR 3—whatever you want to call it—does get snow in the winter and had snow as late as April in 2008. According to the ranger, the road is plowed and is open year-round. Good to know! How else would you get to Mormon Lake in the wintertime? ●

There's not much going on at Mormon Lake. We think we found the lake, but we're not sure.

to Flagstaff and Prescott, it's an easy escape from the oppressive heat of the desert. We expected more traffic, especially RVs and campers. The posted speed limit is 50 miles per hour, and one could theoretically ride comfortably 15 or 20 miles over that (not that we encourage or condone speeding).

There wasn't much going on at Mormon Lake and we had a difficult time finding the actual lake. In fact, we're not positive we did find it. We found a town called Mormon Lake, but the lake looks more like marshland that has been overtaken by the surrounding grasslands. The town is a quaint example of small-town, high-alpine living. There are some services, including gas, lodging, and a country store; you'll have to leave the main road and do a little loop through the town and around the "lake" to get to them. If you feel like parking your bike for a while, you can rent a horse and go for a ride of a different sort.

Once you loop back onto SR 487/FR 3, it's only about 20 miles to I-17. From there, a short hop north to I-40 eastbound will quickly take you to the exit for Walnut Canyon National Monument. Walnut Canyon is another example of the Sinagua

Walnut Canyon National Monument is only ten minutes from Flagstaff and a relaxing end to a great day on the bike.

culture that dominated this region of the country almost 1,000 years ago.

Like other Sinaguan Indians, these people lived in rectangular rooms combined into small villages. In Walnut Canyon, the dwellings are built in natural pockets below the lip of the cliff, mostly facing south and east. Pit houses and freestanding pueblos sit above the rim and back from there were—and, it seems, still are—pockets of deep soil, which allowed the inhabitants to grow crops. Water was scarce and Walnut Creek probably didn't flow year-round but the inhabitants were creative and devised ways to use and conserve what little there was. Most crops were drought resistant and the people ate wild plants as well.

From here, it's an easy ride back the few miles west to Flagstaff. Or you can easily continue on toward another ride in any direction.

NORTHERN NEW MEXICO

Northern New Mexico is famous for both its landscape and its culture, and rightfully so. With innumerable art galleries, funky small towns, old churches, and ancient Indian ruins, it deserves its Land of Enchantment title.

Like southern New Mexico, where remote outposts are situated in the middle of forbidding desert, the mountainous territory of the state's northern half seems to set this place apart from the rest of the world. It's a good place to do your own thing. The population here is an assortment of societal dropouts and outliers, many of them either artists or rednecks, which means most people here are odd but also motorcycle-friendly.

The riding is great, too, so it's not surprising that many residents are also riders. You can see that not only in the number of bikes on the roads, but also in the fact that car drivers seem friendlier here. We lost count of the number of times someone in a car pulled over to let us easily pass on a winding road, obviously aware we could take it faster than they could. Everywhere we went from restaurants to visitor centers, people welcomed us, knowing we were on a bike.

Despite its location in the heart of the Southwest, the territory here is surprisingly green. Much of this area is high elevation, so it's mountainous and forested rather than classic red rock, though the mountains are not as dramatic as the ones to the north in Colorado. If you want classic desert, just head downhill and you'll find plenty.

If you're looking for some culture, this is a great place to spend time. Ancient cultures live in pueblo settlements that preserve the old ways and incorporate modern life. You will pass through many of the nineteen New Mexico pueblos: Taos, Picuris, Sandia, Isleta, San Juan, Santa Clara, San Ildefonso, Nambe, Tesuque, Jemez, Cochiti, Pojoaque, Santo Domingo, San Felipe, Santa Ana, Zia, Laguna, Acoma, and Zuni.

Santa Fe is one of the world's art centers—especially when it comes to Western American art—and is considered America's second-largest art market (after New York). That means the city and its environs are home to hundreds of galleries and thousands of artists. Some of this is serious stuff, with galleries carrying works priced in tens of thousands of dollars. While most of us could never afford most of it (nor could we carry it home on a bike), it's a fun place to stroll around and look at things.

The city also boasts a number of fine museums, including the Georgia O'Keeffe Museum and a renowned opera company. Local artists sell their wares along the sides of the old town plaza. This is a great place to buy something if you want to meet the person who made it and the artists in the square are required to sign their work as a guarantee of authenticity (anywhere in New Mexico look for a signature if you want to buy locally made jewelry. It will often be near or under the stones, which prevents it from being forged later). And if you're interested in gems, a few mines in this region let you go look for yourself, most notably the Harding mine (now owned by the University of New Mexico and open to the public) between Santa Fe and Taos.

The area is also rich in history. Santa Fe is the nation's oldest capital city, and the Palace of the Governors in the middle of town has been a center of government for 400 years.

The hippie types of today pick up on a special feeling that seems to hang in the air. Spirituality of all kinds is evident in a plethora of small-town churches as well as old Catholic missions and even older kiva ruins, where tribes' ancestors worshipped.

RIDE
23

Ride 'Round Gallup

Directions:
south on NM 602 from Gallup
east on NM 53 to I-40
NM 117 through El Malpais National Monument
I-40 west to Gallup

Distance:
160 miles; 210 miles including round-trip along east side
of El Malpais National Monument on NM 117; 220 miles
including round-trip from Grants to Acoma Pueblo
from Gallup to El Morro National Monument: 54 miles
from El Morro National Monument to El Malpais National
Monument: 17 miles
from El Malpais National Monument to Grants: 25 miles
from Grants to Gallup: 64 miles

Time:
a few hours to half a day or more

Services:
Gallup, Grants, and Thoreau

Highlights:
the Zuni people past and present, El Morro National Monument, El Malpais National Monument, beautiful volcanic
and mountainous landscapes

This ride takes you through territory that encompasses geographic history going back millions of years and human history going back hundreds. El Morro National Monument commemorates a travelers' oasis with messages from the past. El Malpais National Monument features some of the region's oldest and most recent volcanic flows, which are easy to see from a couple paved roads.

Hop onto NM 602 out of Gallup, a nice road, wide and smooth. In short order, you leave Gallup in your rearview mirror and what little traffic there was drops off to just you and the occasional pickup truck. Once again you are back in rolling hills with the Zuni Mountains off to your left. This is classic north-

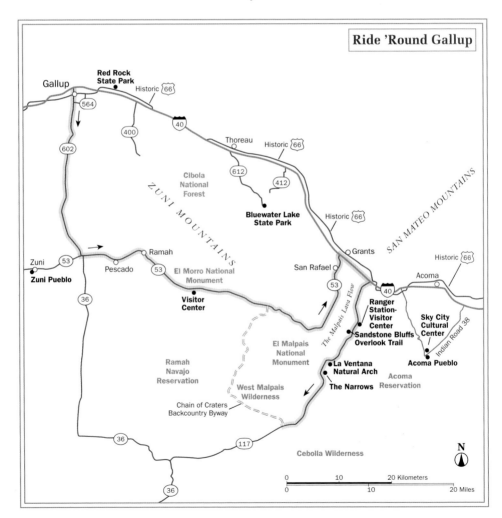

Ride 'Round Gallup

ern New Mexico scenery: juniper and wide-open fields fringed with red rock cliffs. Before long, the road enters the Zuni reservation, Pueblo of Zuni. You will begin to see remnants of old adobe houses not far from the road.

At the intersection of NM 602 and NM 53, you will want to go east (left). In the other direction, the road heads toward the town of Zuni, the center of a culture that has existed in this region for hundreds of years. The Zuni language is unrelated to any other North American dialect and its religious ceremonies—still practiced today—are also unique. This peace-loving tribe has long sustained itself through agriculture and sales of crafts, including pottery and jewelry. The Zuni McKinley County Fair and Rodeo, one of many fairs celebrating native peoples in this area, is held the third weekend in August.

Once on NM 53, you pass through a couple of small towns, Pescado and Ramah. Shortly after passing Ramah, you leave the Pueblo Zuni and enter the Navajo Nation.

This ride's first national monument is El Morro, a vertical sandstone rock formation with a pool of water at its base. This oasis has been a waypoint and a camping spot for hundreds of years and many civilizations, starting with the ancient Puebloans and their Zuni descendants (who called it Atsinna, or "place of

The oasis of El Morro must have been a welcome surprise to its first visitors.

Steve: When I stopped at El Morro, I told the rangers I was doing research for a motorcycle-touring book. After discussing El Morro and El Malpais (both information centers have information about both monuments), one of the rangers told me that if I had time I should seriously think about riding to the Acoma Pueblo, also called Sky City. It's on the Acoma reservation, where one of the rangers lived, and she said the ride up and back is one of the most scenic in the area.

To get there, head east on I-40 from Grants, take exit 102, and go south for about 16 miles to the Sky City Cultural Center, where you can arrange for a tour of Sky City and the Spanish San Esteban del Rey Mission. By the twelfth century, the 75-acre pueblo was established atop a mesa in a beautiful red-rock landscape. With a good defensive position on a 350-foot cliff, it has been inhabited ever since, making it perhaps the oldest continuously inhabited community in the United States. Until recently, it could only be reached by climbing hand-carved stairs (fortunately, now you can ride there).

The walking tour is less than a mile and lasts a little more than an hour (there is some uneven terrain). Photography is tightly controlled on the reservation, where you must purchase a camera permit and get permission before taking any photos of people or their artwork. Video recording is strictly prohibited. The town of Grants also has its own motorcycle rally in July, the Fire and Ice Rally, which spills onto Acoma land. ●

writing on the rocks," which conjures up images of ancient people using this as a kind of bulletin board for each other). Later, the Spanish named it El Morro (The Headland) and added their own inscriptions, so that now the rock contains symbols that mix generations of etched notes.

A short walk takes you from the visitor center to the pool of water at the base of the rock. If you have more time, you can take the Mesa Top Trail loop (2 miles round-trip) from the visitor center past the pool and inscription rock to the top of the mesa for panoramic views of the surrounding countryside as well as the stabilized ruins of Atsinna Pueblo.

Not far down the road is El Malpais National Monument, huge in comparison to El Morro and dedicated more to the geography and geology of the area. We could have spent an entire day and still not been able to see a lot of what it has to offer.

Like much of New Mexico, this land was shaped by volcanic activity, and that history is on display here with lava flows, cinder cones, and lava tubes running through the high desert. The site also includes prehistoric ruins, rock structures, and homesteads. This is a paradise for the rugged individualist, since most of the paths are not well marked and go right through fields of jagged rock or into caves created when the lava cooled. Some hikes are relatively accessible, including the Sandstone Bluffs Overlook trail (closed at dusk), which continues farther to La Ventana natural arch. Short hikes in the Lava Falls area lead to caves and lava tubes.

El Malpais also features a bat cave (ask rangers about it). Hike into it near dusk and you'll see the five or six different species of bats leaving in waves, one kind after another. Some sort of bat etiquette keeps the different species from mixing.

You don't even have to get off the bike to get an idea of the region's interesting features. Two state highways go through the park. NM 53, a scenic byway, follows the northern boundary, beside the El Calderon Lava Flow, the park's oldest at an estimated 115,000 years old. NM 117 goes along the eastern edge and gives good views of the McCarty's Lava Flow. The youngest in the monument, it's only 2,000 to 3,000 years old.

To get to NM 117, take NM 53 to Grants, hop on I-40, and head east to the next exit and south on NM 117. Back near the national monument, there is a ranger station if you need additional information. The south end of NM 117 will intersect with CR 42, also

La Ventana arch is a short hike from the parking lot if you have the time to ride down NM 117 on the east side of the monument.

known as the Chain of Craters Backcountry Byway, a 32-mile dirt road through the monument's western side. It's only recommended for high-clearance vehicles. Use caution and common sense whether doing a short hike or traveling the back roads.

Steve: I was running out of daylight and had to race back to Gallup but I could easily have spent another day exploring this very interesting part of New Mexico. In many places, I-40 is built right over the path of historic Route 66. In Gallup US 66 runs parallel to I-40 on the outskirts of town. The whole area has a strange mix of the modern and all the leftover motels built during the old highway's heyday. I could have spent a few nights photographing all of the neon signs and whatnot remaining from the era before the interstate system stole the thunder from Route 66. ●

RIDE

24

Caldera Loop

Directions:
north on US 285/US 84 from Santa Fe (can also be
reached via US 550 from Albuquerque)
west on NM 96
south on US 550
east on NM 4 and NM 502 back to US 285

Distance:
270 miles

Time:
a long day for the entire loop, especially if you plan to hike

Services:
at Santa Fe and northern suburbs, Española, Cuba, and
Los Alamos

Best Time of Year:
anytime, although roads may be snowy in winter

Highlights:
good cruising roads amid diverse scenery, a chance to look
into the pueblo past and present, the view from the edge
of a giant volcanic caldera, the ruins at Bandelier National
Monument

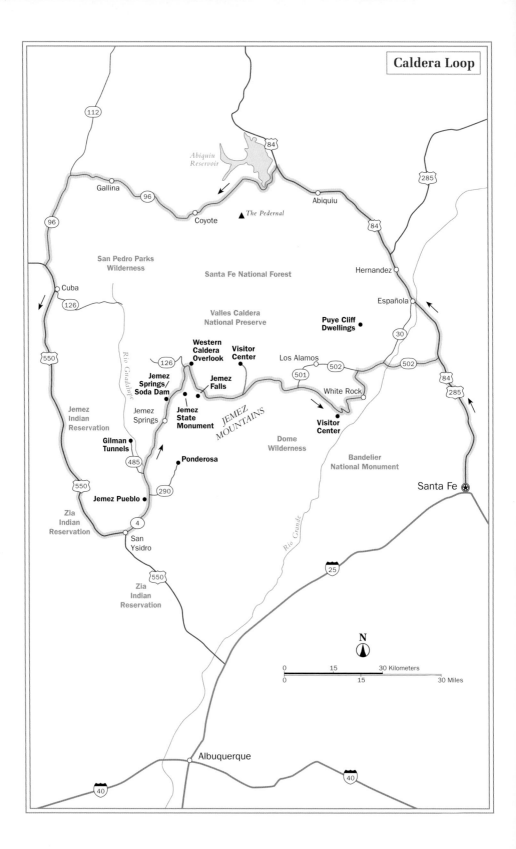

Caldera Loop

112

Abiquiu Reservoir

84

285

Gallina
96
Coyote
▲ The Pedernal
Abiquiu

96
84

San Pedro Parks Wilderness
Santa Fe National Forest
Hernandez

Cuba
126
Valles Caldera National Preserve
Española

550
Puye Cliff Dwellings
30

Rio Guadalupe
Western Caldera Overlook
Visitor Center
Los Alamos
502
502

126
Jemez Springs/ Soda Dam
Jemez Falls
501
84

Jemez Indian Reservation
Jemez Springs
Jemez State Monument
JEMEZ MOUNTAINS
White Rock
285

Gilman Tunnels
485
Visitor Center
Bandelier National Monument
Santa Fe ✪

Ponderosa
290
Dome Wilderness

Jemez Pueblo

Zia Indian Reservation
4

San Ysidro
550

Zia Indian Reservation
Rio Grande

25

N

0   15   30 Kilometers
0   15   30 Miles

Albuquerque

40
40

This is a long ride, made longer by a fair number of stops and potential detours along the way, so plan ahead and know you'll have to make decisions about what to do. It can be done in one long day but if you like side trips, you might want to take two days and plan to stay along the way. Also, with lots of short trails and hot springs on the route, it's a good idea to pack some comfortable shoes, walking clothes, and maybe a swimsuit.

The ride starts out in the suburbs, whether you're coming from Albuquerque (in which case you'd head north on US 550 and join the ride at San Ysidro) or Santa Fe, which is the way we did it. Santa Fe's northern suburbs are actually a series of pueblos, each apparently with its own casino. The stoplights and traffic can get aggravating but you'll just have to grit your teeth and get through it. Environs open up a bit after Española, as US 84 prepares to head out of state to the north. We'll be branching off onto NM 96 at Abiquiu Reservoir, which lies in a broad plain nestled among the red- and yellow-banded mesas once painted by Georgia O'Keeffe. To the south is a distinctive tree-covered mesa, The Pedernal, you may recognize from some of her paintings.

The road is relatively fast, undulating, and easy with wide curves and an occasional small town along the way as it passes through a quintessential Southwestern landscape. (Be careful after

By the time you reach Abiquiu Reservoir, you are finally out of the suburbs and into scenic territory.

a heavy rain, since sometimes the red clay dirt turns to slippery mud that flows across the road.) Climb into foothills stippled with juniper and then ponderosa pine. As you continue southward after the junction with NM 112, and especially after NM 96 merges with US 550, elevation drops and the landscape becomes hotter and drier. Cuba is a good place to refuel and get a bite to eat.

At Cuba a short spur, NM 126, takes you into the mountains of the San Pedro Parks Wilderness. It could cut some of the mileage we're about to put on to the southeast, except that NM 126 becomes a four-wheel-drive dirt road. So remain on US 550 unless you want a little out-and-back scenic ride. The turnoff to reach the north entrance of Chaco Culture National Historical Park, with ruins of impressive Ancestral Puebloan architecture, is 50 miles north on US 550. All roads into the park are unpaved; this entrance road is the best maintained and includes a mere 13 miles of gravel.

US 550 is a well-maintained four-lane highway. You will find yourself on the edge of a broad valley that stretches off to the west, filled with surreal-looking pointed remnants of volcanic cones (Cabezon Peak is particularly striking as it rises up out of the valley). The desert appears endless. You're passing through the Zia and Jemez tribal lands; the Zia originated the round symbol that you see, in yellow and red, all over New Mexico. The two peoples are also known for their beautiful pottery, and you will see places to buy it in many of the towns through here.

At the small town of San Ysidro, continue on NM 4, which will take you northward and back toward the mountains. After just a few miles, you will come upon Jemez Pueblo, nestled among some of the reddest rocks you will ever see. Like many pueblos, this place has been occupied by generations of the same families for hundreds of years. Jemez State Monument combines ancient ruins and those of a seventeenth-century Spanish mission; stop by at the Walatowa Visitor Center for information on it (the ancient village itself is rarely open to the public) and the rest of the attractions along this stretch of the ride, officially called the Jemez Mountain National Scenic Byway.

In Jemez Pueblo, you can sit on the porch at the Sun Clan Cafe and eat a breakfast burrito with sausage, eggs, cheese, potatoes, and chiles.

Steve: On my way from Santa Fe to Gallup, I stopped in at the Sun Clan Cafe in Jemez Pueblo. On our ride through town the day before, I noticed there were a few bikes parked out front, usually a good sign. The cafe advertises burritos, tostadas, beverages, and lots more—and even has a drive-up window if you are in a hurry and want to ride with a burrito in one hand. I had the breakfast burrito with sausage, eggs, cheese, potatoes, and chiles. It was one of the best I've ever had, fresh and flavorful. If you stop in, say hi to the owner, Theresa, and ask her if she and her husband have bought bikes yet. He wants to do some touring but she's not sure she can handle her own bike or riding on the back with him. I told her to go for it! ●

The Gilman Tunnels, blasted out of the mountainside in the 1920s for logging, is a quick out-and-back detour up NM 485. The main ride continues along NM 4 to Jemez Springs. Nestled in a canyon and surrounded by forest, this is a good place to stop for a bite. The biker-friendly Los Ojos is a no-nonsense roadside restaurant with bear skins on the walls, a tin ceiling, and a big fireplace.

On the way out of town, keep an eye out for the Soda Dam, where mineral-laden water has added to a natural dam across the river, a tiny bit at a time. Ask the locals about the best hot springs if you want to take a dip or just head to the public mineral bathhouse in town. If you're planning to do a lot of side trips and can't make this whole loop in one day, the relative abundance of small lodging establishments makes this a fine overnight spot.

It's hard to believe you can go so quickly from desert to lush forest, but keep in mind you are actually scaling the outside wall of a giant volcanic caldera. This becomes more obvious after the intersection of NM 4 and NM 126, which is the other side of the unpaved road (now paved again) over the mountain from Cuba. Turn left here and head west for a couple miles to the best viewpoint at the Western Caldera Overlook. Then turn around and come back on NM 4 eastbound. You'll pass by the Jemez Falls turnoff; the 70-foot series of falls is down a 3-mile road off NM 4.

This whole Valles Caldera area, which used to be private land, has been set aside as a national preserve. Everyone is still trying to figure out what that means, since the preserve includes a working cattle ranch and tourism-oriented development is inevitable. For now, it's a paradise for hikers, fishermen, and hunters. Find out more about the area and its history at the small welcome center in the middle of the caldera at the end of a short dirt road that is well maintained and suitable for any bike.

Leaving the edge of the caldera, you head downhill toward Los Alamos with its famous Los Alamos National Laboratory.

It may not look like it at first glance, but the Valles Caldera National Preserve visitor center lies in what used to be the middle of an enormous ancient caldera.

Stop at the visitor center and inquire about taking a tour if you plan ahead and have time—or check out the interactive Bradbury Science Museum in town, which includes a replica of Little Boy, the second atomic bomb created as part of the Manhattan Project.

The most impressive sight of this area is another few miles down the road. Bandelier National Monument is a well-preserved collection of thirteenth-century cliff houses tucked into the natural pockmarks along the rock faces. The oblong holes in the cliff walls would look strange enough without the addition of ancient human housing. Plan at least a

You'll have to climb a series of ladders to reach Alcove House, located 140 feet above the canyon floor. If you aren't afraid of heights, it's worth the climb.

couple of hours for your visit, since most of the dwellings are along a mile-long paved trail through the park. If you'd like to stay longer or avoid the afternoon heat (which can reach high 90s in the summer), either do this at the beginning of this ride rather than the end or make it a separate day trip from Santa Fe or Albuquerque. More ruins are north of here, just off NM 30 at Puye Cliff Dwellings, managed by the Santa Clara Pueblo.

One final stop before heading back to the big city: After you leave Bandelier, follow signs in the Los Alamos suburb of White Rock to the White Rock Overlook, with picturesque views into the Rio Grande Valley far below.

When you get back to Santa Fe, be sure to try out some of the town's Mexican and New Mexican restaurants (Thomasitas, Bonitas, Marias), and local favorites Coyote Café and the Cowgirl.

RIDE

25

Ring Around Taos

Directions for Enchanted Circle Scenic Byway:
north on US 64 from Taos to Eagle Nest
west and south on NM 38 to Questa
south on NM 522 to Taos

Directions for Wild Rivers Back Country Byway:
north on NM 522 from Questa
NM 378 to the Wild Rivers Recreational Area

Distance:
about 111 miles

Time:
allow a good half day depending on whether you plan to
hike at the Wild Rivers Recreation Area

Services:
at Taos, Angel Fire, Red River, and Questa

Best Time of Year:
spring and fall

Highlights:
cultural and culinary delights of Taos; dramatic views of
mountains, including Wheeler Peak, the highest peak in
New Mexico; the fun and friendly ski resort town of Red
River; the scenic confluence of two wild rivers

This ride explores the Enchanted Circle Scenic Byway, which goes from Taos to Eagle Nest to Questa and back to Taos, making a loop around Wheeler Peak, the highest mountain in New Mexico.

Taos is a small town with a big reputation. It's known as a place to buy art, a second home, and good food—which might make it sound like a haven for snooty rich people. It's not. Instead, Taos is a place where generations of families have weathered the ups and downs of fate, where traditional beliefs and ways still have pull, and where you can find both a good cup of coffee and a cheap burrito.

Nestled at the base of the Taos and Sangre de Cristo Mountains, Taos sits at nearly 7,000 feet, which means it makes for a cool escape in the summer (and it can be chilly in winter, though daytime temperatures are usually above freezing). Its 5,000 residents are mostly laid-back artsy and outdoorsy types who enjoy the finer things.

The Taos Pueblo, listed as both a National Historic Landmark and a UNESCO World Heritage Site, is believed to be the oldest

For many people visiting Taos, the only view of the Rio Grande is from the Rio Grande Gorge Bridge.

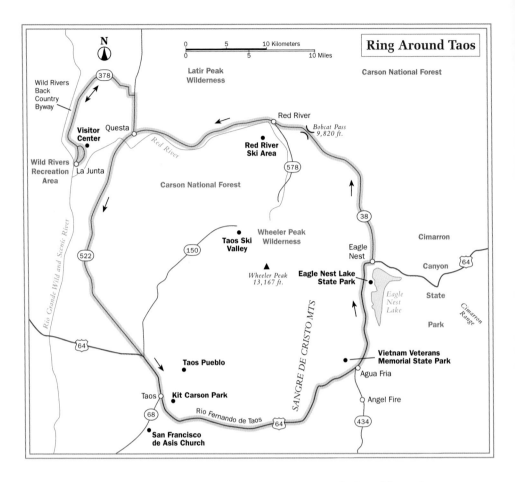

Map labels (within image):

Ring Around Taos

N

0 5 10 Kilometers
0 5 10 Miles

Latir Peak Wilderness

Carson National Forest

378

Wild Rivers Back Country Byway

Visitor Center

Questa

Red River

Bobcat Pass 9,820 ft.

Red River Ski Area

578

Wild Rivers Recreation Area

La Junta

Red River

Carson National Forest

38

Wheeler Peak Wilderness

Cimarron

Taos Ski Valley

150

Eagle Nest

Canyon

64

522

Wheeler Peak 13,167 ft.

Eagle Nest Lake State Park

Eagle Nest Lake

State

Cimarron Range

Rio Grande Wild and Scenic River

Park

64

Taos Pueblo

SANGRE DE CRISTO MTS

Vietnam Veterans Memorial State Park

Agua Fria

Taos

Kit Carson Park

68

Rio Fernando de Taos

64

Angel Fire

434

San Francisco de Asis Church

---

continually inhabited village in America. People lived here for a thousand years, and they still do—which means visitors have to respect the privacy and culture of the occupants. As the pueblo's literature says, "each home is privately owned and occupied by a family and is not a museum display to be inspected with curiosity." It's open most days from 8 a.m. to 4:30 p.m. (except for a few weeks in late winter and early spring). Admission is $10 per person and $5 per camera and includes a walking-tour map that will give you an idea of what you're seeing as you go through. For a different cultural experience, head to the Taos Mountain Casino, also owned by the Taos Indians.

If you're looking for more history, the Kit Carson Home and Museum celebrates the famed mountain and military man. Just south of town, the thick-walled San Francisco de Asis Church,

Christy: New Mexico is full of pueblos, a name for ancient and modern Native American settlements. You will get a better understanding of history if you visit at least one or two. At many pueblos, visitors have to register themselves and their cameras, pay a small fee, and ask permission before taking pictures. The rules might seem odd, considering you're essentially visiting someone's neighborhood. But most neighborhoods don't have streams of curious tourists wanting to look into their windows and take pictures of their family members. You can see why residents can sometimes be touchy about where you go and what you photograph. The rules are a practical compromise: Occupants figure if they're going to let people into their homes (which are traditionally considered sacred places), they might as well get some compensation. Seems a fair trade to me. ●

built in about 1800, is one of the state's most-photographed adobe structures. There are also a bizillion art galleries, featuring everything from homemade arts and crafts to giant sculptural pieces. If you're hungry, you'll find bakeries, coffee shops, and restaurants of all kinds (most of them are along the main drag). About half of them feature some element of New Mexican cuisine flavored with the state's famous red and green chiles.

Now, for the ride. The Enchanted Circle is a very popular day trip, and you'll have plenty of two-wheeled company as you make the loop around New Mexico's tallest mountains, including 13,107-foot Wheeler Peak.

Starting at Taos, follow signs and stay on US 64. At the south end of town, it branches off to the left (heading east, or uphill). Much of the land next to the road is private and you'll see lots of cabins nestled in the woods. The road winds upward into a small canyon. You might have to be patient on the twisty road if there's traffic ahead, but you will get chances to pass.

About 15 miles from Taos, you come out into an open valley surrounded on all sides by hills. This area is a year-round recreation and relaxation mecca. Throughout this ride, you'll see tons of RV parks and fishing holes and meadows perfect for winter snowmobiling. And, consistent with its "Enchanted Circle" name, this territory inspires people: For a place with not many permanent residents, there sure are a lot of churches, church camps, and religious retreats. Keep left at the curve onto NM 38.

One must-do stop along this route is the Vietnam Veterans Memorial State Park. It's just past Agua Fria and near Angel Fire, though directions to it aren't really necessary: You can see it from miles around. Clinging to the edge of the foothills, the bright white edifice rises up like a giant wind-filled sail.

Continuing on NM 38, you pass Eagle Nest and Eagle Nest Lake State Park, with yet more outdoor recreation going on. Wheeler Peak rises to the west, one of many pyramid-shaped mountaintops in the middle of the Enchanted Circle. Past a few more churches, RV parks, and vacation homes, you hit Bobcat Pass, the highest point on this ride at nearly 10,000 feet (there are seven 9,000-plus-foot passes on this ride). From here, the road starts dropping down again into another canyon, and soon you arrive at Red River.

Nestled in a valley at the base of the mountains whose colorful ores give the river its hue, Red River has an energetic but old-fashioned feel, with a number of preserved Victorian-era structures. It's an entertaining combination of skiers, anglers, cowboys, miners, and motorized-vehicle fans. When they get to the main drag through town, they're all interested in the same thing: having a good time. This place has a pretty high per-capita number of bars and restaurants, many of which feature live music. Given all that, some making this tour choose to stay the night. Since most lodgings are ski oriented, there should be options during motorcycle season. But check ahead to be sure.

After you've stopped in Red River for lunch or dinner, head the rest of the way down the canyon. That big operation taking out much of the hillside on your right is the Molycorp molybdenum

The names of fallen soldiers, laid in brick, line the path of the Veterans Memorial Walkway at the Vietnam Veterans Memorial State Park.

You might wonder why there's a veterans memorial out here. The story of its origins is sad and touching. Jeanne and Victor Westphall had the memorial built in honor of their son, Victor David, a Marine lieutenant who died in Vietnam in 1968. The Westphalls (both of whom now lie buried at the site) wanted to commemorate the sacrifices of soldiers in the war and create a place where all kinds of people could feel peace. Built just months after their son's death, it was one of the first permanent monuments honoring those who served in an unpopular war that was still going on. "All we wanted to do was assure that our son, and all his buddies, were properly recognized," Victor Westphall wrote later.

The Westphalls got support for the memorial from government and veterans' organizations, raising funds for a visitor center with informational displays and photos of the dead, often brought in person by family members. It's open from 9 a.m. to 5 p.m. daily, with tours on Saturday (the site itself is always open). Inside the high, curved walls, the chapel features a window that looks out over the valley. ●

mine (try saying that three times fast). You'll find yourself on a broad, flat area at the base of the mountains and soon roll into the town of Questa. Although it's not as scenic as Taos or Red River, it does have pretty much anything a traveler needs: hotels, groceries, gas, and a number of bars and restaurants (including the biker-friendly El Monte Carlo).

From here, you can either go straight back to Taos or take the detour to Wild Rivers Recreation Area, which in 1968 was the first section of river ever to be designated a National Wild and Scenic River. This is a nice side trip from either this ride or on its own from Taos.

To get to the Wild Rivers Recreation Area from Questa, go north on NM 522 and continue about 3 miles to the turnoff for NM 378. The turn is marked, but not well. Although the whole of NM 378 is officially a scenic byway, much of the ride to the canyon is anything but scenic—mostly crumbling adobe and shabby single wides scattered around a dusty sagebrush plain.

The good stuff doesn't begin until you get into the recreation area itself. When you enter (there's a $3 fee), you're greeted by a notice that says, VERTICAL CLIFFS ALONG RIM. KEEP SAFE DISTANCE.— always a good sign (pun intended). And that's the whole point of this spot. It's a chance to stand (or ride, for that matter) along the edge of a cliff and look down. Unlike the Grand Canyon and a lot of canyons in the West, this one isn't particularly colorful. The rock here is ancient black volcanic basalt, which makes it look more burned out than carved.

Taking in the scene may be as simple as riding out to La Junta (The Junction) Point, where, at the end of a short, paved trail, you can see the Rio Grande and Red Rivers meet in the canyon below you. Other views are just off the road as you go to or from the point.

If you're feeling energetic or adventurous, you can see one of the most fascinating aspects of the canyon, the petroglyphs carved onto boulders at the bottom of Big Arsenic Springs Trail. The problem is, they're at the bottom of the canyon—which is 800 vertical feet and more than a mile away. The steep hike

The La Junta Trail leads to the confluence of the Red and Rio Grande Rivers.

doesn't seem so bad on the way down but is a real trial on the way back up. Take your time and check out the informational plaques along the way about some of the things you'll see on the hike, which leads down into a relatively lush riparian area with plants including everything from 500-year-old trees to poison ivy (Helpful: a sign identifying poison ivy. Not helpful: You don't see it until you get pretty close to the real thing). You can do the hike on your own or, if you time it right, with a guided group. They

If you want to do this side trip and the rest of the Enchanted Loop in one day, you might want to reverse direction of the ride from the way we've described it here. We hiked to the bottom of the canyon and back out in late summer, and by noon the temperature was brutal. Your other option would be to do the hike in late afternoon and hope for a summer rainstorm to cool things off a bit. But do not get started too late—this being in the middle of nowhere, there are no streetlights! ●

Well-hidden rocks covered in ancient petroglyphs lie at the bottom of Big Arsenic Springs Trail.

usually leave in the morning. Ask about this at the visitor center if you're interested.

Don't try this hike in your riding boots and *do* bring plenty of water. Check in at the visitor center first; the staff there can give you pointers on how to find the petroglyphs, which are intentionally not marked in order to protect them from vandalism. The hike and the search at the bottom are worth it when you marvel at the human and animal figures cavorting on the rock faces.

Head back to Questa the way you came, then south on NM 522 back to Taos. On the way, if you'd like to get a look at the opposite side of the mountains you just circumnavigated, take NM 150 to Taos Ski Valley. The top of its highest lift reaches nearly 12,000 feet but the base is a mere 9,000, similar to that at Bobcat Pass.

High Roads Around Santa Fe

Directions:

south on NM 518/NM 76 from Taos to Santa Fe

north on US 84/US 285 to Tierra Amarilla

east on US 64 back to Taos

Distance:

from Taos to Santa Fe via High Road to Taos: about 77 miles

from Taos to Santa Fe via NM 68: about 70 miles

from Santa Fe to Tierra Amarilla: 98 miles

from Tierra Amarilla to Taos: 85 miles

Time:

half to a full day

Services:

at Taos, Penasco, Truchas, Santa Fe, Española, and Tierra Amarilla

Best Time of Year:

May through September

Highlights:

colorful historic towns, the Rio Grande Gorge, a gorgeous ride across a high plateau

How do you get to Santa Fe? There are actually several ways, all different. Starting in Taos, you could take winding roads that give you a taste of mountainous rural New Mexico. For high-plateau scenery and terrific views, take US 84 and US 64. We do this as a loop, with a couple options thrown in, but you could also incorporate any combination of these roads as part of a point-to-point trip.

First, the High Road to Taos Scenic Byway linking Taos and Santa Fe: If you haven't had enough of the mountains by the time you want to leave Taos, take NM 518 and follow signs to Espanola (for some reason, they don't say you're also headed for Santa Fe). The road climbs into the Carson National Forest, sur-

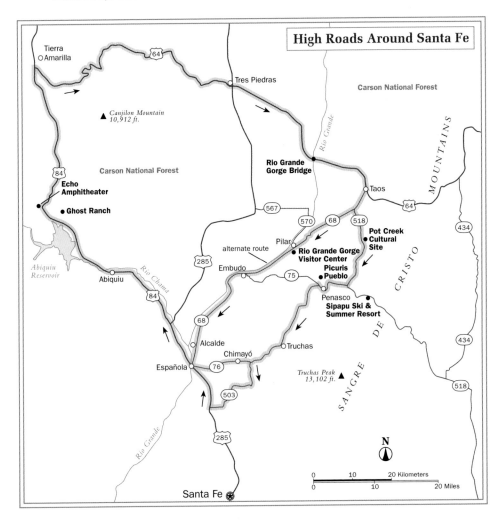

rounded by endless evergreen trees and the occasional small town. Most of the towns have friendly dives where you can stop in for rest and refreshment if you need to, but not much else. This ride is more about the history of these places: Some of the structures, families, and traditions have been here for many generations.

Nine miles south of Taos on NM 518, you'll pass the Pot Creek Cultural Site, with some ruins and picnic areas, then ride through the Picuris Pueblo of the Tiwa tribe. You can learn of the culture at the museum/ gift shop, or check out the tribe's buffalo herd, one of five

The High Road to Taos is typical of northern New Mexico roads: curvy and scenic—and with a crumbling shoulder and occasionally rough surface.

herds owned by various New Mexico pueblo communities.

For a short time, you'll be going in what feels like the wrong direction on NM 75; follow signs for NM 76 (if you go the actual wrong direction, you'll ultimately hit Sipapu Ski & Summer Resort). On NM 76, you're through the most confusing parts of this ride and you can relax a bit.

Christy: Watch signs closely; some of the intersections are not well signed, and I ended up having to turn around a couple times to find my way. That's even harder when the road is so twisty that you could be facing north as you make a turn that will ultimately take you south. Although these are considered state highways, they often feel more like rural roads. ●

This structure must have one of the best views of any outhouse in the country.

Truchas is the next town of any size. Its sleepy streets still retain signs of its Spanish origins, but today it is home to artists (some of whom have used building walls as canvases) and farm animals (by law, vehicles must yield to livestock on the road, so watch out). Look eastward into the mountains for views of 13,000-foot-plus Truchas Peak.

NM 76 and 503 meet at the historic fort town of Chimayó. The old settlement features a town plaza that goes back to the Spanish era (the only fortified plaza remaining in the Southwest); the Santuario de Chimayó, a church where people have long gone to experience the healing powers of the local soil; and the tasty Rancho de Chimayó restaurant.

From here, you can either stay on NM 76 or take NM 503 to the intersection with US 84/US 285. Sometimes NM 503 is so narrow that it's hard to imagine one car driving on it, much less two passing each other. Beware: The surface is not only narrow and winding but also sometimes rough, and gravel strewn as it goes through even more tiny towns, hugging the hillsides. Closer to Santa Fe, dramatic views begin to emerge to the south and west—layers of red-rock cliffs and ridges going on for miles, then Santa Fe nestled in the foothills of the Sangre de Cristo Mountains at the Rockies' southernmost tip.

Your low-road option from Taos to Santa Fe is NM 68, easy to pick up as it dissects Taos. About 5 miles south of town, it begins to drop into the Rio Grande Gorge.

Because the Rio Grande is a National Wild and Scenic River through here, there is a lot of activity on and around it and plenty

Steve: Before hitting NM 68, I made a quick stop at our hotel, the Taos Plaza Indian Hills Inn, where I spoke with owner John Slenes—an unofficial tour guide for the Taos region if there ever was one (he gives motorcyclists an enthusiastic welcome). He told me to be careful on this stretch of NM 68. During heavy rain, the road can become impassable due to mudslides and boulders rolling off the hillside.

As I entered the gorge, I saw a sturdy barrier on the east (uphill) side of the road, constructed of large wood timbers I'd say were 8 feet or longer and a heavy steel mesh fence. I assume it was built to prevent the rocks on the hillside from ending up in the road. The hill was almost an exact 45-degree angle and was peppered with an array of rocks and boulders of all sizes, many of which had rolled down the slope and into the massive fence. Some of the boulders were large enough to strain the fence where it met the hillside, and others had bent or broken the timbers. Luckily, the boulders remained on the uphill side. ●

of pullouts for scenic views of the river and the rafters and boaters below. On summer weekends, vehicles of all kinds, some towing rafts, pull into and out of traffic and compromise visibility. The speed limit is 45 miles per hour on most stretches—which, given the amount of activity, is probably safe. Vehicles tend to bunch up into groups, minimizing passing opportunities.

The Rio Grande Gorge Visitor Center is just south of Pilar, where NM 68 meets NM 570. It's about 28 miles from Taos to the hamlet of Embudo. To join up with the High Road to Taos ride from here, just take NM 75 east to NM 76.

Staying on NM 68, you veer away from the Rio Grande, and the terrain starts to open up as the road makes its way south to Española. About 8 miles north of Española, you enter the town of Alcalde, one of a series of Indian reservations.

When you get to Santa Fe, take a ride through the central square, with Palace of the Governors in the background.

Whether you take the high road or the low road, if you come into Santa Fe from the north, you will connect with US 84/US 285, a four-lane highway at times resembling an interstate and at other times a suburban thoroughfare with stop lights and a full complement of gas stations, fast-food restaurants, and gambling

After a few miles, you'll see signs for Ghost Ranch, pointing you toward the home of Georgia O'Keeffe. One of America's most famous artists, O'Keeffe painted this scenery for decades and now the ranch is used as a convention center and school for artists. In addition to straightforward courses in, say, painting, you can also take An Inner Journey: Still the Mind, Open Your Heart. Or you can just enjoy your own journey and appreciate for yourself the scenery O'Keeffe loved so much. ●

opportunities. Casinos aplenty greet you, each touting its own steak specials, slots, and B-list entertainers.

Now for the second half of this loop. Heading back north from Santa Fe, stay on US 84 past Abiquiu Reservoir (the turnoff for ride 24) and continue north on a good road flanked by beautiful pink-tinted cliffs.

Sagebrush and desert give way to forest and farmland as the road gently rises. You're getting a chance to see from below the scenery you'll soon be above.

At Tierra Amarilla, take the right (east) onto US 64. It winds upward, pulling you onto a big mountain with seemingly endless curves. Come prepared for both chilly temperatures and water on the road. If you encounter either, chances for shelter are scarce: There's not a single town between the turnoff to US 64 and Tres Piedras on the other side.

The road skirts aspen-covered hillsides, with speed limits ranging from 35 to 55 miles per hour, although most bikes can comfortably push those limits (not that we condone speeding). Traffic tends to be refreshingly light, but watch out for varmints.

A touring father-and-son duo takes a break to put on some rain gear atop the US 64 plateau.

We were riding these parts in monsoon season while a hurricane in the Gulf of Mexico spun off moisture into the Southwest. We rode in rain of varying severity for four days from Moab through the Four Corners area all the way to Santa Fe.

We saw a lot of unprepared riders on US 64 who either didn't know it was monsoon season or didn't care. A thunderstorm covered half the mountain, and even once we reached the flatter terrain of the valley between it and Taos, the rain poured down in sheets. A lot of riders looked miserable in their baseball caps and T-shirts. ●

Animals of all of all shapes and sizes seem to love running across the road here.

Be sure to stop and check out the amazing vistas from the overlook just before you get to the top. The cliffs to the north are almost surreal in their drama. From here, the road straightens out a bit as you pass through alpine meadows before you start dropping again on the east side of another pass. The ranger station on the east side of the mountain can provide information on weather and a lot of other subjects, no matter what direction you're headed.

Leaving the lush green forests of the mountains, the road drops you into a huge wide-open valley and the dusty, ramshackle little town of Tres Piedras. From here, US 64 stretches off toward Taos. There's no shelter and no services from here to Taos, unless you count the rest stop at the Rio Grande overlook—just sagebrush plain stretching across the valley floor from mountain to mountain.

Things start to get interesting again when the road rises a bit on the outskirts of Taos and passes a handful of funny-looking buildings featuring a mishmash of architectural styles (turrets, for example). These are the "Earthships" of the Greater World community, environmentally friendly houses made of reused materi-

A small visitor center provides information about Earthships, strange, environmentally friendly homes that dot the landscape outside Taos.

als including old tires. They use solar power and are specially designed for optimal airflow. A sign points the way to "solar survival tours" where, for a few dollars, you can find out more.

The other notable sight on the way to Taos is the Rio Grande Gorge Bridge, the third-highest bridge in the United States at 650 feet above the river. With a beautiful view of the river below and a rest area on the west side, it's a stop worth making. Apparently, a few lonely souls have jumped off, but we recommend strongly against that.

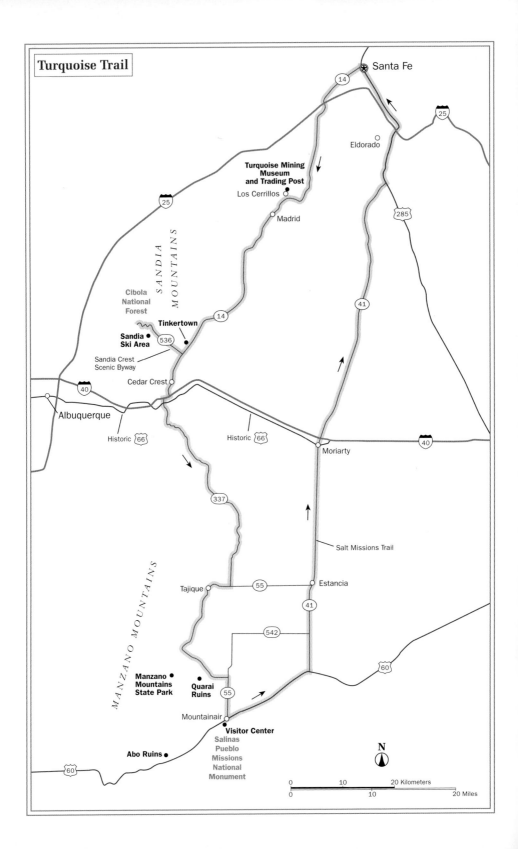

Turquoise Trail

Santa Fe

14

25

Eldorado

**Turquoise Mining
Museum
and Trading Post**

Los Cerrillos

285

Madrid

S A N D I A   M O U N T A I N S

25

Cibola
National
Forest

Tinkertown

**Sandia
Ski Area**

536

14

Sandia Crest
Scenic Byway

41

Cedar Crest

40

Albuquerque

Historic 66

Historic 66

Moriarty

40

337

Salt Missions Trail

M A N Z A N O   M O U N T A I N S

Tajique

55

Estancia

41

542

60

**Manzano
Mountains
State Park**

**Quarai
Ruins**

55

Mountainair

Visitor Center

Salinas
Pueblo
Missions
National
Monument

Abo Ruins

60

N

0   10   20 Kilometers

0   10   20 Miles

RIDE

27

Turquoise Trail

Directions:
south on NM 14 from Santa Fe to I-40
south on NM 337 to Tajique
south on NM 55 to Mountainair
east on US 60 to junction with NM 41
north on NM 41 to US 285

Distance:
234 miles

Time:
one long day

Services:
at Santa Fe, Madrid, Cedar Crest, Tajique, Mountainair,
Estancia, and Moriarty

Best Time of Year:
anytime except the middle of winter

Highlights:
old mining towns along the Turquoise Trail, well-preserved
pueblo ruins, downtown Santa Fe

It's easy to reach NM 14 from Santa Fe, and it gives you a good feel for just how many artists congregate in this part of the world. In town, they sell their creations in the crowded city center, but out here, their shops and galleries are spread out along the roadsides, sometimes agglomerated in small towns that also feature good places to eat or grab a cup of coffee.

You can do this ride from either Santa Fe or Albuquerque, depending on what you want to see and what time of day you want to see it. We were based in Santa Fe. From the Santa Fe town center, Cerrillos Road eventually becomes the Turquoise Trail road, a national scenic byway. Otherwise, you can reach it from I-25. Much of the excitement comes in the first (northern) half of the ride, with a lot of potential stops, so plan accordingly.

Just south of Santa Fe, the ride starts to meander through rolling ranching territory (and also passes the state pen). The road is a good, straight 55 miles an hour most of the way, through rolling pink juniper-dotted hills punctuated by houses. You'll see some volcanic remnants and weird rock formations typical of the Santa Fe outskirts.

The road's nickname comes from its history: People were digging the blue-green rock out of hillsides since before the Spanish arrived in the 1500s and in a few small operations, they still are (this area is also full of old gold, silver, and lead mines). In fact, this area lays claim to being the oldest continually mined site on the North American continent. For the most part, tourism has taken over from mining as the primary industry and many artists make their homes along here. As with other artsy parts of New Mexico, you will likely see some of them along the roads, painting en plein air (outdoors). If you or anyone in your group is a shopper, especially for jewelry, be sure to pack some extra cash and leave room in your saddlebags.

A taste of the small-town life out here comes soon, in the form of the town of Los Cerrillos (the name means "little hills"). The town's gravel roads are laid out in a grid, and at one corner of it is the Turquoise Mining Museum and Trading Post owned by Todd and Patricia Brown, who started building the place in 1975.

Stop in at the Turquoise Mining Museum and Trading Post in Los Cerrillos. The owner is one of the area's authorities on turquoise mining.

Although you won't necessarily know unless you ask, Todd Brown is one of the area's authorities on turquoise mining and works a small mine of his own to make the jewelry sold in his store. You can also buy other rocks and novelties—fossils to antiques to bundles of sage—from inside and outside New Mexico.

Madrid (featured prominently in the biker-buddy movie *Wild Hogs*) is upscale compared to its neighbors, with a chichi Main

Madrid is slightly more upscale than neighboring towns and very biker friendly.

Street filled with art galleries and coffee shops. The galleries carry New Mexico artists' work as well as a lot brought in from elsewhere. With plenty of breakfast, lunch, and snack places, it's a nice stop.

After Madrid, the road climbs into foothills. You'll see a few railroad freight cars that have been converted into homes, some with presumably original graffiti. Stay on NM 14 and you'll climb farther, until you reach the intersection with NM 536, the Sandia Crest Scenic Byway (watch closely for the turnoff if you're coming from the north, as it's not very well signed).

As the name implies, the road takes you to the crest of the mountain, from which you can see for miles—if visibility's good. If it's not good at the bottom, be assured it won't get any better at the top—and this is not the kind of road you want to be on in bad weather.

The Sandia Crest road is a popular ride for locals and visitors alike and if tight, twisty turns are your thing, this is the ride for you. Beware: The road is generally good, but sometimes the surface is not in great condition, with gravel on some of the curves. A lot of accidents happen along here, so this might not be the best time to figure out just how fast you can take a curve signed for 20 miles per hour. If there wasn't so much traffic, it would be a great road to ride hard. Under any circumstances, just watch out for obstacles—including sport bike riders pushing their limits. There is a dirt road that leads to the other side of the mountain (where it's paved again on the Albuquerque side), but it's not suitable for most bikes.

Either before or after your ride up the scenic byway, stop in at Coffee at Dawn, just down the road in Cedar Crest. You're almost guaranteed to run into fellow riders, most of whom will be happy to give you advice (as will the kindly proprietor). It's open until noon during the week and 2 p.m. on weekends.

Continue south on NM 14 and follow signs for NM 337 if you want to take on the second half of this trip (you can also easily take I-40 to Albuquerque if you're headed that direction). This circle is officially called the Salt Missions Trail, referring to the

The entrance sign to Tinkertown gives some indication but can't prepare you for the weirdness inside.

Before you tackle the crest, stop at Tinkertown, one of those classic roadside museums that is the result of one man's dedication (or insanity, depending on how you look at it). A mere $3 gets you in. Ross Ward started carving the thousands of wooden figurines here in 1962 and spent the next thirty years creating miniature scenes of everything from circuses to Old West saloons, many of which have moving parts you can activate by the touch of a button. The building itself is built of glass bottles and concrete. One of many hand-painted signs throughout the labyrinth says, I DID ALL THIS WHILE YOU WERE WATCHING TV, and another one quotes Thomas Edison: INVENTION CONSISTS OF IMAGINATION AND A SCRAP HEAP. ●

Quarai Ruins, one of three sets of ruins preserved in the Salinas Pueblo Missions National Monument.

ruins scattered throughout this former hub in the regional salt trade. The road is an undulating 55 miles per hour, with a few small towns nestled in the foothills of the Manzano Mountains, which rise to the west (Tajique is one of the few with services). The main industries seem to be ranching and selling firewood.

The big attraction here is the Quarai Ruins, well-preserved examples of the Ancestral Pueblo cultures that once thrived here, and there's lots of information about the area's history in exhibits and explanatory panels throughout the compound. There are actually three sets of ruins, and this is the northernmost. The Salinas Pueblo Missions National Monument, with its visitor center, is in Mountainair. The Abo Ruins are southwest of here on US 60. You can easily visit them all if you're planning to head back to Albuquerque via US 60. These settlements, which have served different purposes over the years, are perched on a strategic spot at the edge of the mountains. From here, native peoples headed east to collect salt deposits to sell down the trail.

We go east from Mountainair, then north on NM 41 (you can either connect with US 60 in Mountainair or head north from Punta near the Quarai Ruins, cross the valley on NM 542 and connect at Estancia). Estancia is a decent-size town with all amenities, including many restaurants—a surprising number of which offer live music—and some basic stores. We took this route because it's a relatively quick ride, on straight, fast road, to Santa Fe. If you're staying the night in Albuquerque, you could take this road north and then connect with I-40. Either way, expediency is about all this part of the ride has going for it, as things get flat and wide open with very little scenery save for some private ranches sprawling across the desert prairie pretty much all the way to the Santa Fe suburbs.

About Santa Fe itself: The city's layout can be kind of confusing. Freeways go around it to the west and south, but to get around the city itself, you'll need a map. To get a sense of direction, remember that this is an old city and it's not organized according to what we're often used to seeing in the West. It's arranged in a

Santa Fe is rightfully proud of its status as one of the world's prominent art centers. The city hosts huge art auctions that draw collectors from all over the world. Galleries stock works of all kinds, some of it costing tens or even hundreds of thousands of dollars. But you don't have to pay a lot to get some original art here—especially if you're interested in jewelry or pottery.

The artists settled in front of the Palace of the Governors are required by law to sell only locally made goods, usually by them or their relatives. Each artist signs his or her work to verify authenticity, although sometimes the signature isn't easy to spot. Ask if you're not sure. More booths and carts are scattered along the surrounding streets; these aren't as strictly regulated as those at the palace.

If you want to view but not buy, look into the city's many fine museums, including the Georgia O'Keeffe Museum near the town center. Her work means a lot more when you've been touring the area she depicts in her paintings. ●

No one knows how Santa Fe's Loretto Chapel stairway stays up without support.

spread-out grid system; Santa Fe is like a wheel with the downtown historic area as its hub. The Paseo de Peralta makes an inner loop around downtown, and other major roads run out from there like spokes, eventually joining the freeway on the outskirts of town.

Although it can be confusing, downtown Santa Fe is well worth finding, since most of the city's attractions are clustered there in the space of a few blocks. Everything revolves around the vibrant central square, which is lined with vendors selling their handmade wares. Although street parking can be a huge hassle in a car, it's much easier to find a spot to squeeze a bike into.

The Palace of the Governors—with its long, distinctive colonnade—was built by the Spanish in 1609, when they ruled this territory. This same building continued to function as a center of government for the next 400 years or so. Now it serves as the state's official history museum. For a $6 admission fee, you can tour permanent and rotating exhibitions of art and artifacts from New Mexico history.

The city's famous churches rise nearby: San Miguel Mission, built in 1610 and one of the oldest church buildings in the country; the Romanesque-style St. Francis Cathedral, which Pope Benedict called the "cradle of Catholicism" in the Southwest; and Loretto Chapel, with its mysterious spiral staircase (it has no supports on the inside or outside of the stairway, so no one knows how it stays up).

SOUTHERN ARIZONA

If you want desert, southern Arizona is the place for you. Here, the cacti grow tall, the light is long, and the weather is almost always warm and dry—making this good territory for riding most of the year. It's also a gateway to Mexico and the scene of some wild history, especially during the quick-draw era.

Like northern Arizona, the southern half of the state is partly carved up into Indian reservations. The biggest belong to the Apache Nation (on the eastern side) and the Tohono O'odham Nation, the southern edge of which crosses the Mexican border west of Tucson. It occupies an area the size of Connecticut.

Southern Arizona is mostly relatively flat desert occasionally interrupted by mountains that reach nearly 8,000 feet. And while people sometimes tend to see the desert as barren, this part of the Southwest has a huge range of diverse plants and animals.

At the center of the state, Phoenix is a sprawling urban center with a major airport and every amenity you could want or imagine, including lots of bike and accessory outlets and plenty of places to buy parts or get something fixed. Places like Liberty Motorcycle Rental in Tempe are more than happy to set you up and give suggestions and advice.

Phoenix is the biggest city in the Southwest, with all the delights (great shopping, restaurants) and the headaches (traffic, sprawl) of an urban center. We tend to like staying in midsize cities, which are also plentiful here. As in northern Arizona, we found that small or medium-size towns around here tend to have big, fun-loving personalities.

If you prefer an urban setting and enjoy the nightlife that comes with it, be sure to find your way to motorcycle-friendly parts of the metropolitan area such as Scottsdale. With its own identity apart from Phoenix, it has a thriving bar and restaurant scene year-round. Come the end of March and beginning of April, riders from all over converge for Arizona Bike Week—which actually goes more like ten days if you include pre-rally events (go to www.azbikeweek.com for more information). Since spring is the best time of year to visit anyway (the desert is blooming and temperatures haven't hit 100 yet), you might want to mark your calendar.

It does get blisteringly hot in Phoenix in the summer, generally 10 to 15 degrees hotter than other parts of the state. The thermometer can spike between 115 and 120 degrees (we've seen 105 degrees as early as mid-May), so we recommend heading to higher elevations for an easy escape from the heat.

RIDE 28

Fort Apache Loop/Salt River Canyon

Directions:
south on US 60 from Show Low
east on SR 73 to Fort Apache Historic Park
south on US 60 to Globe
north on SR 188 to SR 87, then to Payson

Distance:
from Show Low to Fort Apache: 38 miles
from Fort Apache to Globe: 88 miles
from Globe to Payson: 85 miles

Time:
half to a full day, depending on time at stops

Services:
at Show Low, Whiteriver, Pinetop, Globe, small towns on the shores of Roosevelt Lake, and Payson

Best Time of Year:
early spring to late fall; higher elevations can be cool and rainy into April, while lower elevations are hot in summer, when Tonto National Monument is closed.

Highlights:
Fort Apache Historic Park, Salt River Canyon's S curves and spectacular views, Tonto National Monument

This ride takes you through some well-traveled and well-loved motorcycle country, with some intriguing historic attractions along the way. With mountains and deserts, you'll get a variety of scenery as well as a taste of Wild West past and present.

We start at Show Low, a classic motorcycle stop and one of many medium-size towns that seems built to cater to motorcyclists, with more restaurants and roadhouses than you'd expect in a town of about 12,000 people. And its 6,400 feet in elevation makes it one of Arizona's cooler spots.

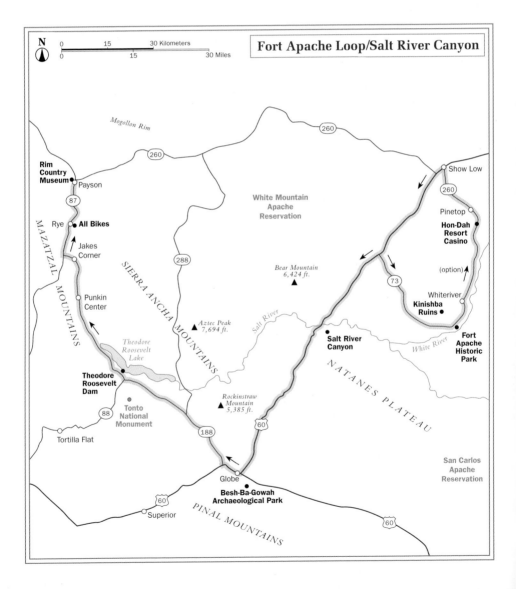

Fort Apache Loop/Salt River Canyon

This female pooch took a liking to us on our tour of Fort Apache. From the looks of her, she must have had pups stashed somewhere.

A giant swath of land just south of Show Low belongs to the Apaches, and this ride gives you a chance to see some of the territory they have considered their sacred home for hundreds of years. Whiteriver is the largest town in the 2,600-square-mile reservation and Pinetop is a recreational area replete with golf courses, lounges, motels, and the sprawling Hon-Dah Resort Casino complex. (*Hon-dah* means "welcome" or "be our guest." It doesn't mean you'll get a discount if you roll in on a Gold Wing.)

You can see Fort Apache via a loop from Show Low or as a detour from a point-to-point ride. Take AZ 260 south out of Show Low and connect with SR 73 at Hon-Dah, then continue south— or take US 60 southward for about 20 miles, turn off at SR 73 and head east.

Unlike most parks of its kind, Fort Apache Historic Park gives the history of whites and American Indians from the Indian perspective. The exhibits at the fort, all run by the White Mountain band, preserve items from both their own history and that of the whites who built the fort. You can tour the parade grounds and some of the preserved buildings surrounding them; pay the $3

The Apaches have been known, especially in old Western movies and cowboy novels, as a "warlike" people. You would be warlike, too, if a bunch of armed strangers moved in and took over your ancestral land. But unlike many other tribes (including many in this part of the world), this band of Apaches managed to stay on their ancestral lands by working with, rather than against, the white invaders.

At Fort Apache, white soldiers established a settlement in 1870 and recruited local Apaches to serve as scouts when fighting other bands. Their service proved a mixed blessing: On one hand, they did keep their beloved territory. On the other, they had to join forces with the invaders to do it. (The 1948 movie *Fort Apache,* starring John Wayne and directed by John Ford, was filmed in Monument Valley to the north of here, so the movie's landscape looks nothing like these mountains. *Broken Arrow,* with Jimmy Stewart, is a more nuanced look at the struggles between whites and Apaches.) ●

admission fee at the Culture Center before you look around (don't take any photos without express permission). The center also houses exhibitions depicting Apache culture and work by local artists and musicians.

Admission to the museum and fort also gets you into the Kinishba Ruins National Historic Landmark, a couple miles north of here. Kinishba is the ruins of a large village originally occupied from about 1250 to 1400. At its busiest, its 500 or so rooms may have housed as many as 1,000 people—a big town back then. Depending on the condition of the unpaved road to the ruins, they may or may not be accessible by motorcycle. Ask about road conditions at the main building.

Now, for US 60 and the ride toward Globe. US 60 through here is a great motorcycle road, curving but fast, with several upcoming bends visible at any given time. It's a good, well-banked ride that

Salt River Canyon is often referred to as a miniature Grand Canyon—for good reason.

comes down off the Mogollon Rim and into Salt River Canyon. The landscape starts off forested with lots of juniper and gets more desert-y and less vegetated as you head toward lower elevations, with views out across miles of juniper-covered red-rock mesas.

The road clings to the sides of the mountain, offering wide vistas of sky and landscape. Striated cliffs drop down into the river valley below and the light changes around every turn. A couple pullouts provide great views. Old, rusted vehicles beneath them testify to the lack of guardrails in some places (leaving us to wonder: are those vehicles there accidentally or intentionally?). Watch for big vehicles on some of the tighter curves; you'll see lots of trailer-towing tourists and semitrucks.

The road plunges a dramatic, switchback-filled 2,000 feet into Salt River Canyon. There's a small interpretive center at the bottom, where you can check out the river up close and even dip your toes in if you're feeling hot, before getting back on the bike and climbing again on the other side. Multiple pullouts allow you to look out across the vista.

At the top, the road unfolds southbound again on rolling hills, where for as far as the eye can see, there are no towns, no farmhouses—just wide-open expanses. The land to the north of the river is part of the White Mountain Apache Reservation, while the 2,900-square-mile San Carlos Apache Reservation is on the south side.

As you descend again into Globe, you reach more traditional desert landscape. Globe is a typical old mining town, looking a little tired these days but offering plenty of services. Like most of the many small casinos scattered around Arizona, the Apache Gold Casino just east of Globe is a possible place to meet some friends for a little indoor recreation. If you want to spend some time (this could be a base for ongoing rides, including more desert exploration to the east), you can also see the spot's boom-and-bust history through a self-guided walking tour of downtown. Or, if you'd like to go farther back in time, take in the Besh-Ba-Gowah Archaeological Park just southeast of Globe. Along with

a museum, the park takes you through lots of ruins from an 800-year-old settlement.

After Globe, we headed north on SR 188 toward Tonto National Monument. This stretch of highway—known at the Apache Trail—begins in Globe, follows SR 188 past Tonto National Monument, and heads west on a well-maintained but unpaved section of SR 88 to Tortilla Flat and Apache Junction (the Tortilla Flat section is covered in ride 29). The monument is an easy detour from the highway.

Traveling northwest on SR 188, you'll see an increasing number of saguaro cacti dotting the hillsides. Theodore

It's a short and paved but fairly steep walk to the lower ruins of Tonto National Monument.

Roosevelt Lake, on the east side of the road, is a major recreational and water storage reservoir for the folks in the Phoenix area. It's hard to believe a massive urban zone is just on the other side of the Four Peaks and Superstition Wilderness areas, which serve as a barrier between Phoenix and this remote-feeling territory.

Be sure you stop off at the pullout just south of the Tonto monument, where you can get views of the upper Tonto ruins that you can't get from the lower ruins. If you choose to, you'll be visiting them in a few minutes.

On the day we were at Tonto National Monument, ranger Jenny Shrum captured a Gila monster in the parking lot just outside the visitor center. Scientists know relatively little about these rare, elusive, and well-camouflaged creatures and are studying them to learn more about their habits. Before Shrum released the Gila monster back into the wild, a microchip was embedded under its skin so scientists can monitor its movements.

The poisonous lizards have a fearsome reputation (they are the only venomous lizards native to North America and can grow up to 2 feet long). But they are relatively slow moving, so your chances of getting bitten are minimal—a doctor remarked in 1899 that "a man who is fool enough to get bitten by a Gila monster ought to die. The creature is so sluggish and slow of movement that the victim of its bite is compelled to help largely in order to get bitten." If you happen across one, count yourself lucky, observe it from a safe distance, and let it go on its way. Do not harass or attempt to kill it, since the animals are protected by state law in both Arizona and Nevada. ●

At the monument, a short, steep trail leads to the lower Tonto ruins, a group of cliff dwellings from the thirteenth century that have been partially restored to give an idea of what they looked like in their heyday. As they did with the other cliff dwellings scattered around here, the Salado Indians chose this site strategically: Not only did it give them an expansive view of the valleys below, but it was also shaded in the afternoon—and even in the thirteenth century, things must have gotten very hot. They do now, too, and that means this is not a place to visit on a summer afternoon. In fact, the ruins are closed during summer because of heat and rattlesnakes. This is a great place for viewing wildlife as well as human activity and you may see anything from butterflies to Gila monsters on your visit.

If you want to get a closer look at the more spectacular upper ruins, you'll have to make a reservation (you'll also have a longer and more strenuous hike, which means starting earlier in the morning).

Leaving Tonto behind, SR 188 is an easy, undulating 55 miles per hour past the Roosevelt dam (see ride 29) and along the shores of the lake, where you'll see campgrounds and boat launches as well as a few places to eat, relax, and refuel at hamlets with names like Punkin Center and Jakes Corner. Leaving the lake, the road climbs steadily upward toward the cliffs at the edge of the Mogollon Rim.

About 10 miles south of Payson, SR 188 joins with SR 87, the Beeline Highway. If you're heading to the big city from here, SR 87 southbound makes a quick ride to Phoenix. We opted instead to go back to the cool mountains and stay in Payson. You'll ride through a valley surrounded by mountains on a road that looks different depending on conditions and the time of day and year.

On our way, we stopped at All Bikes in Rye, about 8 miles south of Payson. All Bikes is the place where old bikes go to die—or to be reborn. If you're on a motorcycle or bicycle or care about anything with wheels, you must at least stop by and take a look around. Here, Ron Alder and his girlfriend Cori have amassed an amazing collection of old motorcycles, bicycles, cars, golf carts, helicopters . . . you get the idea. The place is something between a shop and a museum.

Ron spends his days fixing old contraptions or building new ones out of old parts (the day we were there, he was rebuilding a late 1980s Harley Sportster for a woman in Los Angeles). He makes his living selling things to people around

Ron Alder, owner of All Bikes, works on one of the many bikes in his yard that are in various stages of repair.

the country but cares a lot more about the contraptions themselves than making money. If you're curious, ask about the 1880s wooden bicycle wheel they have in their collection—or anything else that strikes your fancy—and you might make a connection with this character. If you want a part or piece from just about anything with two wheels, this is the place to inquire about it. Since the climate doesn't promote rust, some of the old chrome looks like new.

Payson serves as a base for travelers wanting to explore the Mogollon Rim (find out more about the area at the Rim Country Museum in Green Valley Park, which features the "oldest forest ranger station and residence still standing in the Southwest").

Like other little towns throughout Arizona, Payson has a couple good restaurants and drinking establishments (often, they are the same places). We ate some of the best steak of our lives, drank good beer, and heard some very entertaining karaoke at the Buffalo Bar and Grill right on the highway. The woman at the front desk of our hotel recommended it to us but warned that things can get pretty rowdy after about 10 p.m. on the weekends. It was a Thursday, and apparently the weekend starts on Thursday in Payson. Our kind of place! You could stay in bigger cities, but we like towns the size of Payson and Globe—big enough that you'll find supplies and maybe even a repair shop, but small enough that you get a sense of community and an authentic sample of life in the Wild West.

RIDE

29

Tortilla Flat

Directions from Payson:

SR 87 (Beeline Highway) south to junction with FR 204 (Bush Highway)

FR 204 to junction with FR 207 (Usery Pass Road)

left/south on FR 207, which becomes Ellsworth Road

Ellsworth Road left onto Brown Road, which becomes SR 88 (Lost Dutchman Boulevard/Apache Trail)

Directions coming from the west:

US 60 through Mesa to AZ 88 exit

north on AZ 88

Distance:

from Payson to Mesa: 78 miles

from Mesa to Tortilla Flat: 37 miles

from Tortilla Flat to SR 188: 26 miles

Time:

half a day

Services:

in and around Phoenix, Tortilla Flat (limited), and along Roosevelt Lake

Best Time of Year:

anytime, although it can get hot in summer

Highlights:

a biker-friendly outpost at Tortilla Flat, an exciting gravel-switchback challenge, Roosevelt Dam

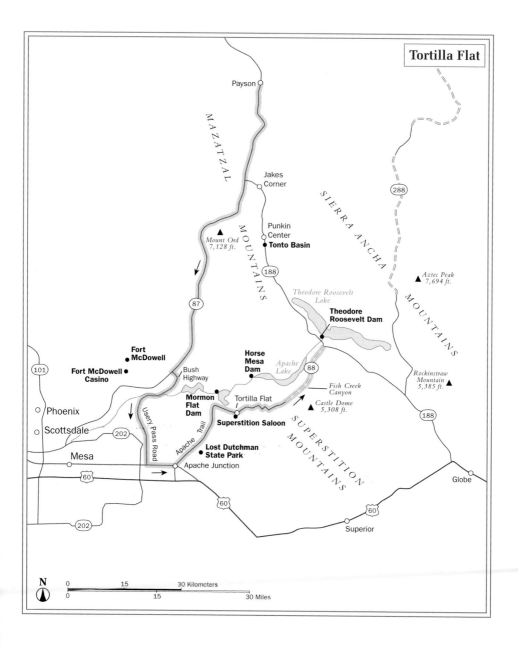

Tortilla Flat is one of the Phoenix area's most popular rides. It's quick, it's fun, and it lets you choose your level of excitement, with a possibility for gravel switchbacks on the way back down.

We started in Payson and headed toward Phoenix on SR 87, a fast road (appropriately nicknamed the Beeline Highway) with some nice hills and plenty of big sweeping turns that allow you to pull back the throttle and lean. SR 87 eventually dumps you down into flat, suburban desert. Be aware of all the cross traffic once you start to hit traffic lights. Motorists turning left in front of you aren't very good at judging your speed. From here, it can be hard to figure out where to turn to get on the road to Tortilla Flat—and construction is happening so fast, it probably won't get easier.

From SR 87, you can take FR 204 (Bush Highway) toward Saguaro Lake, then connect with FR 207 (Usery Pass Road) southbound toward Apache Junction, which is where you want to end up. The road may be a bit slower, but it's more direct than the mazelike route through town and has the added benefit of getting you off the freeway sooner. Otherwise, continue into town and take the Apache Junction exit from Mesa. If you need a break, stop at the Fort McDowell Casino (on SR 87 about 5 miles beyond the turnoff for the Bush Highway) on a strip of Indian reservation land northeast of Phoenix. It's a popular gathering spot.

Once you're in Apache Junction, take SR 88 (also known as Lost Dutchman Boulevard in town, then Apache Trail—the roads all seem to have at least two names each around here, which doesn't help the confusion), following signs for Tortilla Flat.

The Apache Trail road, an official National Forest Scenic Byway, follows an aboriginal route into the mountains, through a pass long used by Indians and later traders. With its narrow switchbacks, it isn't recommended for the faint of heart or for large trailers, although that doesn't stop many from pulling them up to Canyon Lake at the top. The lake has a marina and a replica sternwheeler steamboat, *Dolly*, that takes tourists around the lake.

On your way to Tortilla Flat, you'll pass Lost Dutchman State Park. The Dutchman, Jacob Waltz (he was actually German) is the subject of a favorite Arizona legend. Waltz grew famous for what was rumored to be a huge cache of gold hidden somewhere in these mountains—and for his violent reaction to anyone who tried to loot his treasure. He supposedly killed several people who tried to find it. Almost immediately after his death, various maps began to appear, purportedly leading to the Dutchman's gold stash. Although only bits of evidence have surfaced over the years, some optimists are still actively seeking Waltz's fortune here. ●

Nestled in the mountains and right next to the lake is Tortilla Flat itself, essentially a strip of shops and eateries along the road. This is a tourist trap, for sure, but it's also a quintessential motorcycle destination, so you should definitely plan to stop. You'll find plenty of bikes parked in front of the Superstition Saloon—actually, pretty much anywhere.

Continuing east, the road gradually climbs as you leave Tortilla Flat behind. Five miles down the road, the pavement ends, with SR 88 turning to hardpack and gravel through Fish Creek Canyon. Follow it to an overlook just as it gets ready to descend down the other side of the hill. This is where you have to decide how brave you're feeling. For anyone who enjoys a challenging gravel ride, the canyon can be a lot of fun, especially if you're not inclined to backtrack the way you came.

This is a well-maintained gravel road that sees a lot of use, but it's steep in places and the switchbacks can be a little tight at times, so watch your speed and keep your hand off the front brake. The first big descent you'll encounter drops you about 750 feet of elevation in about three-quarters of a mile. Although it's mostly downhill from the west after that initial descent, it's sometimes difficult to tell whether you are gaining or losing elevation

It may not always be this difficult to find a spot for your bike, but the Superstition Saloon is a popular stop for riders.

Steve: The saloon was packed when we got there. We didn't want to wait for a table, so we headed over to the bar. At the Superstition, rather than "belly up," you "saddle up" to the bar—when you get there, you'll know what I mean. My meal wasn't bad (buzzard wings, the Arizona desert's really big version of chicken wings), but I wish I had known about the burgers before we ordered. Unfortunately, we already had our food when our bartender told me the place was known for its burgers and chili. I love good burgers and I always like to eat an establishment's signature food. But there's always next time! ●

because the road is consistently undulating. Coming in from the east wouldn't be much different until the final ascent.

Going either direction, you'll want to feel comfortable with your bike-handling skills on dirt and gravel. This road is doable for all but the biggest and heaviest bikes and the low-slung choppers you see a lot of in this part of the country. Most bikes will be fine if they take the steepest curves slowly. If you're on a bike with an air-cooled engine, it's probably not a good idea on a 100-degree day, since the heat can be hazardous to your health and could kill your engine if you're going this slowly for this long. If you have any questions about whether conditions are OK, ask at Tortilla Flat. Whether you take the ride on going up or down, you're rewarded with panoramic views of cliffs, cacti, and, in spring, wildflowers blanketing the slopes.

At the end of the gravel road, just before you reach SR 188, you'll drive past the Theodore Roosevelt Dam, which was the world's tallest masonry dam until the original structure was covered by new concrete in 1996. The dam was built up 77 feet, to 357 feet high, after engineers determined that a flood could

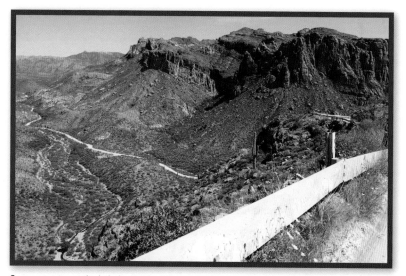

Once you get past the hairpins on the hill, the ride through Fish Creek Canyon is a series of small roller coasters.

send water over the top of the previous version (the new dam also raised the lake level to store water for another million people).

At the dam (where SR 188 used to cross right over the top), you can either go south toward Globe and Tonto National Monument or north to recreational towns along the lake. Heading north, Roosevelt Lake Bridge (built when the road was relocated from the top of the dam) is the longest two-lane, single-span, steel-arch bridge in North America. From here, you can go south on SR 188 toward Globe and US 60 or north toward SR 87, both of which connect back to Phoenix.

The original Theodore Roosevelt Dam was built from 1903 to 1911 out of blocks of stone carved from nearby canyons and lifted using block and tackle (and a lot of human sweat). It was dangerous work: forty-one people died during construction. The town of Roosevelt, where many of the workers lived, was swallowed by the lake after the dam was finished. Informative panels make this dam overlook worthy of a quick stop. ●

**RIDE
30**

Day Trips Around Tucson

Directions:
west on Speedway Boulevard to Gates Pass Road or AZ 86
to Saguaro National Park
east on Tanque Verde Road through Tucson; connects with
Catalina Highway east of town

Distance:
about 125 miles for both Saguaro National Park and Mount
Lemmon

Time:
a half day to a full day (several short rides, each two hours
or more)

Services:
throughout Tucson, limited (no fuel) in national park and on
Mount Lemmon

Best Time of Year:
spring, summer, and fall

Highlights:
the sights of Tucson, the desert flora and fauna, a cool ride
up a green mountain in the middle of the desert

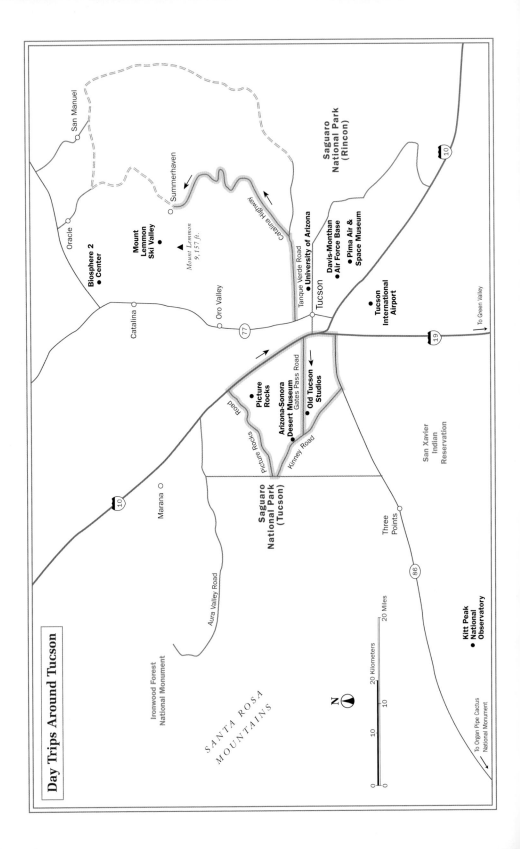

Day Trips Around Tucson

San Manuel

Oracle

Biosphere 2
● Center

Catalina

Oro Valley

77

Summerhaven

Mount
Lemmon
Ski Valley

▲ *Mount Lemmon*
9,157 ft.

Catalina Highway

Tanque Verde Road

University of Arizona

Tucson

Davis-Monthan
Air Force Base

● Pima Air &
Space Museum

Saguaro
National Park
(Rincon)

10

● Tucson
International
Airport

19

To Green Valley

Picture Rocks
Road

● Picture
Rocks

Arizona-Sonora
Desert Museum

Gates Pass Road

● Old Tucson
Studios

Kinney Road

San Xavier
Indian
Reservation

Marana

10

Saguaro
National Park
(Tucson)

Three
Points

86

SANTA ROSA
MOUNTAINS

Aura Valley Road

Ironwood Forest
National Monument

N

20 Miles

20 Kilometers

10

10

0

0

● Kitt Peak
National
Observatory

To Organ Pipe Cactus
National Monument

Like many cities in the Southwest, Tucson is a sprawling maze surrounding a small, historic downtown. Although it's got the restaurants, museums, and other attractions you'd expect of a college (University of Arizona) town with a vibrant past, we thought Tucson's appeal lay much more in its surroundings. With so many other great towns in the Southwest, it stacked up mostly as a place for suburban families, retirees, and others desiring a quiet lifestyle. Nevertheless, with a dearth of any other cities nearby, it's your best bet for a southern Arizona base.

These are actually a couple short trips you could do in a day or on the morning or evening of a longer ride. First, we head out to Saguaro National Park. The park actually comprises two sections, on the east (Rincon) and the west (Tucson) side of town.

Christy: As we hit Tucson from the north, we found that every single exit from I-10 was closed. We later learned the city was in the middle of a major road project to improve its on- and off-ramps and bridges. If there was advance warning of this, we didn't see it. Instead, we had to go all the way to the south end of town, get off the freeway, turn around, and go back north again—only to find the northbound exits were all closed as well. We turned around again when we could, north of Tucson, and this time managed to get onto the frontage road and find a hotel.

When we wanted to visit the downtown area—on the opposite side of the freeway—we discovered mostly closed underpasses. We've never seen such inconvenience—why close an entire city's worth of highway exits? They couldn't keep at least a few open for poor tourists wanting to get into town? Needless to say, we weren't very happy with Tucson by the time we finally got to our hotel. The unintended consequences of "progress" seemed to be a common theme in Tucson, a city that can't seem to keep up with its growing pains. ●

A forest of saguaro blankets the hillsides in Saguaro National Park near Tucson.

The eastern side isn't motorcycle accessible, whereas the western side has a fun road right through it. Plus, many short walks and hikes take you out among the cacti.

The saguaro, Arizona's state symbol, is the largest cactus species in the world. It can be up to 50 feet tall and weigh 8 tons. A lot of that is water, since the cacti store rare rainfall and use it in drier times. In the spring, you may see white flowers atop the cacti. The national park lets you enjoy whole forests of the giant plants and their ecosystems.

Follow the signs for the national park and the Arizona-Sonora Desert Museum. You can either start off on AZ 86, on the southwestern edge of town, or follow signs for Gates Pass Road and Old Tucson Studios. We did the latter and were rewarded with impressive views coming out of the pass (Old Tucson Studios is an Old-West movie set that caters to tourists with daily live shows, musicals, and trail rides).

The entrance is about 5 miles from the western edge of town, and the visitor center is just past that. Admission is $5. The desert museum is a comprehensive and well-appointed look at the plants, animals, and natural history you might encounter on your rides through the Southwest. Plan at least a couple hours for a tour. Go to www.desert museum.org to find out more before you go.

There's not a lot of glitz here, just a whole lot of cacti and a road that winds through them and hilly territory. It makes an 8-mile loop just past the visitor center and there are lots of places to stop and take a look if you desire

A docent holds a Harris's hawk at the entrance of the Arizona-Sonora Desert Museum. Plan to spend several hours when you visit.

(bring water). This park is especially impressive early or late in the day, when the cacti's shadows make them look even stranger. To exit the park, either return the way you came or go northbound after the park loop, connect with Picture Rocks Road, and head through the suburbs back into town.

Organ Pipe Cactus National Monument, another large cactus preserve, is accessible via a long ride across the Tohono O'Odham Nation on AZ 86 or IR 15. This is a long trip on flat, straight, remote roads, so it would only be suitable for extreme cactus enthusiasts. And if that's not enough plant worship for you, Ironwood Forest National Monument is just west of the Saguaro National Park via Avra Valley Road. Its special plant is the ironwood tree; it has some petroglyphs and ghost towns. There's not a lot else going on. Like a lot of places around here, it's great for solitude but its other charms are less obvious. ●

It's 112 miles each way to see more cacti. Feel free if you are so inclined.

It just doesn't seem right to find a ski resort in the mountains near Tucson.

Our second Tucson day trip takes you up Mount Lemmon, which juts up from the valley to an elevation of more than 9,000 feet. That makes it a welcome escape from the heat in the summer and a convenient ski resort in winter.

Take Tanque Verde Road through Tucson and connect on the eastern edge with the Catalina Highway. The scenery along the 27-mile ride goes through multiple climate zones, from desert zone to pine forest (the equivalent of going from Mexico to Canada). As with other areas around here, you will see an astonishing array of bird life as you ride up into the hills. Every turn leads to a view of different plats or oddly shaped rock formations just off the side of the road. Don't forget cool-weather gear and make sure you gas up before you go.

An official scenic byway, the highway is in pretty good condition, well banked with lots of curves. Because it's so curvy and very popular, the speed limit is a mere 35 miles per hour. Keep an eye out for tar repairs snaking across the road.

When you get to the top, you can almost forget that this is just a small oasis in the middle of the enormous desert. A tiny town called Summerhaven is nestled here in the mountains (a fire in 2003 burned through much of this area, but it is slowly recovering). There's some food and a gift shop, but not much else. You may also see the telescopes that make up the observatory up top. The mountain used to be home to a military radar base and an emergency radar tracking station for space shuttles. Now, astronomy buffs use the telescopes to survey the skies.

There is a dirt road down the "back" side of the mountain, but it can be rough in places. Dual-sport bikers do ride it, but inquire about conditions before you give it a try. If you have a lot of time, the road connects with AZ 77, which you could take all the way to Globe (see ride 25) or back to Tucson—a route that would take you past the giant geodesic terrarium of Biosphere 2, a science research and teaching center where people calling themselves "Biospherians" experimented with creating an indoor ecosystem independent from the outside world. Now, visitors can walk through and check out the indoor jungle, crop fields, and million-gallon "ocean."

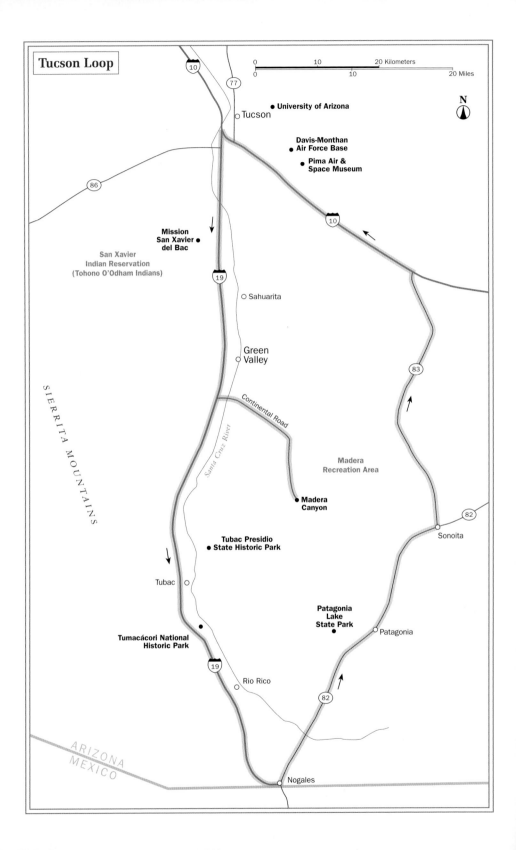

Tucson Loop

University of Arizona

Davis-Monthan
Air Force Base

Pima Air &
Space Museum

Tucson

10

77

86

Mission
San Xavier
del Bac

San Xavier
Indian Reservation
(Tohono O'Odham Indians)

19

Sahuarita

Green
Valley

Continental Road

Santa Cruz River

SIERRITA MOUNTAINS

Madera
Recreation Area

Madera
Canyon

83

82

Sonoita

Tubac Presidio
State Historic Park

Tubac

Patagonia
Lake
State Park

Patagonia

Tumacácori National
Historic Park

19

Rio Rico

82

ARIZONA
MEXICO

Nogales

0   10   20 Kilometers
0   10   20 Miles

N

RIDE

31

Tucson Loop

Directions:

south on I-19 from Tucson

north on SR 82 to junction with SR 83

north on SR 83 to junction with I-10

Distance:

182 miles, less if you skip Madera Canyon

from Tucson to Nogales: 98 miles

from Nogales to Patagonia: 20 miles

from Patagonia to Tucson: 64 miles

Time:

little more than a half day, depending on stops

Services:

at Tucson, Green Valley, Tubac, Rio Rico, Nogales, and Patagonia

Best Time of Year:

anytime

Highlights:

Spanish and Indian history; shopping, eating, and sightseeing around Tubac; a potential side trip across the border into Mexico (be sure to bring your passport!)

This ride takes you south from Tucson to the Mexico border and back. Do some research in advance if you plan to make a foray through Nogales into Mexico. Border controls and customs rules change and you'll want to be on top of things before you go. If you decide to stay on the American side, there's still plenty to see.

From Tucson, I-19 takes you south toward the border, with some interesting sights along the way. Sadly, the road itself isn't much more than a straight, hot freeway with a few gradual shifts in direction but at least it makes an easy way to get from one point to another.

Once you've cleared the suburbs and retirement communities, you pass through San Xavier, one of several sections of the Tohono O'odham Nation, parts of which are scattered around southern Arizona. This section is home to the beautiful 300-year-old San Xavier del Bac Mission, the "White Dove of the Desert." Soon, you'll pass Green Valley, site of many retirees as well as the ASARCO Mineral Discovery Center mining museum and the Titan Missile Museum, a deactivated missile silo (open 9 a.m. to 5 p.m., closed Monday and Tuesday in summer). At Green River, you'll see signs for the Madera Recreation Area, which starts at East Continental Road through town and makes a quick and pleasant out-and-back, especially if you're in the mood for a picnic or just a break from the desert floor.

Madera is a popular spot among the locals for hiking and bird-watching. We spotted all kinds of birds, including many birds of prey. A feeding station at Santa Rita Lodge is open to the public and is an easy chance to see some of the canyon's many hummingbird species as well as Mexican jays, house finches, white-breasted nuthatches, and woodpeckers. Since it's so beloved by locals, the canyon can get busy, especially in summer. Watch out for slow-moving hikers and their equally slow vehicles. ●

The road rises toward the peaks of the Santa Rita Mountains, surrounded by private haciendas, bed-and-breakfast establishments, and guest cabins. The mountains—one of several isolated ranges, called Sky Islands, that rise up suddenly out of the flat southern Arizona desert—are much cooler than the valley and can even get snow into springtime. At the end of the 13-mile-long road, take a short hike to an overlook for great views.

Continuing south on the highway, make another quick stop at Tubac, where working artists now occupy former Spanish military housing at an eighteenth-century fort.

This is just a sample of the crazy yard art you'll find in Tubac. The artists are happy to ship your purchase if you can't carry it home on your bike.

It's a nice place to stop for lunch or at least some good coffee from Ben Wahz Brew Hahz, where the proprietor was trained as a Harley mechanic and can give you the local lowdown. We'll warn you that you might also find some appealing souvenirs made by artists in residence or imported from Mexico. They're usually willing to ship if you don't have room in your saddlebags for their handmade pottery.

Two historic sites lie just outside Tubac: Tubac Presidio State Historic Park and Tumacácori National Historical Park. Tubac Presidio was a Pima Indian village that later grew to support the Spanish who moved in to Christianize the population starting in the late 1600s. Tumacácori was the site of the regional Jesuit mission (its full name, San José de Tumacácori, comes from Spanish and O'odham words meaning "Saint Joseph of the Rocky Flat

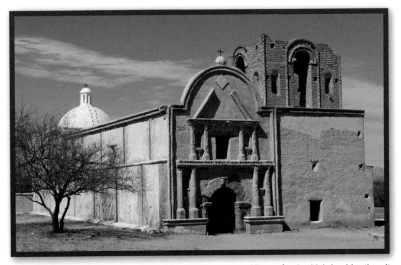

Feel free to wander the grounds and discover the history of Tumacácori, which is older than it first appears.

Place"). The Spanish quashed revolt attempts in 1751 and to prevent further rebellion made the Tubac site into a military garrison—the first in what is now Arizona—the next year.

Now, Tumacácori houses the visitor center for three groups of mission ruins in the area. The ones here are open to the public. The other two, San Cayetano de Calabazas, and Los Santos Ángeles de Guevavi, are only accessible via guided tours that must be booked in advance. Call (520) 398-2341 if you're interested.

The two sites are fairly similar: Both are open 9 a.m. to 5 p.m. daily, both cost $3, both have small museums and gift shops, and both feature paved paths leading past old adobe structures. (Pick up self-guided tour brochures on-site.) If your time is limited, don't feel guilty about choosing to visit just one or the other.

The ride continues toward Mexico (as you can tell by the metric signposts along the highway), through arid territory that has never been kind to humanity. This has long been the site of slave trade, Spanish conquest, and now border crossings by illegal immigrants and drug dealers. While this isn't the most lawless point along the border, that feeling does seem to ratchet up a bit as you go farther south.

While it used to be possible to cross into Mexico or Canada by foot or vehicle without a passport, the United States has tightened restrictions in recent years. You can get into Mexico without a passport but you might have a hard time getting back—Border Control will want to see one. Customs rules allow you to bring $400 worth of goods back into the United States with no tax penalty. ●

Nogales is worth seeing—with some caveats. Many Arizona residents like to go into Mexico occasionally for some shopping and an authentic meal. The main shopping area is right across the border, where the folks selling pottery, baskets, rugs, leather, and jewelry speak English, prefer American dollars, and haggle over prices (the rule of thumb is to try to get the original price down by half). Many visitors park in the lot on the American side and walk in. Given increasing violence in recent years, we can't heartily recommend taking your bike in and leaving it for any length of time. Nor do we recommend riding there at night.

Southern Arizona is an unlikely home to six vineyards, some of which welcome visitors for tastings (go to www.arizonawines.com/southerntrail.html for information). We stopped at the funky Arizona Vineyards, with its colorful collection of old casks and other wine memorabilia, hoping for a taste of some Rattlesnake Red or Desert Dust wine. Alas, it was deserted.

Whether you go into Mexico or not, eventually it will be time to hit the road and head back north. We returned via AZ 82 and AZ 83 for a little change of scenery. The road rises into mountainous territory, past recreational areas, lots of campgrounds, ghost towns, and the hippie, artsy vibe of Patagonia. It's a good place to stop and eat if you didn't in Nogales and the last location with reliable services before you return to the Tucson area. Near town, Patagonia-Sonoita Creek Preserve is one of the best birding spots in the Southwest, home to more than 200 species of birds and plants plus rare fish and frogs.

Our colors matched it, so we had to stop for a tasting. But we found no one to serve us.

As the road rolls along the hillside, it gets more curvy, with lots of pullouts and hiking trailheads, then descends again into full-on desert before connecting with I-10, which will take you back to Tucson (consider stopping at the Pima Air & Space Museum, one of the world's largest aviation museums, on Valencia Road just south of Davis-Monthan Air Force Base). If you're done with Tucson and want to explore Tombstone and other areas to the east, stay on AZ 82, which hangs a right about 10 miles north of Patagonia. We'll cover that area in ride 32.

RIDE
32

Tombstone Tour

Directions:
east on I-10 from Tucson
south on AZ 90 or AZ 80 to Bisbee

Distance:
about 200 miles round-trip to Tucson, depending on exact route
from Tucson to Benson: 50 miles
from Benson to Bisbee: 54 miles
from Bisbee to Chiricahua National Monument: 73 miles
from Chiricahua National Monument to Tucson: 117 miles

Time:
half a day to a day, depending on how far you go and how many stops you make

Services:
in Tucson, Benson, Bisbee, Tombstone, and Willcox

Best Time of Year:
spring or fall

Highlights:
Kartchner Caverns, Chiricahua National Monument, some of the most famous towns and territory of the Wild West, mining history and modern chic at Bisbee

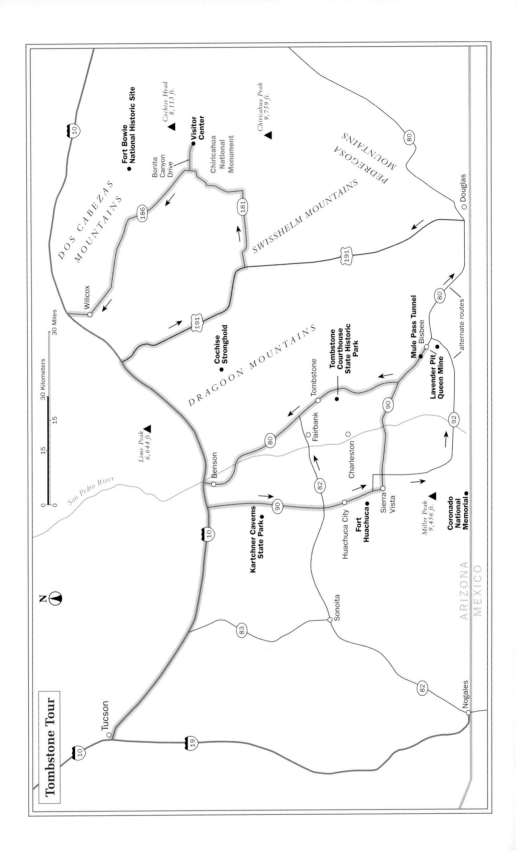

Tombstone Tour

With a lot to see and much of it easily accessible from the highways, this is a popular area for bikers as well as tourists. The scenery is much like that all over southern Arizona: arid, with sweeping vistas and the occasional gritty mountain range dropped into the middle of the valley. It's the sort of trip you take not so much for the riding itself but for all the things to see along the way.

The number of roads and the diverse natural or historical sites through here give you a lot of options. Since many of the roads connect with each other, you might want to make it into a series of mini-loops. One possibility for a day trip is to make a loop from I-10, traveling down AZ 90, turning around at Bisbee and returning via AZ 80. The attractions on this loop alone can easily take up a whole day or just a few hours, depending on your interests.

Take I-10 southeast from Tucson for about 25 miles to the junction with either AZ 90 or AZ 80, which are a couple miles apart. Close to the highway near where both of these roads branch off (it's technically on AZ 80), Benson is a nice little town with all services and a number of restaurants, convenience stores, and small motels. It could make a better base for exploring this area than impersonal Tucson. These small towns take great pride in both their history and their hospitality.

AZ 90 will take you to Kartchner Caverns State Park and Huachuca City ("city" is stretching it). This is wide-open territory that feels more hilly than mountainous. But there's a lot going on in these hills. At Kartchner Caverns, 9 miles south of I-10, water drips down and continues to build ever-growing formations in a "live" limestone cave. It's open daily year-round and offers two options for 1 1/2-hour tours (the Big Room tour is only available Oct 15 to Apr 15. If you're there in August or September, a visit is a little cheaper). You might want to call in advance and reserve a spot for a tour if you want to make sure you get one (call 520-586-2283).

Whichever road you choose south of I-10, it's easy to go back and forth between them (they eventually merge just north of Bisbee) via AZ 82 and AZ 92, both of which cross the San Pedro River and surrounding nature conservation area. On AZ 82, you'll pass by the ghost town of Fairbank and the Santa Cruz de Terrenate Presidio National Historic Site (try saying that three times fast). It's not much more than a few remnants of adobe walls from a short-lived fort established here in the 1700s and it's only accessible via a 2-mile gravel road that may or may not be in good condition.

AZ 92 is even more remote and goes past the ghost town of Charleston. Ghost towns throughout here give you an idea of just how populated the area once was, with hordes arriving to try to make their fortunes—and usually failing, giving the place a still-evident sense of hope gone bad.

If you go south on AZ 92 rather than going east toward AZ 80 or staying on AZ 90 toward Bisbee, the road takes you to Coronado National Memorial, a small forested area on the east slope of Miller Peak that commemorates the Spanish explorers who first made their way through here hundreds of years ago. There's not much else out here in terms of civilization.

The famous gunfighter hangout of Tombstone lies about 20 miles south of I-10 on AZ 80. Like Kartchner Caverns, it's an easy jog from the interstate if you're headed eastbound and don't have much time to spend. It has made the most of its fame as the site of the legendary gunfight featuring Wyatt Earp and Doc Holliday in 1881, where about thirty shots were fired in thirty seconds—no mean feat back then. For years, Tombstone has catered to tourists almost to the point of kitsch. Almost.

Tombstone goes all out to lure visitors, and part of its repertoire is a series of festivals during slow times, especially fall. If you're in town during Labor Day weekend, Tombstone plays host to a "rendezvous of gunfighters" during which gunfight reenactors dress up and show off. More shootouts—along with parades and live music—happen during Helldorado Days, which as of 2009 has been going on for eighty years. You get the idea that Tombstone has been honing its tourist appeal for a long time.

Either before or after your Tombstone visit, check out the old mining town of Bisbee, a good place to stop for lunch. On the

Christy: Tombstone, despite its cheesy elements, has a definite aura of authenticity. Maybe it's the fact that it's out here in the middle of the rough desert, or maybe it's just a general reflection of the tenacity of people who live here. Whatever the reason, it's easy to absorb.

The best thing to do is just suspend disbelief, jump in, and enjoy the tourist experience. Watch men in nineteenth-century-style trench coats and hats meander up and down the dusty streets. Visit the offices of the *Tombstone Epitaph,* printed here since 1881. Stop in at a gift shop and buy something hopefully not made in China. Have a chuckle at the Historama, a diorama display of Tombstone history that hasn't changed much in the past few decades (it's still narrated by Vincent Price). Drink at the Bird Cage Theatre, where prostitutes used to display themselves in enclosures hanging from the ceiling. Stop by at the Tombstone Courthouse, now an official state historical park.

And, if you won't feel cheated by the idea of paying to see what's behind the big fence in the middle of town, fork over the $5.50 and watch a reenactment of the gunfight (daily at 2 p.m.—if you miss it, don't worry; gunfight reenactments seem to happen all over town, all the time). Just outside town is Boothill Graveyard, some of whose crumbling headstones are still legible: HERE LIES LESTER MOORE, 4 SLUGS FROM A 44, NO LES, NO MORE. To get there, follow the signs. You have to walk a bit and pay a small admission fee. ●

way, you'll pass through Mule Pass Tunnel, the longest tunnel in Arizona until the I-10 tunnel was built through Phoenix. Once the site of intense mining that plumbed its rich mineral deposits (still visible in the red soil), Bisbee has preserved its old downtown as a historic district.

The original men in black were gunning for enemies, not aliens.

It might be hard to believe now, but Bisbee was once the largest town between St. Louis and San Francisco, with a population of 25,000 around 1910. Its past lives on in its preserved Victorian buildings and mine remnants as well as the massive Lavender Pit mine, last carved in 1975. Like Tombstone (and a lot of the historic towns in the Southwest), Bisbee hosts many festivals and events, many catering to an affluent crowd. You could spend a lot of money here. Or, just grab a beer and relax for a while before returning to the bike.

From here, you can return to I-10 or try out some of the straight, remote roads to the east. US 191, which picks up just north of the Mexico border about 30 miles east of Bisbee, could be a shortcut to the Chiricahua ("cheer-i-cow-ah") National Monument (buy gas in Bisbee, the last town for a long time).

The monument is easier to access from I-10 (take AZ 186 about 35 miles east of Benson) and could be another day trip or another out-and-back for those traveling east in general. Be sure you're full up on gas and snacks if you go. Located in the middle

Called the Land of Standing-Up Rocks by the Apaches, Chiricahua National Monument offers a striking and rugged sense of beauty.

of nowhere, the monument contains a volcanic area where spikes of volcanic rock rise far into the air. There's a visitor center at the entrance; beyond that, a 6-mile scenic drive winds upward among the pinnacles. The narrow, winding, 25-mile-per-hour road rises along steep canyons and under a few overhanging rocks, so ride with caution.

SOUTHERN NEW MEXICO

With an economy based on ranching, mining, and government research (into astronomy and other sciences—and some say alien life), southern New Mexico doesn't seem to have much of a tourism economy compared with other parts of the West. This can be good or bad; on one hand, it can be hard to find amenities and services in these spread-out, hardscrabble towns. On the other hand, it offers both unparalleled wide-open spaces and plenty of examples of old-fashioned small towns the likes of which are hard to come by these days.

Here, it's wise to gas up when you can. It might also be wise to carry a small container of fuel with you, which would give you added flexibility. Also be sure to pack snacks, lots of water, and layers of clothing—altitudes range from 4,000 to 10,000 feet, so be prepared for temperature changes.

This is prime wildlife viewing territory and birding heaven. You'll see all kinds of raptors, including Harris's hawk, golden (and occasionally bald) eagles, red-tailed hawks, and a host of smaller birds. You also may meet an occasional bear, and wolves were reintroduced here a few years back. Mostly, you'll spot foxes and coyotes and plenty of deer. What you won't find is much in the way of humanity—making this a destination for anyone seeking solitude. Or aliens.

RIDE
33

Coronado Scenic Trail Loop

Directions:
north on US 180 from Silver City, New Mexico, to junction
with NM 78
west on NM 78 to Guthrie, Arizona
north on US 191 to Alpine

Distance:
211 miles
from Glenwood to Clifton: 57 miles
from Clifton to Alpine: 96 miles
from Alpine to Glenwood: 58 miles

Time:
half a day

Services:
at Clifton, Hannagan Meadow (seasonal), Alpine, and
Glenwood

Best Time of Year:
late spring, summer, and fall

Highlights:
historic old mining towns, a cool escape from the desert
heat with expansive views and sweeping curves, some of
the best high alpine riding anywhere

Although this ride doesn't offer much in terms of civilization, it is a great combination of scenery and roads that seem made just for riding.

From Silver City, New Mexico, US 180 heads out to the northwest. It's a good cruiser road, with long, open stretches that feature views of the Gila and Aldo Leopold Wilderness Areas in the

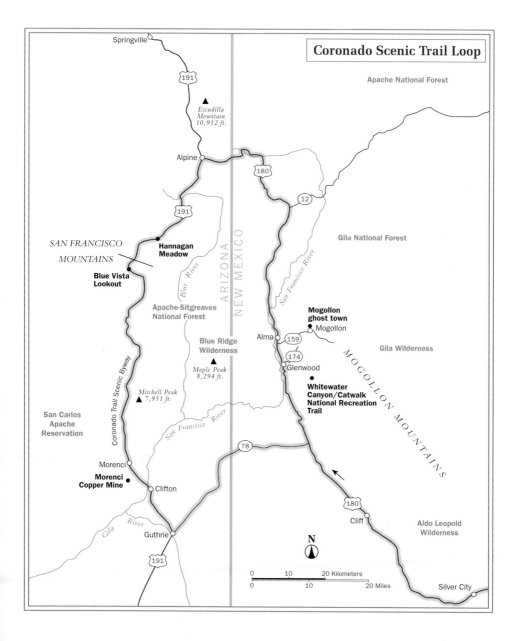

The Catwalk National Recreation Trail takes you along the site of a mining pipeline built into this canyon.

Glenwood's main attraction is Whitewater Canyon and its Catwalk National Recreation Trail. It's a lovely, steep but well-maintained hike that starts off with a level walk along the metal catwalks miners first built next to a pipeline bringing water down the canyon to run the ore-processing mill at the mouth. The hike is definitely worth doing, even if you go only partway up the 1.1-mile trail. Unfortunately, the 5-mile paved ride from town involves two river crossings where water runs right over the road, year-round. (This is odd, given the numerous bridges over the river on the hike itself.) It can be a trickle or run almost a foot deep. Ride until you get to the first crossing and if you can handle that one, you can do the second, which occurs just short of the trailhead. Otherwise, hitch a ride (the ranger station just down the road from Glenwood on US 180 might be able to hook you up) or skip it. ●

craggy mountains to the east. The Leopold Vista pullout explains who Leopold was and how he was instrumental in founding the Gila Wilderness Area—America's first territory so designated.

If you need to refuel, do so at Glenwood, a small town with a gas station and a couple restaurants, including the locally popular Blue Front Bar & Cafe. As do many of the towns in this area, it also boasts a couple of shops, including some selling the locally produced Udder Delight Goat's Milk Soap. Both Butch Cassidy and Geronimo are said to have hidden out in the canyons around here.

Up the road is Mogollon, a fairly well-preserved old mining town that can give you some idea of what these places might have looked like a hundred years ago. The folks there will be happy to sell you souvenirs or rock art.

One of the must-do rides in this region is the US 191/US 180/ NM 78 loop through mountainous western New Mexico and eastern Arizona. You can start at any of the little towns through here; as with most rides in these parts, make sure you fuel up before you go. Depending on the local economy and the time of year, there may not be many chances. US 191 from Clifton to Alpine is probably better done south to north, which saves the good parts for last.

We started and ended in Glenwood and headed south first along US 180 toward the turnoff to NM 78 and Clifton. NM 78 is an undulating, mostly straight road with gentle ups and downs. Roads are fairly straight and cover rolling grasslands and juniper. The distance between Clifton and Alpine is the longest without year-round services, so fuel up in Clifton if you haven't yet. Avoid spending too much time in this modern mining town with all services but no charm. Activity is centered around the giant pit of the Morenci copper mine, which cuts into the ground in a dry landscape at the base of the beautiful mountains (you can stop off at the "scenic" overlook to see the full extent). Get past it early into the ride, since it is so depressing you'll want some time to recover after you see it.

Even in a region dominated by mining, Clifton must be very proud of its heritage. It's the only place we've ever seen a "scenic view" of a mine.

After Clifton, the road turns northward and starts a long ascent through mountainous territory, ultimately skirting the edge of a mesa and giving riders a wide view out to the peaks and valleys to the west. This is a great road, with tight hairpins interspersed with long, sweeping curves and vast vistas. It is also technically closed to big vehicles towing trailers—though one may pop around a corner, so be alert nonetheless.

Heading north on US 191, the road (known starting at Clifton as the Coronado Trail Scenic Byway) climbs several thousand feet, up among mountain peaks. You'll find a lot of tight curves between long, fast ones. It can get chilly and snow may persist into April. If it's been wet or you're traveling in early spring, you might want to check in with one of the local ranger stations (in Glenwood, Clifton, or Alpine) to find out about conditions.

From the Blue Vista Lookout, you're about ten minutes from Hannagan Meadow; as its name implies, it is a green, high-alpine meadow when not covered by feet of snow. The lodge and scattered cabins cater to those wanting to get away from everything and indulge in some high-alpine solitude or recreation. Some

Once you're through the Chase Creek area just north of Clifton, be ready for a lot of great high-alpine riding.

Be sure to stop at the Blue Vista Lookout for a rest and to enjoy uninterrupted views of the surrounding countryside. Besides the whistling of the wind, if you are extremely lucky, you might hear the faint howl of a wolf. The Mexican gray wolf once roamed in much of present-day Arizona, New Mexico, Texas, and Mexico. Seeing the wolf as a threat to livestock, governments organized programs to kill them and by the 1970s, only a few were left in the wild. Wolves were captured in Mexico and bred in captivity while wildlife managers determined where to reintroduce the wolves. They chose the remote Blue Range Wilderness, inside the loop of this ride, and eleven wolves were released here in 1998. A field team keeps track of the wolves and coordinates efforts between the various federal, state, local, and tribal entities that all work together to keep wolves here safely. There are now an estimated fifty or so wolves roaming in this area. ●

Snow can linger on the edge of the Coronado Trail even in the middle of April. And you haven't yet reached the highest elevations of this ride.

services aren't open in the off-season, which runs from November into April.

From Hannagan Meadow, you'll descend about 2,000 feet to the town of Alpine, a rugged little mountain town surrounded by forest and next to a reservoir. It's a relatively (for this part of the world) good-size town; it has services and is a good option to refuel and get snacks if you're low on either. Not surprisingly, it's a haven for hunters and fishermen.

From here, you can head south on US 180, which continues through high-alpine forests until it eventually drops back into the valley north of Alma, New Mexico, and Glenwood a few miles down the road which will complete the loop.

If you're heading for northern New Mexico, take NM 12, which branches off to the northeast about 20 miles east of Alpine. It also starts out in the mountains and gets even higher (passing several historic mining towns) before connecting with US 60 at Socorro.

We were headed for Arizona, so we went west and took US 60 to Show Low. On the way, Springerville is good-size town with plenty of services and lots of thriving restaurants and motels.

RIDE
34

Gila National Forest/Cliff Dwellings

Directions:
north on NM 15 from Silver City
southeast on NM 35
east on NM 152
west on NM 152 back to Silver City

Distance:
218 miles, including Caballo
from Silver City to Gila Cliff Dwellings: 45 miles
from Gila Cliff Dwellings to San Lorenzo: 44 miles
from San Lorenzo to Hillsboro: 35 miles
from Hillsboro to Caballo (if the gas station in Hillsboro is closed): 38 miles round-trip
from Hillsboro to Silver City: 56 miles

Time:
better part of the day, depending on how much time spent at Gila Cliff Dwellings

Services:
at Silver City and Caballo

Best Time of Year:
spring, summer, and fall

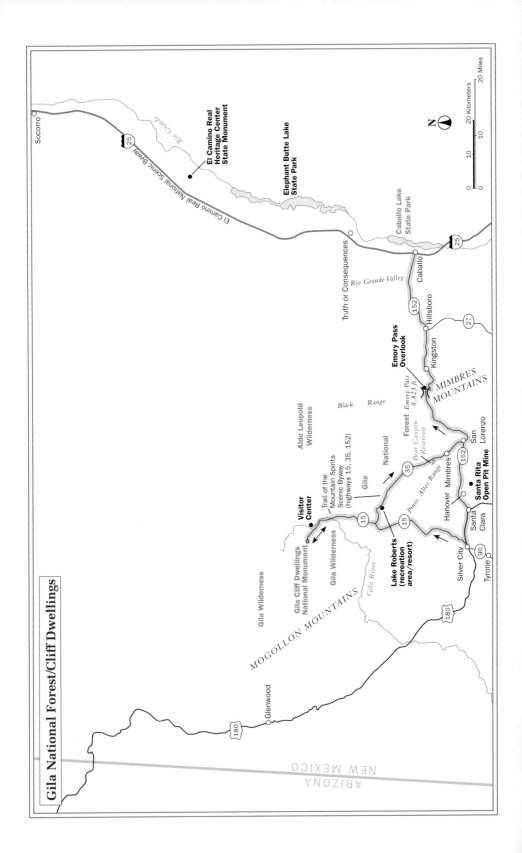

Gila National Forest/Cliff Dwellings

Highlights:

Gila National Forest, Gila Wilderness, Gila Cliff Dwellings
National Monument, many turns through classic high alpine
forest, with views of old mining towns

Silver City is a good base for exploring this area. A former and currently successful mining town, it has all kinds of services, including several auto parts stores, so it's a good place to make sure your ride is in shape as well as to get some food and any other supplies you're missing.

Silver City has a never-say-die attitude you'll see reflected in its past and present. As its name implies, it boomed as a silver mining hotspot. After the 1893 crash in silver values, it remade itself into a refuge for tuberculosis patients. Then, it worked to become the site of Western New Mexico State College, which it did in 1963. Using the buildings originally built for a former "normal school," the college sits attractively nestled into the hillside. These days, miners are digging out valuable copper from open-pit mines.

The small historic downtown is worth a look and is home to a surprising number of good restaurants, including the Buffalo Bar and Nancy's Silver Cafe. Check out the Silver City Brewing Company, with its walls covered with patron-decorated coasters, or the popular Red Barn Steak House and Lounge. This is a motorcycle-friendly town, where you can expect many of the residents to show a polite interest in your bike.

The roads to and from the cliff dwellings, all part of the Trail of the Mountain Spirits National Scenic Byway, form something of a triangle, with NM 15 running fairly directly north from Silver City. Be sure to top off the tank before leaving Silver City, because it could be a while before you see another open gas station. This ride may not look long on a map, but very few of these stretches offer flat-out riding, so plan to take a day.

Signs warn that drivers should expect the 44-mile road from Silver City to Gila Cliff Dwellings National Monument to take two hours, but since you're on a bike, it probably won't take you that long. That doesn't mean the road is easy; the signs also warn of SHARP CURVES AHEAD and truly this drive is full of more hairpins than a Dolly Parton wig. When the signs say 10 miles an hour, you're going to have to slow down at least to 15 or so. Some of the turns are decreasing radius as you swing around, and some of them have the added fun of gravel at the sharpest points.

As soon as you climb into the mountains, you'll notice more juniper trees and then ponderosa pine (the Gila National Forest is home to one of the world's largest ponderosa pine populations). The air is clean and wonderfully scented and the road weaves through classic high-alpine forest. The road follows a stream until it rises to the spine of the mountain, where you'll find yourself on a mountaintop surrounded by craggy vistas.

The road is generally in good condition. It can be rough and you'll find a few potholes, especially (inconveniently) on turns and dips. You probably won't encounter a lot of traffic, and slower vehicles generally seem happy to let bikes pass. You'll ride through a mix of public and private lands, with an occasional summer cabin off the road. Dipping back into the forest, you'll experience some serious downgrades, so again, be careful going around the curves or you could easily find yourself heading right off a cliff.

Just before you get to the national monument (and after you pass the little recreation town of Lake Roberts, with its cabins, seasonal motels, and swimming pools) you'll see the Wilderness Lodge and Hot Springs, a potential place to relax and take a soak if you're feeling road weary.

The national monument marks the end of private land and the beginning of the Gila Wilderness, a massive area with no roads or settlements that can only be penetrated on foot or on the back of a horse or burro.

There's a $3 fee to enter the monument, which is definitely worth a look. The cliff dwellings are a rare chance to climb up,

You can walk right into the homes of an ancient civilization at Gila Cliff Dwellings National Monument.

via a short trail, right into ancient homes built into the side of a cliff out of handmade brick and mortar. Volunteer guides will ask you to leave any food or drink (except water) at the trailhead, for good reason: They don't want visitors to attract wolves or bears. Yes, this is that kind of territory.

The moderately difficult but brief hike takes you up to the ruins, where a community of about forty people lived at any given time about 700 years ago. Like many ancient bands that lived in the Southwest, not much is known about them except that they lived here, built this home, and left for reasons unknown.

Return the same way you came, but this time, leave via NM 35, the other route south from Lake Roberts. NM 35 is more gentle than NM 15, although it still offers its share of curves. You'll pass through the dusty little town of Mimbres, which doesn't seem to have much going for it. The gas station there may or may not be open.

From the farming hamlet of San Lorenzo (also gas-station-free), turning left onto NM 152 will take you on the next leg of the scenic drive. The turnoff onto NM 152 is not well marked, but take the main (striped) road out of town—there aren't many other options. The road rises, levels out, then climbs again into more hard turns through forested country with lots of camping areas beside the road.

Below you are the old mining towns of Kingston (which closed down in the silver market bust of 1893) and Hillsboro, which feels like a once-attractive little town turned rundown art-

Views from Emory Pass Overlook stretch from the old mining towns of Kingston and Hillsboro all the way to the historic Rio Grande Valley and the Caballo Mountains.

Be sure to stop at the Emory Pass Overlook; from here, you can see all the way to Caballo Lake, which is New Mexico's largest (given the relative scarcity of lakes in New Mexico, that might seem akin to, say, the highest peak in Florida). There's a marker here telling the sad history of the Chiricahua Apaches who lived in this region when the white man came; they were rounded up as prisoners of war in 1886 and moved to Florida; then Alabama; then to Fort Sill, Oklahoma, before moving back to reservations in their homeland. The Native Americans who lived in this area, members of the Warm Springs band, were never allowed to return to their homeland. ●

ist commune. When we passed through, it seemed to be pretty much boarded up and for sale. Depending on the season and overall economic conditions, the gas station and restaurants of Hillsboro may or may not be open. They weren't on a late afternoon in April 2008; even the gas pumps had locks on them. To refuel, you may have to drive out along the wide-open desert to a small RV park and convenience store at the junction with I-25.

NM 152 is part of the Geronimo Trail National Scenic Byway and it and SR 27, which goes south at Hillsboro, constitute the Lake Valley Back Country Byway. But given the flat, windy, monotonous quality of the roads and terrain, we didn't see much to warrant the official byway designation. Then again, we were also at the end of a long day and, having not seen an open gas station since Silver City, worried about running out of fuel and having to hike these roads on foot. So that might have colored our view.

We returned to Silver City, completing the triangle. On the way back to Silver City, you'll pass the giant mining operations at Hanover, with the Santa Rita Mine's multicolored tailings piles making for a strangely beautiful, devastated landscape. This and

The Santa Rita Mine dominates the landscape along NM 152 near Hanover.

the Tyrone mine south of town are keeping Silver City booming while many of its cousins have failed.

Another option, if you're headed northbound anyway toward Albuquerque, is to take I-25 through a long swath of true desert. This stretch of road has been a trading and travel route for hundreds of years (and many ethnicities of people) and is one of the longest and oldest such trails in the country, a history celebrated at the El Camino Real International Heritage Center just south of Socorro. This is pretty remote territory; it's no wonder the site of the National Science Foundation's very large array of telescopes is just west of Socorro (it's open for free self-guided tours daily from 8:30 a.m. until sunset). It's also the reason the military conducted the first test of an atomic weapon in this region; Trinity Site is at the north end of the White Sands Missile Range, to the east of I-25.

Socorro, the next good-size town north of Truth or Consequences (at the intersection with US 60), preserves its Spanish history along a 3-mile stretch downtown officially called the Socorro Historical District Scenic Byway. If you do go this way, plan to stop at the Owl Bar in San Antonio, 10 miles south of Socorro, and taste its famous green chile cheeseburger.

You'll ride alongside the lake and pass through Truth or Consequences, which changed its name from Hot Springs in 1950 when the eponymous game show offered to tape from the first town that would rename itself after the show. (Obviously, these people were not too attached to the former name.) The show followed through. Host Ralph Edwards, who died in 2005, continued to visit every year for the next five decades. ●

APPENDIX: MOTORCYCLE DEALERSHIPS (BY MAKE AND STATE)

APRILIA

Arizona

Arizona Superbike
3245 N. Arizona Ave., Ste. E-8
Chandler, AZ 85225
(480) 898-0559
www.azsbk.com

Motohouse KTM Aprilia
16251 N. Cave Creek Rd., No. 6
Phoenix, AZ 85032
(602) 765-8100
www.motohouseaz.com

Renaissance Motorcycles
4411 E. Speedway Blvd.
Tucson, AZ 85712
(520) 747-2647
www.renmoto.com

Sierra Cycles
2137 E. Fry Blvd.
Vista, AZ 85635
(520) 459-2589
www.sierracycles.com

Ton-Up Motorcycles
2729 E. Indian School Rd.
Phoenix, AZ 85016
(602) 778-6687
www.tonupmotorcycles.com

Colorado

Beemers & More Motorcycles Works
800 Stockton Ave.
Fort Collins, CO 80524
(970) 221-1014
www.beemersandmore.com

Erico Motorsports
2855 Walnut St.
Denver, CO 80205
(303) 308-1811
www.ericomotorsports.com

Fay Myers Motorcycle World
9700 E. Arapahoe Rd.
Denver, CO 80202
(303) 744-6632
www.faymyers.com

Pike's Peak Motorsports
5867 N. Nevada Ave., Ste. 1
Colorado Springs, CO 80202
(719) 278-2300
www.pikespeakmotorsports.org

Sportique Scooters
2506 Spruce St.
Boulder, CO 80302
(303) 402-1700
www.sportiquescooters.com

Sportique Scooters
431 E. Pikes Peak Ave.
Colorado Springs, CO 80903
(719) 442-0048
www.sportiquescooters.com

Sportique Scooters
3211 Pecos St.
Denver, CO 80211
(303) 477-8614
www.sportiquescooters.com

Sportique Scooters
4346 S. Broadway
Englewood, CO 80113
(303) 477-8614
www.sportiquescooters.com

Nevada
Michael's Reno Powersports
10828 S. Virginia St.
Reno, NV 89511
(775) 825-8680
www.michaelsreno.com

Pat Clark Motorsports
2495 E. Sahara Ave.
Las Vegas, NV 89104
(702) 432-0650
www.patclarkmotorsports.com

New Mexico
ATV Mountain Cycle
2140 E. U.S. Hwy. 180
Silver City, NM 88061
(877) 755-0707
www.atvmountaincycle.com

Desert Greens Equipment
4850 Pan American Fwy. NE
Albuquerque, NM 87109
(800) 801-0311
www.desertgreensequipment.com

Utah
Aprilia/Vespa of Orem
45 W. University Pkwy.
Orem, UT 84058
(801) 765-0167
www.vespa-utah.com

Salt Lake Motorsports
1077 S. Main St.
Salt Lake City, UT 84111
(801) 478-4000
www.saltlakemotorsports.com

Spinners of Utah
1361 E. Red Hills Pkwy., Ste. C
St. George, UT 84770
(435) 674-5664
www.spinnersofutah.com

BMW

Arizona
BMW Motorcycles of Scottsdale
14870 N. Northsight Blvd., Ste. 100
Scottsdale, AZ 85260
(480) 609-1800
www.goaz.com

Iron Horse Motorcycles
3444 E. Grant Rd.
Tucson, AZ 85716
(520) 327-0773
www.ironhorsemotorcycles.com

Victory BMW
1701 N. Arizona Ave.
Chandler, AZ 85225
(480) 899-9113
www.victorybmw.com

Colorado
BMW of Denver
2910 S. Havana St.
Aurora, CO 80014
(303) 755-6400
www.bmwofdenver.com

BMW Motorcycles of Colorado
    Springs
1394 S. Twenty-first St.
Colorado Springs, CO 80904
(719) 635-3004
www.pikespeakmotorsports.org

Grand Junction BMW
2747 Crossroads Blvd.
Grand Junction, CO 81506
(970) 245-0812
www.bmwgj.com

Foothills BMW/Triumph Motorcycles
1435 Wadsworth Blvd.
Lakewood, CO 80214
(303) 202-1400
www.foothillsbmw.com

Northern Colorado Euro Motorcycles
6002 Byrd Dr.
Loveland, CO 80538
(970) 679-1600
www.bmwducati.com

Nevada
BMW Motorcycles of Las Vegas
6675 S. Tenaya Way
Las Vegas, NV 89113
(702) 454-6269
www.bmwoflasvegas.com

Sierra BMW Motorcycles
1380 Kleppe Lane
Sparks, NV 89431
(775) 355-0655
www.sierrabmw.com

New Mexico
Sandia BMW Motorcycles
6001 Pan American Fwy. NE
Albuquerque, NM 87109
(505) 884-0066
www.sandiabmwmotorcycles.com

Santa Fe BMW
2578 Camino Entrada
Santa Fe, NM 87505
(505) 474-0066
www.santafebmw.com

Utah
BMW Motorcycles of Salt Lake City
215 N. Redwood Rd.
North Salt Lake, UT 84054
(801) 936-4600
www.bmwmotorcyclesofsaltlake.com

BUELL

Arizona
Arrowhead Harley-Davidson/Buell
16130 N. Arrowhead Fountain
    Center Dr.
Peoria, AZ 85382
(623) 247-5542
www.arrowheadharley.com

Chandler Harley-Davidson
6895 W. Chandler Blvd.
Chandler, AZ 85226
(480) 496-6800
www.chandlerharley.com

Grand Canyon Harley-Davidson
Old Hwy. 66
Bellemont, AZ 86015
(928) 774-3896
www.grandcanyonhd.com

Grand Canyon Harley-Davidson
10434 S. Hwy. 69
Mayer, AZ, 86333
(928) 632-4009
www.grandcanyonhd.com

Hacienda Harley-Davidson
15600 N. Hayden Rd.
Scottsdale, AZ 85260
(480) 905-1903
www.haciendaharleydavidson.com

Harley-Davidson Buell of Tucson
7355 N. I-10 Frontage Rd.
Tucson, AZ 85743
(520) 792-0111
www.tucsonharley.com

Metro Motorsports
6161 W. Bell Rd.
Glendale, AZ 85308
(602) 843-5000
www.ridenow.com

RideNow Powersports
1346 E. Florence Blvd., Ste. 2
Casa Grande, AZ 85222
(520) 316-9368
www.ridenow.com

RideNow Powersports
3333 N. Arizona Ave.
Chandler, AZ 85224
(480) 503-3333
www.ridenow.com

RideNow Powersports
13690 W. Test Dr.
Goodyear, AZ 85338
(623) 214-6400
www.ridenow.com

RideNow Powersports
17202 N. Cave Creek Rd.
Phoenix, AZ 85032
(602) 992-8620
www.ridenow.com

RideNow Powersports
15380 W. Bell Rd.
Surprise, AZ 85374
(623) 474-3740
www.ridenow.com

RideNow Powersports
4375 W. Ina Rd.
Tucson, AZ 85741
(520) 579-3939
www.ridenow.com

RideNow Powersports
7075 E. Twenty-second St.
Tucson, AZ 85710
(520) 757-9141
www.ridenow.com

Sierra Vista Harley-Davidson
176 W. Fry Blvd.
Sierra Vista, AZ 85635
(520) 458-9500
www.sierravistaharley.com

Colorado
Big Sky Harley-Davidson
4258 Tenth Ave. S.
Great Falls, CO 59405
(406) 727-2161
www.bigskyharley.com

Colorado Springs Harley-Davidson
2180 Victor Place
Colorado Springs, CO 80915
(719) 591-7594
www.coloradospringsharley
    davidson.com

Grand Junction Harley Davidson/
    BMW
2747 Crossroads Blvd.
Grand Junction, CO 81506
(970) 245-0812
www.gjharley.com

Pike's Peak Motorsports
5867 N. Nevada Ave., Ste. 1
Colorado Springs, CO 80918
(719) 278-2300
www.pikespeakmotorsports.org

Nevada
Carson City Harley-Davidson
2900 Research Way
Carson City, NV 89706
(775) 882-7433
www.carsoncityhd.com

Henderson Harley-Davidson
1010 W. Warm Springs Rd.
Henderson, NV 89014
(702) 456-1666
www.hendersonhd.com

Kawasaki of Las Vegas
3850 N. Rancho Dr.
Las Vegas, NV 89130
(702) 656-1955
www.ridenow.com

Las Vegas Harley-Davidson
2605 Southern Ave., Ste. 100
Las Vegas, NV 89169
(702) 431-8500
www.lasvegasharleydavidson.com

Las Vegas Motorcycles
5835 W. Flamingo Rd.
Las Vegas, NV 89103
(702) 871-8910
www.lasvegasmotorcycles.com

Red Rock Harley-Davidson
7100 W. Sahara Ave.
Las Vegas, NV 89117
(702) 876-2884
www.redrockharley.com

Reno Harley-Davidson/Buell
2315 Market St.
Reno, NV 89502
(775) 329-2913
www.renohd.com

RideNow Powersports
6350 Boulder Hwy.
Las Vegas, NV 89122
(702) 451-1121
www.ridenow.com

RideNow Powersports
4120 E. Craig Rd.
North Las Vegas, NV 89030
(702) 214-5380
www.ridenow.com

New Mexico
Barnett's Las Cruces Harley Davidson
2600 Lakeside Dr.
Las Cruces, NM 88005
(575) 541-1440
www.barnettharley.com

Four Corners Harley-Davidson
6520 E. Main St.
Farmington, NM 87402
(505) 325-6710
www.fourcornershd.com

Santa Fe Harley-Davidson
4360 Rodeo Rd.
Santa Fe, NM 87507
(505) 471-3808
www.santafeharley.com

Thunderbird Harley-Davidson
5000 Alameda Blvd. NE
Albuquerque, NM 87113
(505) 856-1600
www.thunderbirdhd.com

Utah
Harley-Davidson of Salt Lake City
2928 S. State St.
Salt Lake City, UT 84115
(801) 487-4647
www.harley-davidsonslc.com

South Valley Harley-Davidson
8886 S. Sandy Pkwy. Dr.
Sandy, UT 84070
(801) 563-1100
www.harley-davidsonslc.com

Zion Harley-Davidson
2345 N. Coral Canyon Blvd.
Washington, UT 84780
(435) 673-5100
www.zionhd.com

DUCATI

Arizona
Phoenix Ducati
5640 N. Seventh St.
Phoenix, AZ 85014
(602) 864-1437
www.ducatisuperstore.net

Renaissance Motorcycle
5844 E. Speedway Blvd.
Tucson, AZ 85712
(520) 747-2647
www.renmoto.com

Colorado
Erico Motorsports
2855 Walnut St.
Denver, CO 80205
(303) 308-1811
www.ericomotorsports.com

Fay Myers Motorcycle World
9700 E. Arapahoe Rd.
Denver, CO 80202
(303) 744-6632
www.faymyers.com

Northern Colorado BMW/Ducati
    Motorcycles
6540 S. College Ave.
Fort Collins, CO 80525
(970) 223-2829
www.bmwducati.com

Rocky Mountain Cycle
412 N. Chelton Rd.
Colorado Springs, CO 80909
(719) 591-9700
www.rockymtncycleplaza.com

Nevada
Big Valley Motorsports
2225 Market St.
Reno, NV 89502
(775) 322-4311
www.ducatireno.com

Southern Nevada Harley-Davidson
Sales
2605 Southern Ave.
Las Vegas, NV 89109
(702) 431-8500
www.lasvegasharleydavidson.com

New Mexico
R & S Yamaha Ducati
3305 Juan Tabo NE
Albuquerque, NM 87111
(505) 292-8011
www.teamrands.com

Utah
Salt Lake Motorsports
1077 S. Main St.
Salt Lake City, UT 84111
(801) 478-4000
www.saltlakemotorsports.com

White Knuckle Motor Sports
889 N. 2000 W.
Springville, UT 84663
(801) 489-0393
www.whiteknucklemotorsports
suzuki.com

HARLEY-DAVIDSON

Arizona
Arrowhead Harley-Davidson
16130 N. Arrowhead Fountain
Center Dr.
Peoria, AZ 85382
(623) 247-5542
www.arrowheadharley.com

Bobby's Territorial Harley-Davidson
2550 E. Gila Ridge Rd.
Yuma, AZ 85365
(928) 782-1931
www.territorialhd.com

Buddy Stubbs Anthem Harley-
Davidson
41715 N. Forty-first Dr.
Anthem, AZ 85086
(623) 465-1122
www.anthemhd.com

Buddy Stubbs Arizona Harley-
Davidson
13850 N. Cave Creek Rd.
Phoenix, AZ 85022
(602) 971-3400
www.buddystubbshd.com

Chandler Harley-Davidson
6895 W. Chandler Blvd.
Chandler, AZ 85226
(480) 496-6800
www.chandlerharley.com

Chester's Harley-Davidson
922 S. Country Club Dr.
Mesa, AZ 85210
(480) 894-0404
www.chestershd.com

Grand Canyon Harley-Davidson
I-40 exit 185
Bellemont, AZ 86015
(928) 774-3896
www.grandcanyonhd.com

Grand Canyon Harley-Davidson
138 S. Montezuma
Prescott, AZ 86303
(928) 778-2241
www.grandcanyonhd.com

Grand Canyon Harley-Davidson
320 N. Hwy. 89A, Ste. 1
Sedona, AZ 86336
(928) 204-0020
www.grandcanyonhd.com

Grand Canyon Harley-Davidson Shop
10434 S. Hwy. 69
P.O. Box 1035
Mayer, AZ 86333
(928) 632-4009
www.grandcanyonhd.com

Hacienda Harley-Davidson
15600 N. Hayden Rd.
Scottsdale, AZ 85260
(480) 905-1903
www.haciendaharley-davidson.com

Harley-Davidson of Tucson
7355 N. I-10
Eastbound Frontage Rd.
Tucson, AZ 85743
(520) 792-0111
www.tucsonharley.com

Mother Road Harley-Davidson
2501 Beverly Ave.
Kingman, AZ 86409
(928) 757-1166
www.motherroadhd.com

Sierra Vista Harley-Davidson Shop
176 W. Fry Blvd.
Sierra Vista, AZ 85635
(520) 458-9500
www.sierravistaharley.com

Superstition Harley-Davidson
2910 W. Apache Trail
Apache Junction, AZ 85220
(480) 346-0600
www.superstitionhd.com

Colorado
Aspen Valley Harley-Davidson
2302 Devereux Rd.
Glenwood Springs, CO 81601
(970) 928-7493
www.aspenhd.com

Black Canyon Harley-Davidson
87 Merchant Dr.
Montrose, CO 81401
(970) 252-0900
www.gjharley.com

Colorado Springs Harley-Davidson
2180 Victor Place
Colorado Springs, CO 80915
(719) 591-7594
www.coloradospringsharley
    davidson.com

Durango Harley-Davidson
750 S. Camino Del Rio
Durango, CO 81301
(970) 259-0778
www.durangoharley.com

Freedom Harley-Davidson
8020 W. Colfax Ave.
Denver, CO 80214
(303) 238-0425
www.freedomh-d.com

Grand Junction Harley-Davidson
2747 Crossroads Blvd.
Grand Junction, CO 81506
(970) 245-0812
www.gjharley.com

Greeley Harley-Davidson
3010 W. Twenty-ninth St.
Greeley, CO 80631
(970) 351-8150
www.wildwestms.com

High Country Harley-Davidson/Buell
3761 Monarch St.
Frederick, CO 80516
(303) 833-6777
www.highcountryharley.com

Mile High Harley-Davidson
16565 E. Thirty-third Dr.
Aurora, CO 80011
(303) 343-3300
www.milehigh-harley.com

Mile High Harley-Davidson
Denver International Airport
    Concourse B
8900 Pena Blvd.
Denver, CO 80249
(303) 342-9021
www.milehigh-harley.com

Mile High Harley-Davidson
6280 E. Pine Lane
Parker, CO 80138
(720) 842-1500
www.milehigh-harley.com

Outpost Harley-Davidson
5001 N. Elizabeth
Pueblo, CO 81008
(719) 542-6032
www.outposthd.com

Pikes Peak Harley-Davidson
5867 N. Nevada Ave.
Colorado Springs, CO 80918
(719) 278-2300
www.pikespeakharleydavidson.com

Rocky Mountain Harley-Davidson
2885 W. County Line Rd.
Littleton, CO 80129
(303) 703-2885
www.rockymountainhd.com

Sun Harley-Davidson
8858 Pearl St.
Thornton, CO 80229
(303) 287-7567
www.sunharleydavidson.com

Thunder Mountain Harley-Davidson
4250 Byrd Dr.
Loveland, CO 80538
(970) 292-0400
www.thundermountainharley.com

Nevada
Carson City Harley-Davidson
2900 Research Way
Carson City, NV 89701
(775) 882-7433
www.carsoncityhd.com

Henderson Harley-Davidson
1010 W. Warm Springs Rd.
Henderson, NV 89014
(702) 456-1666
www.hendersonhd.com

Las Vegas Harley-Davidson
3700 W. Flamingo Rd.
Las Vegas, NV 89103
(702) 252-5130

Las Vegas Harley-Davidson
328 E. Freemont St.
Las Vegas, NV 89101
(702) 383-1010

Las Vegas Harley-Davidson
3790 Las Vegas Blvd. S.
Las Vegas, NV 89109
(702) 891-0530

Las Vegas Harley-Davidson
MGM Grand Hotel
3799 Las Vegas Blvd. S.
Las Vegas, NV 89109
(702) 795-7073

Las Vegas Harley-Davidson
3645 Las Vegas Blvd. S.
Las Vegas, NV 89109
(702) 893-7773

Las Vegas Harley-Davidson
3150 Paradise Rd.
Las Vegas, NV 89109
(702) 943-6822

Las Vegas Harley-Davidson
2605 Southern Ave., Ste. 100
Las Vegas, NV 89169
(702) 431-8500
www.lasvegasharleydavidson.com

Las Vegas Harley-Davidson
c/o Marshall Rousso
Mccarran Airport
5757 Wayne Newton Blvd.
Las Vegas, NV 89111
(702) 736-9493

Red Rock Harley-Davidson
2260 S. Rainbow Blvd.
Las Vegas, NV 89146
(702) 876-2884
www.redrockharley.com

Reno Harley-Davidson/Buell
2315 Market St.
Reno, NV 89502
(775) 329-2913
www.renohd.com

Reno Harley-Davidson/Buell
407 N. Virginia St.
Reno, NV 89501
(775) 323-2453
www.renohd.com

New Mexico
Barnett's Las Cruces Harley-Davidson
2600 Lakeside Dr.
Las Cruces, NM 88005
(575) 541-1440
www.barnettharleylascruces.com

Champion Harley-Davidson
2801 W. Second St.
Roswell, NM 88201
(575) 624-0151
www.championroswell.com

Four Corners Harley-Davidson
6520 E. Main St.
Farmington, NM 87402
(505) 325-6710
www.fourcornershd.com

High Plains Harley-Davidson
4400 Mabry Dr.
Clovis, NM 88101
(575) 769-1000
www.highplainshd.com

Santa Fe Harley-Davidson
4360 Rodeo Rd.
Santa Fe, NM 87507
(505) 471-3808
www.santafeharley.com

Thunderbird Harley-Davidson
5000 Alameda Blvd. NE
Albuquerque, NM 87113
(505) 856-1600
www.thunderbirdhd.com

Utah
Beers Harley-Davidson
2029 W. Hwy. 40
Vernal, UT 84078
(435) 789-5196

Golden Spike Harley-Davidson
892 W. Riverdale Rd.
Ogden, UT 84405
(801) 394-4464
www.goldenspikeharley.com

Harley-Davidson of Salt Lake City
2928 S. State St.
Salt Lake City, UT 84115
(801) 487-4647
www.harley-davidsonslc.com

Saddleback H-D Shop
2359 N. Main St.
Logan, UT 84341
(435) 787-8100
www.saddlebackharley.com

South Valley Harley-Davidson Shop
8886 S. Sandy Pkwy. Dr.
Sandy, UT 84070
(801) 563-1100
www.harley-davidsonslc.com

Timpanogos Harley-Davidson
555 S. Geneva Rd.
Lindon, UT 84042
(801) 434-4647
www.timpharley.com

Zion Harley-Davidson Shop
2345 N. Coral Canyon Blvd.
Washington, UT 84780
(435) 673-5100
www.zionhd.com

HONDA

Arizona
Apache Motorcycles
3618 W. Camelback Rd.
Phoenix, AZ 85019
(602) 973-5111
www.phoenixpowersports.com

Carefree Yamaha
3120 W. Carefree Hwy., No. 5
Phoenix, AZ 85086
(623) 334-8295
www.phoenixpowersports.com

Champion Suzuki
1350 S. Clearview Ave., Ste. 111
Mesa, AZ 85208
(480) 325-1818
www.phoenixpowersports.com

Hales Motors
534 Madison Ave.
Prescott, AZ 86301
(928) 445-5730
www.starislandms.com

Metro Motorsports
6161 W. Bell Rd.
Glendale, AZ 85308
(602) 843-5000
www.ridenow.com

Northland Motorsports
4308 E. Route 66
Flagstaff, AZ 86004
(928) 526-7959
www.northlandmotorsports.com

RideNow Powersports
1346 E. Florence Blvd., Ste. 2
Casa Grande, AZ 85222
(520) 316-9368
www.ridenow.com

RideNow Powersports
3333 N. Arizona Ave.
Chandler, AZ 85224
(480) 503-3333
www.ridenow.com

RideNow Powersports
13690 W. Test Dr.
Goodyear, AZ 85338
(623) 214-6400
www.ridenow.com

RideNow Powersports
17202 N. Cave Creek Rd.
Phoenix, AZ 85032
(602) 992-8620
www.ridenow.com

RideNow Powersports
15380 W. Bell Rd.
Surprise, AZ 85374
(623) 474-3740
www.ridenow.com

RideNow Powersports
4375 W. Ina Rd.
Tucson, AZ 85741
(520) 579-3939
www.ridenow.com

RideNow Powersports
7075 E. Twenty-second St.
Tucson, AZ 85710
(520) 757-9141
www.ridenow.com

Colorado
Apex Sports
327 S. Weber St.
Colorado Springs, CO 80903
(719) 475-2437
www.apexsportsinc.com

Britt Powersports
6235 S. Santa Fe Dr.
Littleton, CO 80120
(303) 794-6367
www.brittpowersports.com

Colorado Powersports Boulder
1880 Fifty-fifth St.
Boulder, CO 80301
(303) 447-3500
www.copowersports.com

Davis Service Center
2380 E. Main St.
Montrose, CO 81401
(970) 249-8161
www.davisservicecenter.com

Fay Myers Motorcycle World
9700 E. Arapahoe Rd.
Denver, CO 80202
(303) 744-6632
www.faymyers.com

Greeley Harley-Davidson
3010 W. Twenty-ninth St.
Greeley, CO 80631
(970) 351-8150
www.wildwestms.com

Hi-Point Motorsports
2802 S. Grand Ave.
Glenwood Springs, CO 81601
(970) 945-5977
www.hipointmotorsports.com

Rocky Mountain Cycle Plaza
412 N. Chelton Rd.
Colorado Springs, CO 80909
(719) 591-9700
www.rockymtncycleplaza.com

Rocky Mountain Cycle Plaza
4106 Outlook Blvd.
Pueblo, CO 81008
(719) 545-5490
www.rockymtncycleplaza.com

RPM Motorsports
1251 Wadsworth Blvd.
Lakewood, CO 80214
(303) 232-7576
www.rpmms.com

Nevada
Big Valley Motorsports
2235 Market St.
Reno, NV 89502
(775) 324-1901
www.ducatireno.com

Carter Powersports
6275 S. Decatur Blvd.
Las Vegas, NV 89118
(702) 795-2000
www.carterpowersports.com

5th Gear Power Sports
420 Thirtieth St.
Elko, NV 89801
(775) 738-8933
www.5thgearelko.com

Kawasaki of Las Vegas
3850 N. Rancho Dr.
Las Vegas, NV 89130
(702) 656-1955
www.ridenow.com

Michael's Cycle Works
2680 S. Carson St.
Carson City, NV 89701
(775) 883-6111
www.michaelscycleworks.com

RideNow Powersports
6350 Boulder Hwy.
Las Vegas, NV 89122
(702) 451-1121
www.ridenow.com

RideNow Powersports
4120 E. Craig Rd.
North Las Vegas, NV 89030
(702) 214-5380
www.ridenow.com

New Mexico
Champion Motorsports
2801 W. Second St.
Roswell, NM 88201
(575) 624-0151
www.championroswell.com

Deming Cycle Center
820 E. Spruce St.
Deming, NM 88030
(575) 546-6963
www.demingcycle.com

Las Cruces Motorsports
2125 S. Valley Dr.
Las Cruces, NM 88005
(575) 524-3626
www.lcmotorsports.com

Motorsport
6919 Montgomery Blvd. NE
Albuquerque, NM 87109
(505) 884-9000
www.abqmotorsport.com

R & S Honda Polaris
1425 Wyoming NE
Albuquerque, NM 87112
(505) 293-1860
www.teamrands.com

Utah
Beers Harley-Davidson
2029 W. Hwy. 40
Vernal, UT 84078
(435) 789-5196

Cache Honda Yamaha
3665 N. Hwy. 91
Hyde Park, UT 84318
(435) 563-6291
www.cachehy.com

Honda Suzuki of Salt Lake
2354 S. State St.
Salt Lake City, UT 84115
(801) 486-5401
www.hondasuzuki.com

Jorgensen's
980 S. Cove View Rd.
Richfield, UT 84701
(435) 896-6408
www.jhsport.com

Newgate Motorsports
3740 S. 250 W.
Ogden, UT 84405
(801) 394-3403
www.newgatemotorsports.com

Steadman's
916 N. Main St.
Tooele, UT 84074
(435) 882-3565
www.steadmans.net

Stephen Wade Powersports
1295 E. Red Hills Pkwy.
St. George, UT 84770
(435) 628-5281
www.swpowersports.com

KAWASAKI

Arizona
Action Motorsports
4125 W. Summit Walk Court
Anthem, AZ 85086
(623) 465-5006
www.actionmotorsportsaz.com

Apache Motorcycles
3618 W. Camelback Rd.
Phoenix, AZ 85019
(602) 973-5111
www.phoenixpowersports.com

Arizona Kawasaki Victory
1015 W. Apache Trail
Apache Junction, AZ 85220
(480) 982-3363
www.arizonakawasaki.com

Carefree Yamaha
3120 W. Carefree Hwy., No. 5
Phoenix, AZ 85086
(623) 581-6060
www.phoenixpowersports.com

Champion Suzuki
1350 S. Clearview Ave., Ste. 111
Mesa, AZ 85208
(480) 325-1818
www.phoenixpowersports.com

Desert Riders Motorsports
212 E. Hwy. 70
Safford, AZ 85546
(928) 348-8844

Hales Motors
534 Madison Ave.
Prescott, AZ 86301
(928) 445-5730
www.starislandms.com

Kawasaki Suzuki of Kingman
2365 Northern Ave.
Kingman, AZ 86409
(928) 757-2480
www.kawasakisuzukiofkingman.com

Kelly's Kawasaki
817 S. Country Club Dr.
Mesa, AZ 85210
(480) 969-9610
www.kellys-kawasaki.com

Metro Motorsports
6161 W. Bell Rd.
Glendale, AZ 85308
(602) 843-5000
www.ridenow.com

Northland Motorsports
4308 E. Route 66
Flagstaff, AZ 86004
(928) 526-7959
www.northlandmotorsports.com

Performance Cycle Center
3741 N. I-10 Frontage Rd., Ste. 101
Tucson, AZ 85705
(520) 622-2780
www.performancecyclecenter.com

RideNow Powersports
1346 E. Florence Blvd., Ste. 2
Casa Grande, AZ 85222
(520) 316-9368
www.ridenow.com

RideNow Powersports
3333 N. Arizona Ave.
Chandler, AZ 85224
(480) 503-3333
www.ridenow.com

RideNow Powersports
13690 W. Test Dr.
Goodyear, AZ 85338
(623) 214-6400
www.ridenow.com

RideNow Powersports
17202 N. Cave Creek Rd.
Phoenix, AZ 85032
(602) 992-8620
www.ridenow.com

RideNow Powersports
15380 W. Bell Rd.
Surprise, AZ 85374
(623) 474-3740
www.ridenow.com

RideNow Powersports
4375 W. Ina Rd.
Tucson, AZ 85741
(520) 579-3939
www.ridenow.com

RideNow Powersports
7075 E. Twenty-second St.
Tucson, AZ 85710
(520) 757-9141
www.ridenow.com

Sierra Cycles
2137 E. Fry Blvd.
Sierra Vista, AZ 85635
(520) 459-2589
www.sierracycles.com

Sunwest Xpress
1017 Hwy. 95
Bullhead City, AZ 84629
(928) 754-5475
www.sunwestxpress.com

Victory Motorcycle of Mesa
833 S. Country Club Dr.
Mesa, AZ 85210
(480) 668-7969
www.victoryofmesa.com

Colorado
Apex Sports
327 S. Weber St.
Colorado Springs, CO 80903
(719) 475-2437
www.apexsportsinc.com

Colorado Powersports Boulder
1880 Fifty-fifth St.
Boulder, CO 80301
(303) 447-3500
www.copowersports.com

Davis Service Center Inc.
2380 E. Main St.
Montrose, CO 81401
(970) 249-8161
www.davisservicecenter.com

Fay Myers Motorcycle World
9700 E. Arapahoe Rd.
Denver, CO 80202
(303) 744-6632
www.faymyers.com

Fremont Motorsports
600 E. Main St.
Florence, CO 81226
(719) 784-9633
www.fremontmotorsports.com

Fun Center
29603 U.S. Hwy. 160 E.
Durango, CO 81301
(970) 259-1070
www.funcentercycles.com

G-Force Powersports
7700 W. Colfax
Lakewood, CO 80214
(303) 238-4303
www.gforcepowersports.com

Grand Prix Motorsports
3105 W. County Line Rd.
Littleton, CO 80129
(303) 761-2471
www.grandprixmotorsports.com

Hi-Point Motorsports
2802 S. Grand Ave.
Glenwood Springs, CO 81601
(970) 945-5977
www.hipointmotorsports.com

Powersports Unlimited
2733 Eighth Ave.
Greeley, CO 80631
(970) 352-7669
www.powersportsunlimited.com

Rocky Mountain Cycle Plaza
412 N. Chelton Rd.
Colorado Springs, CO 80909
(719) 591-9700
www.rockymtncycleplaza.com

Rocky Mountain Cycle Plaza
4106 Outlook Blvd.
Pueblo, CO 81008
(719) 583-9721
www.rockymtncycleplaza.com

Rocky Mountain Kawasaki
645 Frontage Rd.
Longmont, CO 80501
(303) 651-2453
www.rockymountainkawasaki.com

Sun Enterprises
8877 N. Washington St.
Thornton, CO 80229
(303) 287-7566
www.sunent.com

Sun Sports Unlimited
219 W. Hwy. 50
Gunnison, CO 81230
(970) 641-0883
www.sunsportsunlimited.com

Unique Rides
3321 E. Mulberry St.
Fort Collins, CO 80524
(970) 416-5986
www.uniqueridesco.com

Valcom Motorsports of Trinidad
13840 Hwy. 350
Trinidad, CO 81082
(719) 846-9446
www.valcommotorsports.com

Vickery Motorsports
2231 S. Parker Rd.
Denver, CO 80231
(303) 755-4387
www.vickerymotorsports.com

Xtreme Performance Center
826 Park St.
Castle Rock, CO 80109
(303) 660-5302
www.xtreme-performance.com

Xtreme Performance Center
4100 S. Valley Dr.
Longmont, CO 80504
(970) 535-9100
www.xtreme-performance.com

Nevada
Carter Powersports
6275 S. Decatur Blvd.
Las Vegas, NV 89118
(702) 795-2000
www.carterpowersports.com

5th Gear Power Sports
420 Thirtieth St.
Elko, NV 89801
(775) 738-8933
www.5thgearelko.com

Kawasaki of Las Vegas
3850 N. Rancho Dr.
Las Vegas, NV 89130
(702) 656-1955
www.ridenow.com

Michael's Cycle Works
2680 S. Carson St.
Carson City, NV 89701
(775) 883-6111
www.michaelscycleworks.com

RideNow Powersports
6350 Boulder Hwy.
Las Vegas, NV 89122
(702) 451-1121
www.ridenow.com

RideNow Powersports
4120 E. Craig Rd.
North Las Vegas, NV 89030
(702) 214-5380
www.ridenow.com

Sonoma Cycle
405 W. Winnemucca Blvd.
Winnemucca, NV 89445
(775) 623-6888
www.sonomacycle.com

New Mexico
Champion Motorsports
2801 W. Second St.
Roswell, NM 88201
(575) 624-0151
www.championroswell.com

Hester's Motorsports
1190 S. Second St.
Raton, NM 87740
(575) 445-3558
www.hester-motorsports.com

Las Cruces Motorsports
2125 S. Valley Dr.
Las Cruces, NM 88005
(575) 524-3626
www.lcmotorsports.com

Motorsport
6919 Montgomery Blvd. NE
Albuquerque, NM 87109
(505) 884-9000
www.abqmotorsport.com

R & S Kawasaki KTM Suzuki Sea-Doo
9601 Lomas NE
Albuquerque, NM 87112
(505) 292-6692
www.teamrands.com

R & S West Motorcycle ATV Marine
10012 Coors Blvd. NW
Albuquerque, NM 87114
(505) 896-0200
www.teamrands.com

Santa Fe Motor Sports
2594 Camino Entrada
Santa Fe, NM 87507
(505) 438-1888
www.santafemotorsports.com

Utah
Big Boys Toys
2529 N. Hwy. 89
Ogden, UT 84404
(800) 273-9040
www.bigboysutah.com

Cedar City Motor Sports
1579 N. Main St., Nos. 108–109
Cedar City, UT 84720
(435) 867-9111
http://cedarcitymotorsports.com

Delta Sports Center
299 N. Hwy. 6
Delta, UT 84624
(435) 864-3432
www.deltasports.com

Full Throttle Powersports
240 N. Frontage Rd.
Centerville, UT 84014
(801) 292-1492
www.fullthrottlepowersports.com

Newgate Motorsports
3740 S. 250 W.
Ogden, UT 84404
(801) 394-3403
www.newgatemotorsports.com

Renegade Sport 2
1903 S. 800 W.
Logan, UT 84321
(435) 755-7111
www.renegadesports.us

Ron Greene Sports Center
96 S. State St.
Mount Pleasant, UT 84647
(435) 462-2425
www.rongreenesportscenter.com

South Valley Motorsports
11553 S. State St.
Draper, UT 84020
(801) 576-1899
www.southvalleymotorsports.com

Vesco's
370 W. 1175 S.
Brigham City, UT 84302
(435) 734-9424
www.vescos.net

KTM

Arizona
Bernie's Cycle Service
34 E. Southern Ave.
Mesa, AZ 85210
(480) 835-1420
www.ktmaz.com

Gila Valley Cycle & Ski
304 Fifth St.
Safford, AZ 85546
(928) 428-4694
www.gilavalleycycleandski.com

Motohouse KTM Aprilia
16251 N. Cave Creek Rd., No. 6
Phoenix, AZ 85032
(602) 765-8100
www.motohouseaz.com

Northland Motorsports
4308 E. Route 66
Flagstaff, AZ 86004
(928) 526-7959
www.northlandmotorsports.com

Performance Cycle Center
3741 N. I-10 Frontage Rd., Ste. 101
Tucson, AZ 85705
(520) 622-2780
www.performancecyclecenter.com

Premier Motorsports
301 W. Deer Valley Rd.
Phoenix, AZ 85027
(623) 582-1350
www.premierktm.com

Star Island Motorsports
5425 E. Second St.
Prescott Valley, AZ 86301
(928) 445-5730
www.starislandms.com

Colorado
Apex Sports
327 S. Weber St.
Colorado Springs, CO 80903
(719) 475-2437
www.apexsportsinc.com

Craig Powersports
2607 E. U.S. 40
Craig, CO 81625
(970) 826-0060
www.craigpowersports.com

Eagle Motor Works
851 Sawatch Rd.
Eagle, CO 81631
(970) 328-2580

Elite Motorsports
1400 E. Eisenhower Blvd.
Loveland, CO 80537
(970) 461-1022
www.elitektm.com

Fay Myers Motorcycle World
9700 E. Arapahoe Rd.
Denver, CO 80202
(303) 744-6632
www.faymyers.com

Fun Center
29603 U.S. Hwy. 160 E.
Durango, CO 81301
(970) 259-1070
www.funcentercycles.com

Hymark Motorsports
175 E. Spaulding
Pueblo West, CO 81007
(719) 547-3478
www.hymarkmotorsports.com

KTM of Aspen
1107 Hendrick Dr.
Carbondale, CO 81623
(970) 963-6099
www.ktmofaspen.net

KTM of Grand Junction
2314 Hwy. 6 & 50
Grand Junction, CO 81501
(970) 255-8140
www.ktmgj.com

Sun Enterprises
8877 N. Washington St.
Thornton, CO 80229
(303) 287-7566
www.sunent.com

Sun Sports Unlimited
219 W. Hwy. 50
Gunnison, CO 81230
(970) 641-0883
www.sunsportslimited.com

Valcom Motorsports of Trinidad
13840 Hwy. 350
Trinidad, CO 81082
(719) 846-9446
www.valcommotorsports.com

Nevada
5th Gear Power Sports
420 Thirtieth St.
Elko, NV 89801
(775) 738-8933
www.5thgearelko.com

Las Vegas Motorcycles
5835 W. Flamingo Rd.
Las Vegas, NV 89103
(702) 871-8910
www.lasvegasmotorcycles.com

Reno KTM—Nevada Motorcycle
    Specialties
540 S. Rock Blvd.
Sparks, NV 89431
(775) 358-4388
www.nevadaktm.com

New Mexico
New Urban Transport
1800 Central SE
Albuquerque, NM 87106
(505) 247-2698
www.vespaabq.com

R & S Kawasaki KTM Suzuki Sea-Doo
9601 Lomas NE
Albuquerque, NM 87112
(505) 292-6692
www.teamrands.com

R & S West Motorcycle ATV Marine
10012 Coors Blvd. NW
Albuquerque, NM 87114
(505) 896-0200
www.teamrands.com

Santa Fe Motor Sports
2594 Camino Entrada
Santa Fe, NM 87507
(505) 438-1888
www.santafemotorsports.com

Utah

A.D.S Motorsports
284 W. Twelfth St.
Ogden, UT 84404
(801) 393-4561
www.adsmotorsports.com

Beers Harley-Davidson
2029 W. Hwy. 40
Vernal, UT 84078
(435) 789-5196

Delta Sports Center
299 N. Hwy. 6
Delta, UT 84624
(435) 864-3432
www.deltasports.com

Edge Motorsports
14301 S. Minuteman Dr.
Draper, UT 84020
(801) 495-3278
www.get2theedge.com

Escape Motorsports
1480 N. State St.
Provo, UT 84604
(801) 374-0602
www.escapemotorsports.com

Full Throttle Powersports
240 N. Frontage Rd.
Centerville, UT 84014
(801) 292-1492
www.fullthrottlepowersports.com

Renegade Sport 2
1903 S. 800 W.
Logan, UT 84321
(435) 755-7111
www.renegadesports.us

Vernal Sports Center
2029 W. Hwy. 40
Vernal, UT 84078
(435) 789-5196

SUZUKI

Arizona

Action Motorsports
4125 W. Summit Walk Ct.
Anthem, AZ 85086
(623) 465-5006
www.actionmotorsportsaz.com

All-Pro Cycle and Offroad
1770 E. Ash St.
Globe, AZ 85501
(928) 425-2030
www.allprocycle.com

Apache Motorcycles
3618 W. Camelback Rd.
Phoenix, AZ 85019
(602) 973-5111
www.phoenixpowersports.com

Carefree Yamaha
3120 W. Carefree Hwy., No. 5
Phoenix, AZ 85086
(623) 334-8295
www.phoenixpowersports.com

Champion Suzuki
1350 S. Clearview Ave., Ste. 111
Mesa, AZ 85208
(480) 325-1818
www.phoenixpowersports.com

Drew & The Crew Motorsports
806 W. Thatcher Blvd.
Safford, AZ 85546
(928) 348-3302
www.dandcmotorsports.com

Extreme Suzuki
7340 E. McDowell Rd.
Scottsdale, AZ 85257
(480) 970-4800
www.phoenixpowersports.com

Hales Motors
534 Madison Ave.
Prescott, AZ 86301
(928) 445-5730
www.starislandms.com

Kawasaki Suzuki of Kingman
2365 Northern Ave.
Kingman, AZ 86409
(928) 757-2480
www.kawasakisuzukiofkingman.com

Metro Motorsports
6161 W. Bell Rd.
Glendale, AZ 85308
(602) 843-5000
www.ridenow.com

Northland Motorsports
4308 E. Route 66
Flagstaff, AZ 86004
(928) 526-7959
www.northlandmotorsports.com

RideNow Powersports
1346 E. Florence Blvd., Ste. 2
Casa Grande, AZ 85222
(520) 316-9368
www.ridenow.com

RideNow Powersports
3333 N. Arizona Ave.
Chandler, AZ 85224
(480) 503-3333
www.ridenow.com

RideNow Powersports
13690 W. Test Dr.
Goodyear, AZ 85338
(623) 214-6400
www.ridenow.com

RideNow Powersports
17202 N. Cave Creek Rd.
Phoenix, AZ 85032
(602) 992-8620
www.ridenow.com

RideNow Powersports
15380 W. Bell Rd.
Surprise, AZ 85374
(623) 474-3740
www.ridenow.com

RideNow Powersports
4375 W. Ina Rd.
Tucson, AZ 85741
(520) 579-3939
www.ridenow.com

RideNow Powersports
7075 E. Twenty-second St.
Tucson, AZ 85710
(520) 757-9141
www.ridenow.com

Sierra Cycles
2137 E. Fry Blvd.
Sierra Vista, AZ 85635
(520) 459-2589
www.sierracycles.com

Wild West Motorsports
2500 E. Sixteenth St.
Yuma, AZ 85365
(928) 783-8282

Colorado
Altitude Motorsports
16135 Colorado Hwy. 9
Breckenridge, CO 80424
(970) 453-0353
www.jnjmoto.com

Apex Sports
327 S. Weber St.
Colorado Springs, CO 80903
(719) 475-2437
www.apexsportsinc.com

Colorado Powersports Boulder
1880 Fifty-fifth St.
Boulder, CO 80301
(303) 447-3500
www.copowersports.com

Colorado Powersports Denver
2050 W. 104th Ave.
Thornton, CO 80234
(303) 427-9000
www.copowersports.com

Craig Powersports
2607 E. U.S. 40
Craig, CO 81625
(970) 826-0060
www.craigpowersports.com

Davis Service Center
2380 E. Main St.
Montrose, CO 81401
(970) 249-8161
www.davisservicecenter.com

Fay Myers Motorcycle World
9700 E. Arapahoe Rd.
Denver, CO 80202
(303) 744-6632
www.faymyers.com

Fort Collins Motorsports
1800 Southeast Frontage Rd.
Fort Collins, CO 80525
(970) 498-8858
www.fortcollinsmotorsports.com

Fun Center
29603 U.S. Hwy. 160 E.
Durango, CO 81301
(970) 259-1070
www.funcentercycles.com

Grand Prix Motorsports
3105 W. County Line Rd.
Littleton, CO 80129
(303) 761-2471
www.grandprixmotorsports.com

Grand Valley Powersports
2865 N. Ave.
Grand Junction, CO 81501
(970) 263-4600
www.gvpowersports.com

Horizon Motor Sports
314 Chestnut St.
Sterling, CO 80751
(888) 551-3748
www.horizonmotorsportsllc.com

Mountain Powersports
7258 Hwy. 82
Glenwood Springs, CO 81601
(970) 928-0788
www.propolaris.com

OTD Cyclesports
7010 E. Colfax Ave.
Denver, CO 80220
(303) 399-5370
www.otdsuzukidenver.com

Powersports Unlimited
2733 Eighth Ave.
Greeley, CO 80631
(970) 352-7669
www.powersportsunlimited.com

Rocky Mountain Cycle Plaza
412 N. Chelton Rd.
Colorado Springs, CO 80909
(719) 591-9700
www.rockymtncycleplaza.com

Rocky Mountain Cycle Plaza
4106 Outlook Blvd.
Pueblo, CO 81008
(719) 545-5490
www.rockymtncycleplaza.com

RPM Motorsports
1251 Wadsworth Blvd.
Lakewood, CO 80214
(303) 232-7576
www.rpmms.com

Steamboat Powersports
2989 Riverside Plaza
Steamboat Springs, CO 80487
(970) 879-5138
www.steamboatpowersports.com

Xtreme Performance Center
826 Park St.
Castle Rock, CO 80109
(303) 660-5302
www.xtreme-performance.com

Xtreme Performance Center
4100 S. Valley Dr.
Longmont, CO 80504
(970) 535-9100
www.xtreme-performance.com

Nevada
Carter Powersports
6275 S. Decatur Blvd.
Las Vegas, NV 89118
(702) 795-2000
www.carterpowersports.com

E-Lee Suzuki
295 Aultman St.
Ely, NV 89301
(775) 289-3095

5th Gear Power Sports
420 Thirtieth St.
Elko, NV 89801
(775) 738-8933
www.5thgearelko.com

Kawasaki of Las Vegas
3850 N. Rancho Dr.
Las Vegas, NV 89130
(702) 656-1955
www.ridenow.com

Michael's Cycle Works
2680 S. Carson St.
Carson City, NV 89701
(775) 883-6111
www.michaelscycleworks.com

Michael's Reno Powersports
10828 S. Virginia St.
Reno, NV 89511
(775) 825-8680
www.michaelsreno.com

Nevada Suzuki
3475 Boulder Hwy.
Las Vegas, NV 89121
(702) 457-0343
www.suzukiofnevada.com

RideNow Powersports
6350 Boulder Hwy.
Las Vegas, NV 89122
(702) 451-1121
www.ridenow.com

RideNow Powersports
4120 E. Craig Rd.
North Las Vegas, NV 89030
(702) 214-5380
www.ridenow.com

Sonoma Cycle
405 W. Winnemucca Blvd.
Winnemucca, NV 89445
(775) 623-6888
www.sonomacycle.com

New Mexico
ATV Mountain Cycle
2140 E. U.S. Hwy. 180
Silver City, NM 88061
(877) 755-0707
www.atvmountaincycle.com

Champion Motorsports
2801 W. Second St.
Roswell, NM 88201
(575) 624-0151
www.championroswell.com

Deming Cycle Center
820 E. Spruce St.
Deming, NM 88030
(575) 546-6963
www.demingcycle.com

Desert Cycle
1315 Hamilton Rd., No. A
Gallup, NM 87301
(505) 722-3821

Four Corners Powersports
6520 E. Main
Farmington, NM 87402
(505) 325-6710
www.fourcornerspowersports.com

Las Cruces Motorsports
2125 S. Valley Dr.
Las Cruces, NM 88005
(575) 524-3626
www.lcmotorsports.com

Los Lunas Motorsports
2214 Sun Ranch Village Loop
Los Lunas, NM 87031
(505) 865-1700
www.loslunasmotorsports.com

Motorsport
6919 Montgomery Blvd. NE
Albuquerque, NM 87109
(505) 884-9000
www.abqmotorsport.com

R & S Kawasaki KTM Suzuki Sea-Doo
9601 Lomas NE
Albuquerque, NM 87112
(505) 292-6692
www.teamrands.com

R & S West Motorcycle ATV Marine
10012 Coors Blvd. NW
Albuquerque, NM 87114
(505) 896-0200
www.teamrands.com

Santa Fe Motor Sports
2594 Camino Entrada
Santa Fe, NM 87507
(505) 438-1888
www.santafemotorsports.com

Santa Teresa Motorsports
910 Livingston Loop
Santa Teresa, NM 88008
(575) 589-4980
www.santateresamotorsports.com

Southwest Suzuki
1000 Hwy. 70 W.
Alamogordo, NM 88310
(575) 434-0454

Zia Power Sports
1521 N. Prince St.
Clovis, NM 88101
(575) 762-6169
www.ziapowersports.com

Utah
Beers Harley-Davidson
2029 W. Hwy. 40
Vernal, UT 84078
(435) 789-5196

Big Boys Toys
2529 N. Hwy. 89
Ogden, UT 84404
(800) 273-9040
www.bigboysutah.com

Carbon Emery Motorsports
4510 N. Hwy. 6
Helper, UT 84526
(435) 472-8862

D & P Performance
110 E. Center St.
Cedar City, UT 84720
(435) 586-5172
www.dandpperformance.net

Edge Motorsports
14301 S. Minuteman Dr.
Draper, UT 84020
(801) 495-3278
www.get2theedge.com

Escape Motorsports
1480 N. State St.
Provo, UT 84604
(801) 374-0602
www.escapemotorsports.com

Honda Suzuki of Salt Lake
2354 S. State St.
Salt Lake City, UT 84115
(801) 486-5401
www.hondasuzuki.com

Jorgensen's
980 S. Cove View Rd.
Richfield, UT 84701
(435) 896-6408
www.jhsport.com

Layton Cycle & Sports
60 N. Main
Layton, UT 84041
(801) 544-2241
www.laytoncycle.com

Nelson's Fast Track
1740 S. Hwy. 40
Heber City, UT 84032
(435) 654-5343
www.nftpowersport.com

Ron Greene Sports Center
96 S. State St.
Mount Pleasant, UT 84647
(435) 462-2425
www.rongreenesportscenter.com

Stephen Wade Powersports
1295 E. Red Hills Pkwy.
St. George, UT 84770
(435) 628-5281
www.swpowersports.com

Vernal Sports Center
2029 W. Hwy. 40
Vernal, UT 84078
(435) 789-5196

Vesco's
370 W. 1175 S.
Brigham, UT 84302
(435) 734-9424
www.vescos.net

White Knuckle Motor Sports
889 N. 2000 W.
Springville, UT 84663
(801) 489-0393
www.whiteknucklemotorsports
   suzuki.com

TRIUMPH

Arizona
Arizona Superbike
3245 N. Arizona Ave., Ste. E-8
Chandler, AZ 85225
(480) 898-0559
www.azsbk.com

Euro Motorsports Scottsdale
14880 N. Northsight Blvd.
Scottsdale, AZ 85260
(480) 609-1800
www.goaz.com

Metro Motorsports
6161 W. Bell Rd.
Glendale, AZ 85308
(602) 843-5000
www.ridenow.com

Performance Cycle Center
3741 N. I-10 Frontage Rd., Ste. 101
Tucson, AZ 85705
(520) 622-2780
www.performancecyclecenter.com

RideNow Powersports
1346 E. Florence Blvd., Ste. 2
Casa Grande, AZ 85222
(520) 316-9368
www.ridenow.com

RideNow Powersports
3333 N. Arizona Ave.
Chandler, AZ 85224
(480) 503-3333
www.ridenow.com

RideNow Powersports
13690 W. Test Dr.
Goodyear, AZ 85338
(623) 214-6400
www.ridenow.com

RideNow Powersports
15380 W. Bell Rd.
Surprise, AZ 85374
(623) 474-3740
www.ridenow.com

RideNow Powersports
4375 W. Ina Rd.
Tucson, AZ 85741
(520) 579-3939
www.ridenow.com

RideNow Powersports
7075 E. Twenty-second St.
Tucson, AZ 85710
(520) 757-9141
www.ridenow.com

Triumph Superstore
5640 N. Seventh St.
Phoenix, AZ 85014
(602) 864-1437
www.triumphsuperstore.net

Colorado
Apex Sports
327 S. Weber St.
Colorado Springs, CO 80903
(719) 475-2437
www.apexsportsinc.com

Erico Motorsports
2855 Walnut St.
Denver, CO 80205
(303) 308-1811
www.ericomotorsports.com

Foothills BMW Triumph Motorcycles
1435 Wadsworth Blvd.
Lakewood, CO 80214
(303) 202-1400
www.foothillsbmw.com

Nevada
Freedom Cycle Reno
9726 S. Virginia St.
Reno, NV 89511
(775) 358-3500
www.freedomcyclereno.com

Kawasaki of Las Vegas
3850 N. Rancho Dr.
Las Vegas, NV 89130
(702) 656-1955
www.ridenow.com

Pat Clark Motorsports
2495 E. Sahara Ave.
Las Vegas, NV 89104
(702) 432-0650
www.patclarkmotorsports.com

RideNow Powersports
6350 Boulder Hwy.
Las Vegas, NV 89122
(702) 451-1121
www.ridenow.com

RideNow Powersports
4120 E. Craig Rd.
North Las Vegas, NV 89030
(702) 214-5380
www.ridenow.com

New Mexico
PJ's Motorcycles
12910 Central Ave. SE
Albuquerque, NM 87123
(505) 323-6700
www.pjsmotorcycles.com

Utah
BMW Motorcycles of Salt Lake
215 N. Redwood Rd.
North Salt Lake, UT 84054
(801) 936-4600
www.bmwmotorcyclesofsaltlake.com

VICTORY

Arizona
Arizona Kawasaki Victory
1015 W. Apache Trail
Apache Junction, AZ 85220
(480) 982-3363
www.arizonakawasaki.com

Arizona Victory Phoenix
13401 N. Cave Creek Rd.
Phoenix, AZ 85022
(602) 404-7300
www.arizonavictory.com

Arizona Victory Tucson
1102 N. Anita Ave.
Tucson, AZ 85705
(520) 770-9500
www.arizonavictory.com

AZ West
3198 Sweetwater Ave.
Lake Havasu City, AZ 86406
(928) 680-4151
www.azwestallsports.com

Cochise Motorsports
417 E. Wilcox Dr.
Sierra Vista, AZ 85635
(520) 458-5297
www.cochisemotorsports.com

Flagstaff Hotbike
3122 E. Route 66
Flagstaff, AZ 86004
(928) 773-8668
www.flagstaffhotbike.com

Prescott Valley Motorcycles
6500 E. SR 69
Prescott Valley, AZ 86314
(928) 772-4266
www.pvmotorcycles.com

Victory Motorcycle of Mesa
833 S. Country Club Dr.
Mesa, AZ 85210
(480) 668-7969
www.victoryofmesa.com

Colorado
Colorado Powersports
2050 W. 104th Ave.
Thornton, CO 80234
(303) 427-9000
www.copowersports.com

Fun Center
29603 U.S. Hwy. 160 E.
Durango, CO 81301
(970) 259-1070
www.funcentercycles.com

G-Force Powersports
7700 W. Colfax
Lakewood, CO 80214
(303) 238-4303
www.gforcepowersports.com

Grand Prix Motorsports
3105 W. County Line Rd.
Littleton, CO 80129
(303) 761-2471
www.grandprixmotorsports.com

Rocky Mountain Cycle Plaza
412 N. Chelton Rd.
Colorado Springs, CO 80909
(719) 591-9700
www.rockymtncycleplaza.com

Rocky Mountain Cycle Plaza
4106 Outlook Blvd.
Pueblo, CO 81008
(719) 545-5490
www.rockymtncycleplaza.com

Xtreme Performance Center
826 Park St.
Castle Rock, CO 80109
(303) 660-5302
www.xtreme-performance.com

Xtreme Performance Center
4100 S. Valley Dr.
Longmont, CO 80504
(970) 535-9100
www.xtreme-performance.com

Nevada
Arlen Ness Motorcycles Las Vegas
4020 Boulder Hwy.
Las Vegas, NV 89121
(702) 440-6377
www.arlennesslasvegas.com

Kawasaki of Las Vegas
3850 N. Rancho Dr.
Las Vegas, NV 89130
(702) 656-1955
www.ridenow.com

Reno Cycles & Gear
3445 Kietzke Lane
Reno, NV 89502
(775) 355-8810
www.renocycles.com

New Mexico
Rosedale Motorsports
8994 Fourth St. NW
Albuquerque, NM 87114
(505) 897-1519
www.rosedalemotorsports.com

Santa Teresa Motorsports
910 Livingston Loop
Santa Teresa, NM 88008
(575) 589-4980
www.santateresamotorsports.com

Utah
Biker's World
138 W. State St.
Hurricane, UT 84737
(435) 635-9000
www.bikersworldus.com

Tri City Performance
461 S. 800 W.
Centerville, UT 84014
(801) 298-8081
www.tricityperformance.net

Tri City Performance
1350 S. 2000 W.
Springville, UT 84663
(801) 794-3005
www.tricityperformance.net

YAMAHA

Arizona
Apache Motorcycles
3618 W. Camelback Rd.
Phoenix, AZ 85019
(602) 973-5111
www.phoenixpowersports.com

Carefree Yamaha
3120 W. Carefree Hwy., No. 5
Phoenix, AZ 85086
(623) 334-8295
www.phoenixpowersports.com

Champion Suzuki
1350 S. Clearview Ave., Ste. 111
Mesa, AZ 85208
(480) 325-1818
www.phoenixpowersports.com

Cycle Center
14660 W. Jimmie Kerr Blvd.
Casa Grande, AZ 85222
(520) 836-8739

Desert Recreation Yamaha
315 Long Ave.
Bullhead City, AZ 86429
(928) 754-4391
www.desrec.com

Desert Riders Motorsports
212 E. Hwy. 70
Safford, AZ 85546
(928) 348-8844

Four Seasons Motorsports
16485 N. Hwy. 87
Rye, AZ 85541
(928) 474-3411
www.fourseasonmotorsports.com

Metro Motorsports
6161 W. Bell Rd.
Glendale, AZ 85308
(602) 843-5000
www.ridenow.com

Northland Motorsports
4308 E. Route 66
Flagstaff, AZ 86004
(928) 526-7959
www.northlandmotorsports.com

Outdoor Sports
9100 E. Valley Rd.
Prescott Valley, AZ 86314
(928) 772-0575
www.outdoorsportsaz.com

RideNow Powersports
1346 E. Florence Blvd., Ste. 2
Casa Grande, AZ 85222
(520) 316-9368
www.ridenow.com

RideNow Powersports
3333 N. Arizona Ave.
Chandler, AZ 85224
(480) 503-3333
www.ridenow.com

RideNow Powersports
13690 W. Test Dr.
Goodyear, AZ 85338
(623) 214-6400
www.ridenow.com

RideNow Powersports Phoenix
17202 N. Cave Creek Rd.
Phoenix, AZ 85032
(602) 992-8620
www.ridenow.com

RideNow Powersports
15380 W. Bell Rd.
Surprise, AZ 85374
(623) 474-3740
www.ridenow.com

RideNow Powersports
4375 W. Ina Rd.
Tucson, AZ 85741
(520) 579-3939
www.ridenow.com

RideNow Powersports
7075 E. Twenty-second St.
Tucson, AZ 85710
(520) 757-9141
www.ridenow.com

Walt's Motorsports Marine
1551 S. Palo Verde Blvd.
Lake Havasu, AZ 86403
(928) 855-5019
www.waltsmotorsports.com

Colorado
Apex Sports
327 S. Weber St.
Colorado Springs, CO 80903
(719) 475-2437
www.apexsportsinc.com

Colorado Powersports
1880 Fifty-fifth St.
Boulder, CO 80301
(303) 447-3500
www.copowersports.com

Colorado Powersports
2050 W. 104th Ave.
Thornton, CO 80234
(303) 427-9000
www.copowersports.com

Coyote Motorsports
301 E. Fifty-seventh Ave.
Denver, CO 80216
(303) 293-8000
www.coyotemotorsports.com

Davis Service Center
2380 E. Main St.
Montrose, CO 81401
(970) 249-8161
www.davisservicecenter.com

Fort Collins Motorsports
1800 Southeast Frontage Rd.
Fort Collins, CO 80525
(970) 498-8858
www.fortcollinsmotorsports.com

Fremont Motorsports
600 E. Main St.
Florence, CO 81226
(719) 784-9633
www.fremontmotorsports.com

G-Force Powersports
7700 W. Colfax
Lakewood, CO 80214
(303) 238-4303
www.gforcepowersports.com

Grand Prix Motorsports
3105 W. County Line Rd.
Littleton, CO 80129
(303) 761-2471
www.grandprixmotorsports.com

Grand Valley Powersports
2865 N. Ave.
Grand Junction, CO 81501
(970) 263-4600
www.gvpowersports.com

Greeley Harley-Davidson
3010 W. Twenty-ninth St.
Greeley, CO 80631
(970) 351-8150
www.wildwestms.com

Hi-Point Motorsports
2802 S. Grand Ave.
Glenwood Springs, CO 81601
(970) 945-5977
www.hipointmotorsports.com

Mountain Tech Yamaha
22495 Hwy. 285
Nathrop, CO 81236
(719) 395-0438
www.mountaintechbv.com

Peak Motorsports
2901 Adcock Blvd.
Alamosa, CO 81101
(719) 587-4039
www.peakmotorsportsonline.com

Rocky Mountain Cycle Plaza
412 N. Chelton Rd.
Colorado Springs, CO 80909
(719) 591-9700
www.rockymtncycleplaza.com

Rocky Mountain Cycle Plaza
4106 Outlook Blvd.
Pueblo, CO 81008
(719) 545-5490
www.rockymtncycleplaza.com

Silverthorne Power Sports
128 W. Tenth St.
Silverthorne, CO 80497
(970) 513-1119
www.silverthornepowersports.com

Sun Sports Unlimited
219 W. Hwy. 50
Gunnison, CO 81230
(970) 641-0883
www.sunsportsunlimited.com

Unique Rides
3321 E. Mulberry St.
Fort Collins, CO 80524
(970) 416-5986
www.uniqueridesco.com

Vickery Motorsports
2231 S. Parker Rd.
Denver, CO 80231
(303) 755-4387
www.vickerymotorsports.com

Xtreme Performance Center
826 Park St.
Castle Rock, CO 80109
(303) 660-5302
www.xtreme-performance.com

Xtreme Performance Center
4100 S. Valley Dr.
Longmont, CO 80504
(970) 535-9100
www.xtreme-performance.com

Nevada
E-Lee Suzuki
295 Aultman St.
Ely, NV 89301
(775) 289-3095

5th Gear Power Sports
420 Thirtieth St.
Elko, NV 89801
(775) 738-8933
www.5thgearelko.com

Kawasaki of Las Vegas
3850 N. Rancho Dr.
Las Vegas, NV 89130
(702) 656-1955
www.ridenow.com

Michael's Cycle Works
2680 S. Carson St.
Carson City, NV 89701
(775) 883-6111
www.michaelscycleworks.com

Michael's Reno Powersports
10828 S. Virginia St.
Reno, NV 89511
(775) 825-8680
www.michaelsreno.com

Moto Zoo
1190 Lockspur St.
Pahrump, NV 89060
(775) 537-1600

RideNow Powersports
6350 Boulder Hwy.
Las Vegas, NV 89122
(702) 451-1121
www.ridenow.com

RideNow Powersports
4120 E. Craig Rd.
North Las Vegas, NV 89030
(702) 214-5380
www.ridenow.com

Sonoma Cycle
405 W. Winnemucca Blvd.
Winnemucca, NV 89445
(775) 623-6888
www.sonomacycle.com

New Mexico
Alamogordo Cycle Center
21070 Hwy. 70 W.
Alamogordo, NM 88310
(505) 437-8189
www.zianet.com/acc

Bobby J's Yamaha
4724 Menual Blvd. NE
Albuquerque, NM 87110
(505) 884-3013
www.bjsyamaha.com

Champion Motorsports
2801 W. Second St.
Roswell, NM 88201
(575) 624-0151
www.championroswell.com

Deming Cycle Center
820 E. Spruce St.
Deming, NM 88030
(575) 546-6963
www.demingcycle.com

Four Corners Powersports
6520 E. Main
Farmington, NM 87402
(505) 325-6710
www.fourcornerspowersports.com

Hester's Motorsports
1190 S. Second St.
Raton, NM 87740
(575) 445-3558
www.hester-motorsports.com

R & S Yamaha
3305 Juan Tabo Blvd. NE
Albuquerque, NM 87111
(505) 292-8011
www.teamrands.com

Rio Yamaha
1390 N. Main St.
Las Cruces, NM 88001
(575) 527-2200
www.rioyamaha.com

Santa Fe Motor Sports
2594 Camino Entrada
Santa Fe, NM 87507
(505) 438-1888
www.santafemotorsports.com

Sunland Park Yamaha
159 Sunland Park Dr.
Sunland Park, NM 88063
(575) 589-7433
www.sunlandparkyamaha.com

Utah
Big Pine Sports
340 N. Milburn Rd.
Fairview, UT 84629
(435) 427-3338
www.bigpinesports.com

Cache Honda Yamaha
3765 N. Hwy. 91
Hyde Park, UT 84318
(435) 563-6291
www.cachehy.com

317

Careys Cycle
4450 S. 700 W.
Riverdale, UT 84405
(801) 394-3469
www.careyscycle.com

Cedar City Motor Sports
1579 N. Main St. Nos. 108–109
Cedar City, UT 84720
(435) 867-9111
http://cedarcitymotorsports.com

Delta Sports Center
299 N. Hwy. 6
Delta, UT 84624
(435) 864-3432
www.deltasports.com

Freedom RV & Sports Center
396 S. Main
Gunnison, UT 84634
(435) 528-7244

Full Throttle Powersports
240 N. Frontage Rd.
Centerville, UT 84014
(801) 292-1492
www.fullthrottlepowersports.com

Jorgensen's
980 S. Cove View Rd.
Richfield, UT 84701
(435) 896-6408
www.jhsport.com

Layton Cycle & Sports
60 N. Main St.
Layton, UT 84041
(801) 544-2241
www.laytoncycle.com

Moab Powersports
1082 S. Hwy. 191
Moab, UT 84532
(435) 259-7800
www.moabpowersports.com

South Valley Motorsports
11553 S. State St.
Draper, UT 84020
(801) 576-1899
www.southvalleymotorsports.com

Steadman's
916 N. Main St.
Tooele, UT 84074
(435) 882-3565
www.steadmans.net

Stephen Wade Powersports
1295 E. Red Hills Pkwy.
St. George, UT 84770
(435) 628-5281
www.swpowersports.com

Vesco's
370 W. 1175 S.
Brigham, UT 84302
(435) 734-9424
www.vescos.net

Weller Recreation
2972 N. 900 E.
Kamas, UT 84036
(435) 783-4718
www.wellerrec.com

INDEX

Dixie National Forest, 51, 155
Dixon, Maynard, 68
Dolly steamboat, 246
Dolores (CO), 96, 97, 99
Dolores River, 99, 106
Dry Fork Creek Canyon, 16–17
Ducati dealers, 293–94
Duchesne (UT), 3, 5–6, 7, 8
Duck Creek Village (UT), 41–42
Dulce (CO), 107, 112
Dunton Hot Springs, 99
Durango (CO), 89, 91, 94–95, 107–8,
    113, 125, 127, 130, 134
Durango & Silverton Narrow Gauge
    Railroad, 93–94
Durango-Dulce Loop tour (CO), 106,
    107–13

E
Eagle Mountain (UT), 30
Eagle Nest Lake State Park, 210
Eagle Nest (NM), 206, 207, 210
Earthships, 222–23
El Camino Real International
    Heritage Center, 288
El Malpais National Monument,
    193, 194, 197
El Morro National Monument,
    193, 194, 195–97
Elberta (UT), 30
elevation, xv
Ely (NV), 27, 32–34
Emory Pass Overlook, 286
Enchanted Circle Scenic Byway.
    See Ring Around Taos tour
    (NM)
Escalante (UT), 39, 46, 47, 49
Escalante River Gorge, 49
Española (NM), 199, 215, 219
Estancia (NM), 225, 231
Eureka (UT), 30
Evanston (WY), 3, 10

F
Farmington (NM), 117, 133, 135
fee areas, xix
Fish Creek Canyon, 247
Fisher Towers (UT), 62
Flagstaff (AZ), 161, 166, 167, 169,
    174, 175, 183, 188, 190

Flagstaff/Camp Verde Loop tour
    (AZ), 183–90
Flagstaff/Sedona/Prescott tour
    (AZ), 174–82
Flaming Gorge Reservoir, 17–18, 19
Fort Apache Historic Park, 235,
    237–38
Fort Apache Loop/Salt River
    Canyon tour (AZ), 235–43
Fort Uintah, 6
Fort Verde State Historic Park, 185
Four Corners tours
    about: regional overview, 115
    Cortez-Aztec-Ignacio Loop, 132,
        133–39
    Four Corners Trail, 116–24
    Gallup to Canyon de Chelly, 140,
        141–48
    Mesa Verde National Park,
        125–31
Francis (UT), 10
Fred Harman Art Museum, 108–9
Fredonia (AZ), 161, 163–64

G
Gallup (NM), 141, 142, 193,
    194, 198
Gallup to Canyon de Chelly tour
    (AZ, NM), 140, 141–48
Ganado (AZ), 141, 147
Gateway (CO), 97, 104–5
gear, xvi–xvii
Georgia O'Keeffe Museum,
    192, 231
Geronimo Trail National Scenic
    Byway, 287
Ghost Ranch, 220
Ghost Town Gear, 180
ghost towns, 31, 54, 62, 79, 93, 157,
    255, 263, 268
Gila monsters, 241
Gila National Forest/Cliff Dwellings
    tour (NM), 281–88
Gila Wilderness Area, 275–77, 284
Gilman Tunnels, 203
Glenwood (NM), 274, 276, 277
Globe (AZ), 235, 238, 240, 243, 250
Goosenecks State Park, 74
Grand Canyon National Park, 161,
    163, 167–73

ABOUT THE AUTHORS

Christy Karras has spent much of her life living in and writing about the West. She has covered a wide range of topics including arts, outdoors, and travel for publications such as the *Seattle Times* and the *New York Times*.

She is the author of *More than Petticoats: Notable Women of Utah,* as well as the second edition of *Scenic Driving: Utah.* Before leaving her day job to focus on books, she was an editor at *Wasatch Journal* magazine and a reporter for the *Salt Lake Tribune* and The Associated Press.

She is passionate about traveling to new places and getting to know their history and culture, which entails being one of those people who will stop at every possible roadside attraction and historical marker. She divides her time between the deserts of Utah and the forests of the Pacific Northwest, where she seeks new adventures with her fiancé, Bill.

Whatever she is doing at this moment, she would probably rather be touring.

Stephen Zusy has spent most of his adult life living in or near the Southwest. Having a bit of the vagabond spirit, the list of places he has lived in is long and includes Denver, Tucson, Salt Lake City, and Park City, Utah, all of which have provided plenty of opportunity to travel and recreate in the vast majority of the Southwest.

He has a degree in business and a lifelong passion for photography, a combination that has served him well. Over the past decade and a half, he has worked in real estate, the commercial photography world in northern California, and as a photojournalist at the *Park Record* and the *Salt Lake Tribune.* He has done freelance work for a diverse range of publications and news outlets, including *Getty,* the *Wasatch Journal,* and *Entertainment Weekly.*

He has been a motorcycle enthusiast since he was a child. He spent his youth riding mini-bikes and dirt bikes until he graduated to street bikes—against the wishes of his parents—shortly after graduating from high school. He has ridden all manner and style of motorcycle over the years. There have been only a few times as an adult when he has not owned a motorcycle, and during those times, it never took long for a little twitch to develop in his throttle wrist. There are few sounds he loves more than the roar of a motorcycle engine and no place he'd rather be than on his bike, twisting back the throttle, searching for an endless series of perfectly banked curves.

For now, home is Park City, Utah, but he's considering a move to somewhere he can ride year-round.

Travel Like a Pro

To order call 800-243-0495 or visit thenewgpp.com